Intellectual Property Law in Saudi Arabia

Intellectual Property Law in Saudi Arabia

Second Edition

Mohammed El Said

This book was originally published as a monograph in the International Encyclopaedia of Laws/Intellectual Property Law.

Wolters Kluwer

Published by:
Kluwer Law International B.V.
PO Box 316
2400 AH Alphen aan den Rijn
The Netherlands
E-mail: international-sales@wolterskluwer.com
Website: lrus.wolterskluwer.com

Sold and distributed in North, Central and South America by:
Wolters Kluwer Legal & Regulatory U.S.
7201 McKinney Circle
Frederick, MD 21704
United States of America
Email: customer.service@wolterskluwer.com

Sold and distributed in all other countries by:
Air Business Subscriptions
Rockwood House
Haywards Heath
West Sussex
RH16 3DH
United Kingdom
Email: international-customerservice@wolterskluwer.com

Printed on acid-free paper

ISBN 978-94-035-0325-7

e-Book: ISBN 978-94-035-0221-2
web-PDF: ISBN 978-94-035-0225-0

Printed in the United Kingdom.

The Author

Professor Mohammed El Said (born 1976) obtained his Bachelor's degree in Law from the University of Jordan, Jordan (1998). He completed his LLM in International Business Law from the University of Manchester, UK (1999) and obtained his doctorate in 2005 from the same university for his research into the area of intellectual property and international trade. In 2005, he joined the Lancashire Law School as a Lecturer in International Trade Law. Professor El Said is a qualified solicitor under the Jordanian Bar Association (2001). He also worked as a consultant with leading media organizations in the Middle East and for other international organizations including the United Nations Development Programme (UNDP), the World Intellectual Property Organization (WIPO) and the World Health Organization (WHO). Professor El Said has several books and publications in the area of intellectual property rights. He is the author of *Public Health Related TRIPS-Plus Provisions in Bilateral Trade Agreements: A Policy Guide for Negotiations and Implementers in the Eastern Mediterranean Region*, published by the World Health Organization (WHO) and the International Centre for Trade and Sustainable Development (ICTSD), 2010; *IPRs in Jordan*, Kluwer Law International BV, 2009, *IPRs in Lebanon*, Kluwer Law International BV, 2012, *IPRs in Oman*, Kluwer Law International BV, 2014 and *The Development of Intellectual Property Protection in the Arab World*, The Edwin Mellen Press, 2008. Professor El Said is a legal project lead for Creative Commons project (CC) in Qatar.

The Author

Table of Contents

List of Abbreviations

AIDS	Acquired Immunodeficiency Syndrome
BoG	Board of Grievance
ccTLD	Country-Code Top-Level Domain
FTA	Free Trade Agreement
GCC	Gulf Cooperation Council
GDP	Gross Domestic Product
GI	Geographical Indication
IPRs	Intellectual Property Rights
IS	Islamic State
KACST	King Abdul Aziz City for Science and Technology for patents
LIR	Local Internet Registry
MOC	Ministry of Trade and Commerce
OPEC	Organization for Petroleum Exporting Countries
PBUH	Peace Be Upon Him
PCT	Patent Cooperation Treaty
PLT	Patent Law Treaty
SAR	Saudi Riyal
TRIPS	Agreement on Trade-Related Aspects of Intellectual Property Rights
UAE	United Arab Emirates
UCC	Universal Copyright Convention
UNDP	United Nations Development Programme
UPOV	International Convention for the Protection of New Varieties of Plants
US	United States
USD	United States Dollars
WIPO	World Intellectual Property Organization
WTO	World Trade Organization

List of Abbreviations

Preface

This study consists of a comprehensive description of the Saudi Arabia intellectual property protection regime. Since much of this regime has been shaped by the influence of international and regional agreements on the one hand, particularly the 1883 Paris Convention for the Protection of Industrial Property, the TRIPS Agreement, and the 2006 Gulf Cooperation Council (GCC) Unified Patent and Trademark laws and Agreements, the basic traits and characteristics of the Saudi intellectual property law will be familiar to foreign lawyers, academics, students, policy makers and researchers, to which this work is directed towards.

The international intellectual property conventions are not examined in this monograph, although some represent and are included under a number of the Saudi intellectual property laws and regulations. Rather, this study focuses on the Saudi domestic and national laws and legislations, as it has evolved on the basis of the statutes which implement Saudi Arabia's international commitments and obligations in the intellectual property area. In addition, the study contains reference to the relevant judicial and court decisions issued in the country in this regard. Also, the study contains special reference to Saudi's commitments in the area of intellectual property as a result of signing of some regional trade agreements within the GCC states. However, the monograph, where relevant, makes reference to the provisions and principles of the main regional and international intellectual property agreements and treaties particularly the TRIPS Agreement.

While the Saudi Arabian intellectual property legal theories and principles are largely based on European precedents and international developments, legal practice has a distinct local flavour, not easy to describe and examine in a study of this type. Deep influence of religious norms particularly the Quran and *Shariah* within the Saudi legal regime are highly visible and represent a unique feature of the country's judiciary and legal regime. This should serve as a caveat against all too easy generalizations about the role and status of intellectual property law in developing Arab and gulf countries including the Kingdom of Saudi Arabia.

The law stated in the monograph is as of December 2017.

Preface

Acknowledgements

This work would not have seen the light of the day without the help and support of many colleagues, friends and family.

In particular, I am thankful to the Lancashire Law School, the University of Central Lancashire (UCLAN), United Kingdom for its continuous and valuable support.

I am also thankful to my wife and family for being there for me.

Acknowledgements

General Introduction

§1. General Background

I. Geography

1. The Kingdom of Saudi Arabia (hereinafter 'Saudi Arabia') is an Arab state which occupies the majority part of the Arabian Peninsula and is the largest country in area in the Middle East despite having 95% of its land as desert (twice the size of France and Germany combined). Mountains running parallel to the Red Sea extend along the Arabian Gulf. Below the arid landscape, oil has made this desert kingdom one of the wealthiest nations in the world.[1] In addition to its massive oil reserves (estimated to represent quarter of world's reserves), the country gains its prestigious status from being the custodian of the birthplace of Islam.[2]

Saudi Arabia shares borders with seven countries and three bodies of water.[3] To the west, the Gulf of Aqaba and the Red Sea form a coastal border of almost 1,800 kilometres that extends to the southern part of Yemen and follows a mountain ridge for approximately 320 kilometres extending to Najran. To the north, Saudi Arabia is bounded by Jordan, Iraq and Kuwait. The northern boundary extends almost 1,400 kilometres from the Gulf of Aqaba on the west to *Ras al Khafji* on the Arabian Gulf.

In general, the climate of Saudi Arabia is extremely hot and dry most of the year – with the exception of the Asir Province on the western coast where the weather is slightly milder – Saudi Arabia receives very low annual rainfall in general. Because of the influence of a subtropical high-pressure system, there is considerable variation in temperature and humidity between the summer and winter seasons. The two main differences in the climate of Saudi Arabia can be felt between the coastal areas and the interior.[4] The average summer temperature is about 45°C, but readings of up to 54°C are not unusual. Commonly, the heat becomes intense shortly after sunrise and lasts until sunset. In the winter, the temperature seldom drops below 0°C, but the almost total absence of humidity and the high wind-chill factor make a quite cold atmosphere. In the spring and autumn the heat is temperate; temperatures average around 29°C. The region of Asir along the western coast is influenced by the Indian

1. For more details *see* at http://travel.nationalgeographic.com/travel/countries/saudi-arabia-facts/. Last visited 13 Feb. 2016.
2. *See* http://www.bbc.com/news/world-middle-east-14702705. Last visited 12 Jan. 2016.
3. Kuwait, Iraq, Qatar, Jordan, Yemen, Oman and United Arab Emirates.
4. *See* for more http://www.weatheronline.co.uk/reports/climate/Saudi-Arabia.htm. Last visited 12 Jan. 2016.

Ocean monsoons, usually occurring between October and March. An average of 300 millimetres of rainfall occurs during this period that is about 60% of the annual precipitation. For the rest of the country, rainfall is very low and erratic. The entire year's rainfall may consist of one or two local, heavy cloudbursts or thunderstorms.[5]

Saudi Arabia's Geology is diverse. The country's rocks range in age from the Precambrian to the present day,[6] forming part of a larger unit that includes the Arabian Peninsula (*Al Jazeera Al Arabeyeh*) and is known as the Arabian Plate. According to the Saudi Geological Survey:

> Some Precambrian rocks in this region date back to the Archean (nearly 3 million years ago) but most are Neoproterozoic (1000-540 Ma). It is believed that they originated as volcanic islands or as chains of volcanoes along spreading centers and subduction zones in a Neoproterozoic ocean and against ancient continental margins, and were folded and uplifted toward the end of the Precambrian as a large belt of mountains. The mountains existed between about 680-540 Ma and were part of one of the largest mountain belts ever known to have existed on Earth. By the end of the Precambrian, the mountains had been eroded and only their roots are preserved, exposed in western Saudi Arabia in the Arabian shield.[7]

II. Cultural Composition

2. The Saudi cultural composition has its roots firmly under the Islamic religion. Islam is practised by all Saudis and governs their personal, political, economic and legal lives. As mentioned, Islam was born in Saudi Arabia and thus its birthplace (Mecca) is visited by millions of Muslims every year to perform pilgrimage (*Hajj*). The Prophet Muhammad Peace Be Upon Him (PBUH) is seen as the last of God's messengers (following in the footsteps of previous messengers of God including Jesus, Moses, Abraham, etc.) to bring revelation to mankind. The Quran and the actions of the Prophet (*the Sunnah*) are used as the basis for all guidance in the religion.[8]

In general, the population of Saudi Arabia may be characterized by a high degree of cultural homogeneity. This homogeneity was reflected and shaped by a common Arabic language and in adherence to Sunni Islam. The family plays a big role in the composition of the Saudi society since it represents 'the primary basis of identity and

---

5. *Ibid.*
6. According to National Geographic, Precambrian time covers the vast bulk of the Earth's history, starting with the planet's creation about 4.5 billion years ago and ending with the emergence of complex, multicelled life-forms almost 4 billion years later. The Precambrian is the earliest of the geologic ages, which are marked by different layers of sedimentary rock. Laid down over millions of years, these rock layers contain a permanent record of the Earth's past, including the fossilized remains of plants and animals buried when the sediments were formed. For more *see* National Geographic, at http://science.nationalgeographic.com/science/prehistoric-world/precambrian/. Last visited 12 Jan. 2016.
7. For more *see* http://www.sgs.org.sa/English/Geology/Pages/default.aspx. Last visited 14 Jan. 2016.
8. For more *see* http://www.kwintessential.co.uk/resources/global-etiquette/saudi-arabia-country-profile.html. Last visited 14 Jan. 2016.

status for the individual and the immediate focus of individual loyalty, just as it was among those who recognized a tribal affiliation'.[9]

The country has an increasingly large educated workforce as a result of the country's additional investment levels in that sector particularly with relation to female education. However, as in the case of the majority of countries in the region, activities and investments affiliated with science, technology and research and development remain weak. This explains the reason behind the slow development of the intellectual property protection regime and institutions in the country and the scarcity of literature in this particular field.

III. Political System

3. The modern Kingdom of Saudi Arabia, which was founded in 1932 by Abdul Aziz bin Abd al-Rahman Al Saud (Ibn Saud), is a hereditary monarchy. The Chief of state and government is the King. The King is also the prime minister, chief of state, the head of government and commander in chief of the military of Saudi Arabia. The King's Cabinet, or Council of Ministers, is appointed by the King every four years. There are twenty-two government ministries that are part of the Cabinet.[10]

Administratively, the populated regions are divided into thirteen provinces (*mintaqah*), which are each ruled by a governor. Governors are appointed by the King and usually report directly to him. As been reported, the provincial government oversees the local offices of the central government and municipal officials. In some of the provinces, the governor has chosen to hold a public *majlis* to allow the people to voice their grievances. This is one of the main forms of popular participation in local government affairs. Some of the larger provinces are divided into districts and sub-districts. The district and sub-district governments are subject to the authority of the provincial government.[11] The primary objective of the governor and his administrative staff is the supervision and administration of the region in line with the public policy and regulations of the State. The governor's primary responsibilities include the maintenance of public security, order and stability and the guaranteeing of individual rights and freedoms within the framework of the *Shariah* and governmental regulations, in addition to the promotion of social and economic development in the region.

In 2003, the Saudi King approved the creation of consultative councils on the municipal level whereby half of the officials in these bodies are to be elected by popular vote. A time frame of one year has been dedicated to the establishment of election procedures and institutions, and in 2005 the first democratic local elections in Saudi Arabia were held.[12] Notably, formation of political parties is not allowed in the country.

Although the country enjoys a high degree of internal stability, regional tensions in the aftermath of the Persian Gulf War and the Iran-Iraq war and the rise of Islamic

9. For more *see* http://countrystudies.us/saudi-arabia/21.htm. Last visited 14 Jan. 2016.
10. For more *see* http://www.hziegler.com/articles/political-system-of-saudi-arabia.html. Last visited 15 Jan. 2016.
11. For more *see* http://unpan1.un.org/intradoc/groups/public/documents/un/unpan023182.pdf. Last visited 14 Feb. 2016.
12. *Ibid.*

terrorist organizations in the region including Islamic State (IS) continue to necessitate large defence expenditures.[13] The conflict across the border in Yemen and regional tensions with other countries including Iran coupled with decreasing oil prices in recent months has added to concerns about the financial stability of the country.[14]

4. The Saudi Constitution – referred to as the Basic Law of Governance – is the most important constitutional law in Saudi Arabia.[15] It states that the Quran and the *Sunnah* of the Prophet Muhammad PBUH are the constitution of the country and stresses in Article 7 that Islamic Religious Law '*Shariah*' is the foundation of the Kingdom.[16] The Quran and the *Sunnah* are the sources of the authority of the government and they govern all administrative regulations of the State.[17] The Basic Law of Governance confirms the monarchical royal system of the state and defines the judicial authority, the executive authority and the legislative authority.[18]

The Saudi Basic Law of Governance is divided into a number of parts and sections dealing with the separation and division of powers between various branches (the judiciary, the legislative and the executive branches).

The executive authority consists of the King, the Council of Ministers, local governments, ministry subsidiaries and other public agencies. The legislative authority is shared by the King, the Council of Ministers and the Consultative Council (*Majlis al-Shura*). The legislative authority is referred to in the Basic Law of Governance as the 'regulatory authority' which is empowered to enact laws and regulations.

Part One of the Basic Law of Governance includes a number of general principles emphasizing the Arab and religious Islamic nature and foundations of the state with its capital being Riyadh. The State's official language is Arabic.

Article 55 of the Basic Law of Governance provides that the King shall run the affairs of the nation in accordance with the principles of Islam. The King shall supervise the implementation of Islamic *Shariah* and the general policies of the State and the protection and defence of the country. The King presides over the Council of Ministers.

---

13. According to Business Insider UK, 'Saudi Arabia has one of the best-funded defence forces in the Middle East. The kingdom spends 25% of its budget, or about $80 billion, on its military'. For more *see* http://uk.businessinsider.com/saudi-arabia-spends-25-of-its-budget-on-its-military-2015-12. Last visited 2 Mar. 2016.
14. For more *see* Ahmed Al-Darwish et al., *Saudi Arabia: Tackling Emerging Economic Challenges to Sustain Strong Growth*. Middle East and Central Asia departmental paper series (Washington, D.C.: International Monetary Fund, 2015).
15. *See* the Basic Law of Governance (promulgated by the Royal Decree No. A/90 dated 1 Mar. 1992).
16. Article 1 of the Basic Law of Governance states The Kingdom of Saudi Arabia is a fully sovereign Arab Islamic State. Its religion shall be Islam and its constitution shall be the Book of God and the Sunnah (Traditions) of His Messenger, may God's blessings and Peace Be Upon Him (PBUH). Its language shall be Arabic and its capital shall be the city of Riyadh.
17. Article 7 of the Basic Law of Governance states that Governance in the Kingdom of Saudi Arabia derives its authority from the Book of God Most High and the Sunnah of his Messenger, both of which govern this law and all the laws of the State.
18. Article 44 of the Basic Law of Governance states that the authorities in the State shall consist of: – Judicial Authority; – Executive Authority; – Regulatory Authority. These authorities shall cooperate in the discharge of their functions in accordance with the Basic Law of Governance and other laws. The King shall be their final authority.

The King shall be assisted in the discharge of his functions by the members of the Council of Ministers in accordance with the provisions of the Basic Law of Governance and other laws. The Law of the Council of Ministers shall set forth the power of the Council with respect to internal and foreign affairs and to the organization of the agencies of the government and coordination among them. It shall also set forth the requirements ministers must meet, their powers, accountability and all their affairs. The Law of the Council of Ministers and the powers of the Council shall be amended in accordance with the Basic Law of Governance.[19]

Furthermore, the King shall appoint Vice Presidents of the Council of Ministers and member ministers of the Council of Ministers and shall relieve them by Royal Order. The Vice Presidents of the Council of Ministers and the member ministers of the Council of Ministers shall be considered collectively responsible before the King for the implementation of the Islamic *Shariah* and the laws and the general polices of the State. The King may dissolve the Council of Ministers and reconstitute it. The King shall appoint those who hold the rank of minister and deputy minister and those in Distinguished Grade, and shall relieve them of their office by Royal Order. Ministers and heads of independent agencies shall be considered responsible before the King for the ministries and agencies they head.[20] The law shall set forth the provisions for civil service, including salaries, stipends, compensation, fringe benefits and pensions.[21] The King shall be the Supreme Commander in Chief of all armed forces and shall appoint and terminate the services of officers in accordance with the law.[22] The King may declare the state of emergency in accordance with what is set forth in the law.[23]

As explained, Article 44 of the Saudi Basic Law of Governance highlights the authorities in the State which shall consist of the Judicial Authority, the Executive Authority and the Regulatory Authority. These authorities shall cooperate in the discharge of their functions in accordance with the Basic Law of Governance and other laws. The King shall be their final authority. The Basic Law further reiterates that the source for *fatwa* (religious legal opinion) in the Kingdom of Saudi Arabia shall be the Book of God and the *Sunnah* of his Messenger PBUH. The law shall set forth the hierarchy and jurisdiction of the Board of Senior *Ulema* and the Department of Religious Research and *Fatwa*.[24]

5. Saudi Arabia's judicial system traditionally has been based on the *Shariah* – the Qur'anic laws and the oral teachings of Prophet Muhammad PBUH. Article 46 of the Basic Law of Governance reiterates the independence of the judiciary. There shall be no power over judges in their judicial function other than the power of the Islamic *Shariah*. The right of litigation shall be guaranteed equally for both citizens and residents in the Kingdom.[25]

The judicial system is composed of a Supreme Judicial Council, Courts of Appeals and First Instance Courts. There is also an administrative judicial body known

19. The Basic Law of Governance, Art. 56.
20. *Ibid.*, Art. 58.
21. *Ibid.*, Art. 59.
22. *Ibid.*, Art. 60.
23. *Ibid.*, Art. 61.
24. *Ibid.*, Art. 45.
25. *Ibid.*, Art. 47.

as the Board of Grievances (BoG) affiliated to the King. The Saudi legal system has several administrative committees that adjudicate civil, commercial, administrative and criminal cases.

Although the Basic Law of Governance does not refer to the protection of Intellectual Property Rights (IPRs) explicitly, it ensures the protection of all forms of property,[26] and ensures the protection of cultural heritage.[27]

The courts shall apply to cases before them the provisions of Islamic *Shariah*, as indicated by the Quran and the *Sunnah* and whatever laws not in conflict with the Quran and the *Sunnah* which the authorities may promulgate.[28] There is no system of binding legal precedents, with judges having the power to use independent legal reasoning to reach a decision in any matter. Subject to the provisions of Article 53 of the Basic Law of Governance, the courts shall have jurisdiction to adjudicate all disputes and crimes.[29] The King or whomever he deputizes shall be responsible for the enforcement of judicial rulings.[30] The law shall set forth the composition and jurisdiction of the Supreme Judicial Council, as well as the hierarchy and jurisdiction of the courts.[31]

Appointment and termination of judges shall be by Royal Order, at the recommendation of the Supreme Judicial Council, as set forth by the law.[32] The law shall set forth the structure and jurisdiction of the BoGs.[33] The law shall set forth the final authority, organization and jurisdiction of the Bureau of Investigation and Prosecution.[34]

IV. Population Statistics

6. The population of Saudi Arabia reached approximately 30.77 million in 2015.[35] In general, population growth reported a steady and greater upward trend in certain regions namely Riyadh, Mecca and Eastern Region and Jazan region in a minor way during the last two decades. However, growth rates in Saudi Arabia during the past two decades rank above the general average of 2.37%, registered across the Arab world. The high birth rate and the low mortality rate are the result of dedicated and intensive efforts towards raising the standard of health care in the country. According

26. Article 17 of the Basic Law of Governance states that property, capital and labour are basic constituents of the economic and social structure of the Kingdom. They are private rights which fulfil a social function in accordance with Islamic *Shariah*.
27. Article 29 of the Basic Law of Governance states that the State shall foster sciences, arts and culture, and shall encourage scientific research, protect Islamic and Arabic heritage, and contribute to Arab, Islamic and human civilization.
28. The Basic Law of Governance, Art. 48.
29. *Ibid.*, Art. 49.
30. *Ibid.*, Art. 50.
31. *Ibid.*, Art. 51.
32. *Ibid.*, Art. 52.
33. *Ibid.*, Art. 53.
34. *Ibid.*, Art. 54.
35. For more *see* the Saudi General Authority of Statistics, available at http://www.stats.gov.sa/en/english. Last visited 2 Mar. 2016.

to available statistics, inhabitants from Saudi origins form 72.9% of the population, which comprises 50.1% males and 49.9% females. Foreigners form 27.1% of the population, of whom 69.5% are males and the remaining are females. This increasing number of foreigners may be attributed to the growth of the Saudi economy and interest by foreigners to invest in it accordingly. Others also attribute this to the Saudi's government policy of using its oil revenues to expand general services and build a solid infrastructure.[36]

Saudi Arabia's Domestic population growth rate is expected to be around 1.8% *per annum* between 2010 and 2015 according to the UNDP's 2015 Human Development Report.[37]

§2. Historical Background

7. According to Global Britannica, some archaeological accounts narrate that civilization flourished in the area of modern day Arabia more than 5,000 years ago. Of all the empires that profited from the lucrative trade in frankincense, few have captured the imagination like the Nabataeans, a people of Bedouin origin who developed a specialized capability and knowledge of the trade caravan routes. From their extraordinary rock-hewn cities of Madain Saleh and Petra (in Jordan), the Nabataeans grew wealthy from around 200 BC by exacting tolls and protection money from the caravans. The Nabataeans never really possessed an 'empire' in the common military and administrative sense of the word, but instead established a zone of influence that stretched as far north as Syria and south into the rich Hadaramawt region (Yemen). In the years following the Prophet Muhammed's PBUH death in 632 AD, the territory of what is now Saudi Arabia was nominally ruled from afar by the Umayyad and Abbasid Caliphates, and was saved from obscurity only by the spiritual significance and stature of the holy cities of Mecca and Medina.[38] The emergence of the Arabian Muslims as the founders of one of the great empires of history led the name 'Arab' to be used by these Muslims themselves and by the nations with whom they came in contact to indicate all people of Arabian origin. The very name Arabia, or its Arabic name *Jazīrat al-Arab*, has come to be used for the whole peninsula, which largely includes Saudi Arabia today.[39] The Islamic civilization remained vigorous for centuries, providing stability and advancing human knowledge when most of other parts (including Western Europe) were in a state of chaos and superstition known to historians as the Dark Ages. In the thirteenth century, the Mongol invasions dealt a devastating blow

36. *See* the Saudi Ministry of Foreign Affairs, available at http://www.mofa.gov.sa/sites/mofaen/EServ/VisitingSaudiArabia/aboutKingDom/Pages/KingdomGeography46466.aspx. Last visited 7 Feb. 2016.
37. For more *see* the UNDP, Human Development Report 2013: Work for human development (New York, UNDP 2013).
38. For more *see* http://www.lonelyplanet.com/saudi-arabia/history. Last visited 6 Feb. 2016.
39. For more *see* http://global.britannica.com/topic/history-of-Arabia. Last visited 7 Feb. 2016.

to the Arabs' eastern lands and their empire began to decline.[40] By 1517 the Ottomans, under Salim I, had established their authority over Hejaz and remained in control for large parts with several interruptions and Egyptian involvement in the country until it gained its independence in 1932.[41] On 23 September 1932, the lands under the control of Abdul Aziz were renamed the Kingdom of Saudi Arabia and in 1936 a treaty was signed with Yemen marking the southern borders of the Kingdom for the first time in modern history. King Abdul Aziz Ibin Saud died in November 1953 after more than half a century as leader and king. He was succeeded by his eldest son, Saud bin Abdul Aziz, who devoted a great deal of time to fostering the Kingdom's relations with its neighbours.[42]

Today, Saudi Arabia is a high-income country, with Gross Domestic Product (GDP) per capita estimated at USD 746.2 billion in 2014.[43] The country has an oil-based economy with strong government controls over major economic activities. It possesses about 16% of the world's oil reserves, ranks as the largest exporter of oil and plays a leading role in the Organization for Petroleum Exporting Countries (OPEC). The oil sector accounts for roughly 80% of budget revenues, 45% of GDP and 90% of export earnings. Saudi Arabia is working to support the growth of the private sector in order to diversify its economy and to employ more Saudi nationals. Diversification efforts are focusing various sectors including power generation, telecommunications, natural gas exploration and petrochemical sectors. As part of its effort to attract foreign investment, Saudi Arabia acceded to the World Trade Organization (WTO) in 2005. The government has begun establishing six 'economic cities' in different regions of the country to promote foreign investment and pledged to spend USD 373 billion between 2010 and 2014 on social development and infrastructure projects to advance Saudi Arabia's economic development.[44]

Saudi Arabia started applying the Gulf Cooperation Council (GCC) common external tariff on 5 January 2003. Since 1986, the Saudi Riyal (SAR), the national currency, has been pegged to the US dollar (USD 1 per SAR 3.75 since 1986). With the exception of Kuwait, all GCC countries have their currencies pegged to the US dollar. The sustained stability in domestic prices and the exchange rate over a prolonged period of time has greatly facilitated the growth of the Saudi economy.[45]

Since the mid-1990s, the count has been implementing a development strategy aimed at, *inter alia*, reducing its high dependence on crude oil and natural gas. Designing the path for government policy over the next five years, the Kingdom's 10th Development Plan, which covers the period between 2015 and 2019, places renewed emphasis on

---

40. *See* Jonathan Lyons, *The House of Wisdom: How the Arabs Transformed Western Civilization* (New York, Bloomsbury Press, 2009). *See also* Mohammad El Said, 'The Compatibility of Modern Intellectual Property Protection Norms with Islamic Principles: Lessons from History', *W.I.P.O. Journal* 4, no.1 (2012): 121–128.
41. For more *see* http://www.lonelyplanet.com/saudi-arabia/history. Last visited 7 Feb. 2016.
42. *See* https://www.psaiahf.com/en/about-festival/visitors/history-of-the-kingdom-of-saudi-arabia. Last visited 25 Feb. 2016.
43. *See* http://data.worldbank.org/country/saudi-arabia. Last visited 7 Feb. 2016.
44. For more *see* http://www.indexmundi.com. Last visited 14 Feb. 2016.
45. *See* the WTO, the Working Party on the Accession of the Kingdom of Saudi Arabia, WT/ACC/SAU/61, 1 Nov. 2005.

education and private sector development as the keys to economic diversification.[46] On the macroeconomic level, the government has declared its intention to pursue fiscal and monetary policies that 'contribute to fiscal stability, stimulate economic growth and support social welfare'. In policy terms, this involves improving the efficiency of government expenditure while also increasing the government's non-oil revenues. In general, the Development Plan focuses on the following sectors/paths:[47]

- *Diversification*: As a first step towards greater diversification, the plan envisages raising utilization rates of mineral resources, diversifying sector activities and developing local processing of mining raw materials. The plan aims to increase the contribution of the services sector to GDP, with an emphasis on financial, tourism, transport, engineering, communications and IT services.
- *Knowledge Society*: Underpinning economic diversification is the transition to a knowledge-based economy and society, which constitutes the third objective of the plan. This encompasses a wide array of changes, ranging from greater utilization of the results of scientific research in addressing socio-economic issues to raising the knowledge content of goods and services produced in the Kingdom.
- *Capital Productivity*: In addition to pushing the Saudi economy to become more knowledge-driven, there are other steps the government can take to improve productivity. For instance, in terms of capital productivity, the Kingdom wishes to encourage companies to shift from unskilled labour-intensive business models to those that rely more on capital, advanced technology and skilled labour. To facilitate this, over the course of the plan, the government will streamline the procedures for the establishment and market entry of companies, in addition to developing bankruptcy regulations that also safeguard the rights of creditors.
- *Labour*: In terms of labour productivity, the plan focuses on the country's education and training systems as an avenue for fostering a positive work ethic and enabling workers to deal efficiently with technological developments. This will require 'developing labour market mechanisms and regulations and wage policies in a way that facilitates movement of labour between companies and establishments, as well as between the public and private sectors', according to the language of the plan.
- *Resource Efficiency*: For both economic and environmental reasons, the plan makes conservation of oil resources and rationalization of their use a stated goal. This will be achieved through the promotion of energy efficiency measures and by fast-tracking regulations to spur the use of renewable energy sources for electricity generation and water desalination. Water resources are to be managed according to the National Water Strategy, which anticipates that reclaimed water will increasingly be used for agriculture, while growth in water consumption

46. For more on the plan *see* the Saudi Ministry of Economy and Planning, available at http://services.mep.gov.sa/themes/BlueArc/. Last visited 14 Feb. 2016.
47. The following part is largely based on Saudi Arabia's new development plan shows clear commitment to education and the private sector. http://www.oxfordbusinessgroup.com/analysis/long-game-new-development-plan-shows-clear-commitment-education-and-private-sector. Last visited 14 Feb. 2016.

levels will be contained by reducing the losses in the production, transportation and distribution of water and through stricter enforcement of regulations.

- *Private Sector*: The government has made increasing the contribution and productivity of the private sector one of the principal objectives of the national development plan.

The government expects these measures to increase the level of local content in goods and services provided to the government by the private sector. This, in turn, should boost the private sector's role in creating jobs – particularly for Saudi nationals, which is an overarching aim of the government's medium-term plan.[48]

On 1 December 2005, the country joined the WTO. In order to meet its obligations towards the WTO, Saudi Arabia underwent an over whole of its intellectual property protection regime. This resulted in the revision of most existing intellectual property regimes and the introduction of new protection regimes. Three government authorities have authority to protect and enforce IPRs in Saudi Arabia today: the Ministry of Commerce and Industry for Trademarks, the Ministry of Culture and Information for Copyright, and King Abdul Aziz City for Science and Technology for patents (KACST).

Notably, the General Directorate for Intellectual Property which is based within the Saudi Ministry of Commerce and Industry is the department tasked with monitoring and following up on all developments and activities in the field of IPRs locally and globally. In order to be able to implement this it may suggest any of the following actions:[49]

(1) Proposing an annual plan to support and encourage the innovation and creativity of individuals and institutions in the Kingdom and to encourage and attract foreign investment.
(2) Mobilizing efforts to achieve this in coordination with all relevant authorities, taking into account the other parties actions in this regard and that it should be an integral work of support to benefit the work.
(3) Inviting the Standing Committee for Intellectual Property, which was established by Royal Order No. 1239 dated 22 June 1995, to discuss the annual plan and any emerging issues. If the committee sees fit to also invite representatives of other relevant bodies and submit findings including recommendations.
(4) Submitting the plan and any recommendations the committee or administration sees fit to take necessary guidance, and submit what is necessary to His Majesty for direction.
(5) Conducting field and technical studies related to work in this area.
(6) Activating the technical cooperation programme between the Kingdom and the World Intellectual Property Organization (WIPO) in all aspects of technical advice, training, workshops and seminars and ensure the participation of representatives of relevant government agencies.
(7) Taking advantage of all opportunities for technical cooperation and training at the international level, both from international organizations such as WTO and

48. *Ibid.*
49. According to the Ministry website available at, http://www.mci.gov.sa/en/Agencies/TechnicalAffairs/Departments/Sharq/Pages/default.aspx.

World Customs Organization and Interpol and those available from friendly countries, conferences and seminars related to IPRs and to invite government agencies concerned to participate in and benefit from them.

On the other hand, the Standing Committee on IPRs is the committee which was established by the Royal Decree No. 1239 dated 22 June 1995. It comprises of representatives from the ministries of: Commerce and Industry, Culture and Information, Foreign Affairs, Petroleum and Mineral Resources, Finance (Customs Department), Bureau of Grievances and King Abdul Aziz City for Science and Technology.[50] Responsibilities, the Committee's most important tasks since the Kingdom's membership in the WTO, are the following:[51]

(1) Representing the Kingdom in the Agreement on Trade-Related Aspects of Intellectual Property Rights (TRIPS) Council of the World Trade Organization (WTO), which in addition to many of its considered topics, reviewed the IPRs systems in the Kingdom in February 2007 and like other countries that have preceded it in the WTO membership passed it.
(2) Participating in the negotiations for comprehensive trade liberalization by the WTO's 'Doha Development Agenda', in respect to its field of specialization.
(3) Participating in meetings of various committees of the WIPO to draft agreements that specialize in all branches of this area and the development of previous agreements and mechanisms of action in accordance to the rapid technical and scientific progress in this age.
(4) Studying the possibility of the Kingdom's participation in some of the WIPO agreements which the committee considers important or are imposed by public interest including economic and trade relations with major trading partners.
(5) Monitoring the Technical Cooperation Programme with WIPO which includes technical advice and ongoing technical training and participating in seminars and conferences held in the Kingdom.
(6) Preparing periodic reports on the achievements of agencies and their efforts to combat abuse and the elimination of piracy in this area and using them to refute accusations of production companies. It also seeks to remove the Kingdom from the American 'Special 301' Report which is published in an annual report on behalf of the American Foreign Trade Representatives that impacts trade relations between the two countries and the image of the investment environment in the Kingdom in general.
(7) Following up and studying emerging issues in its area of expertise in accordance to the resolution to form the committee.

50. Headquarters and Chairmanship: It is based at and chaired by the Ministry of Commerce and Industry.

51. According to the Ministry website available at, http://www.mci.gov.sa/en/Agencies/TechnicalAffairs/Departments/Sharq/Pages/default.aspx.

Chapter 1. Copyright and Neighbouring Rights

§1. Sources: Legislation

8. As in the case of the majority of other civil law countries in the Middle East region, the sources of the Saudi copyright protection regime extend to cover a number of fields including legislation, royal decrees, custom, court decisions, Islamic law and *Shariah*, in addition to legal doctrine. However, with similarity with other regional jurisdictions, legislation (in the form of Royal Decrees, Legislations and Regulations) occupies the primary position unlike other sources which are often treated as secondary sources.[52] Primarily, the Saudi Arabian national copyright protection regime has often been subject to the influence of both *Shariah* principles and regional and international treaties and arrangements.

As been discussed elsewhere extensively, legal protections for some form of copyrights have existed in the region for some time. Pre-Islamic era examples are many in this regard, particularly in the area of Arabic poetry and literature through awarding and attributing authors the ownership of their works through the public 'disclosure' and 'recitation' of their poems in social public events and performances in addition to other various works and publications.[53]

The Kingdom of Saudi Arabia was the first GCC country to introduce a copyright law back in 1989.[54] Under the 1989 Saudi Copyright Law, authors of original works of art in literature, science (including computer programs) and culture in general enjoyed legal protection.[55] Rights belonging to the author also included the right to translate, abridge, publish, financially and commercially exploit and reproduce the work.[56] The 1989 Saudi Copyright Law also contained a number of exceptions including educational use, use by public libraries and personal use, etc.[57] The right to financially exploit the work lapses after the period of fifty years from the death of the author or the death of the last author in case of joint works.[58] A protection period of twenty-five years from the date of publication applies to movies, applied artworks and photographs.[59] The 1989 Saudi Copyright Law also had several penalties applicable to cases of copyright infringement.[60]

52. *See* M. El Said, *IPRs in Jordan* (The Netherlands: Kluwer Law International, 2009), M. El Said, *IPRs in Lebanon* (The Netherlands: Kluwer Law International, 2011) and M. El Said, *IPRs in Oman* (The Netherlands: Kluwer Law International, 2013).
53. M. El Said, *The Development of Intellectual Property Protection in the Arab World* (Lewiston: Edwin Mellen Press, 2008).
54. *See* the Saudi Arabian Royal Decree No. M/11 of 1989 Concerning the Protection of Copyrights (hereinafter 'the 1989 Saudi Copyright Law').
55. *See* Art. 3, the 1989 Saudi Copyright Law.
56. *See* Art. 5, the 1989 Saudi Copyright Law.
57. *See* Art. 8, the 1989 Saudi Copyright Law.
58. Article 24.1, the 1989 Saudi Copyright Law.
59. Article 24.2, the 1989 Saudi Copyright Law.
60. *See also* Arts 28–30, the 1989 Saudi Copyright Law.

The 1989 Saudi Copyright Law remained in force until the year 2003, which witnessed the overall revamping of the intellectual property protection regime in the country.[61] Prompted by the country's accession to the WTO, Saudi Arabia introduced a number of intellectual property laws including a copyright law in 2003 as a consequence of the WTO's accession process which was finally concluded in 2005. In accordance with this, Saudi Arabia enacted its most recent Copyright Law by virtue of the Royal Decree No. M/41 of 2.7.1424H (issued 30 August 2003) which went into effect in March 2004 (hereinafter 'the 2003 Saudi Copyright Royal Decree'). The main features of the 2003 Saudi Copyright Royal Decree include:

- more explicit protection for computer software and databases;
- more specific protection for audiovisual works and sound recordings, including protection for a period of fifty years after the first public display or publication;
- legal use of foreign works such as translations and copying was clarified according to the TRIPS Agreement;[62]
- duration of protection of all artistic and literary works is in accordance with the requirements of the Berne Convention; and
- more explicit remedies against the infringement of copyright including border measures and damages.

In addition to the 2003 Saudi Copyright Royal Decree – which is the main statutory source on copyright protection in the country today,[63] there is also the 2004 Implementing Regulations of the Copyright Decree and its subsequent amendment (hereinafter 'the 2004 Implementing Regulations').[64] The 2004 Implementing Regulations contain various provisions related to the processes and procedures mentioned under the 2003 Saudi Copyright Royal Decree.

The inauguration of the 2003 Saudi Copyright Royal Decree represented a major step towards upgrading the country's copyright protection and enforcement regime due to its general compliance with the TRIPS Agreement standards of protection.[65]

The 2003 Saudi Copyright Royal Decree is divided into seven chapters in addition to the definitions section. Chapter I deals with the issue of 'Protected Works'; Chapter II deals with 'Owner's Rights'; Chapter III is dedicated to the subject of 'Rights'; Chapter IV covers the issue of 'Lawful Use' of the Rights; Chapter V is concerned with the 'Scope and Duration of the Protection' of the Rights; Chapter VI provides a number of special provisions dealing with issues including the issue of 'Infringements

61. D. Price, *The Development of Intellectual Property Regimes in the Arabian Gulf States: Infidels at the Gates* (New York: Routledge, 2009).
62. Notably, Art. 1 of the 2003 Royal Decree defines copying as 'Producing a copy or more of one of the literary, artistic or scientific works on a material means, including any sound or visual recording.'
63. The 2003 Saudi Copyright Royal Decree shall supersede the 1989 Saudi Copyright Law issued by the Royal decree No. M/11, dated 19/05/1410 H.
64. Issued by The Minister of Culture and Information's Decision No. (1688/1) dated 10/04/1425H (29 May 2004) and amended by His Excellency's Decision No. (1640) dated 15/05/1426H (22 Jun. 2005).
65. *See* generally M.B. Al Fuzan, *Netham Hemayet Hukok El Muelf*, 1st edn. (Al Riyadh: Maktabet Al Kanon Wa El Ektesad, 2009).

and Penalties' and finally Chapter VII is devoted to deal with 'General and Closing Provisions'.

9. The enforcement of copyright protection in Saudi Arabia is affiliated with the Ministry of Culture and Information.[66] In relation to this, the General Department of Copyrights undertakes the following activities:[67]

(1) Protection of artistic works.[68]
(2) Protection of computer programs.
(3) Control and investigation.
(4) International organizations, training and public relations.

Moreover, the police, public prosecutors, the judiciary, customs officials and employees of the Department of Copyright at the Ministry of Culture and Information nominated to this effect are the competent authorities responsible for enforcing the copyright law and combating piracy in the country. In addition to this, some authorities and administrative procedures are also affiliated with the Ministries of Culture and Information,[69] Justice and Higher Education. As of this date, there are no specialized copyright courts in the country.

There are other laws and regulations pertaining to some anti-piracy measures and copyright enforcement in Saudi Arabia. Examples of these include the following laws and regulations:

(1) Law of King Fahd National Library (promulgated by Royal Decree No. M/9 of 13/5/1410H (12 December 1989), as amended by Royal Decree No. M/2 of 24/3/1417 (9 August 1996).
(2) Anti-Cyber Crime Law (promulgated by Royal Decree No. M/17 on 26 March 2007).
(3) Electronic Transaction Protection Law (promulgated by Royal Decree No. M/8 of 26 March 2007).
(4) Law of Criminal Procedure (promulgated by Royal Decree No. M/39 of 16 October 2001).
(5) The GCC Unified Customs Law No. 10 of 2003.

10. Saudi Arabia has signed and ratified several international and regional trade agreements which contain reference to copyright and other related rights protection. The country's approach is therefore in line with the prevailing practise in the region which follows the principle of the supremacy of international agreements and therefore

---

66. *See* the Saudi Arabian Ministry of Culture and Information, available at http://www.info.gov.sa/copyrights/English/eDefault.aspx.
67. The competent department in the Ministry which exercises the powers granted to the Ministry by the provisions of the Law and these Regulations, including the technical and administrative tasks necessary for implementing their provisions.
68. Article 1 of the 2003 Saudi Copyright Royal Decrees defines artistic works as 'Works which appeal to the sense of beauty of the public, such as painting, colouring, movement, sound, picture, viewing or music.'
69. For more on the Ministry of Culture and Information *see* http://www.info.gov.sa/Sectors.aspx.

treaties and agreements signed by the country are directly applicable within the national legal framework as part of its legal system. The following international copyright-related agreements may be mentioned in this regard:

(1) The Stockholm Agreement of 1967, creating the WIPO, joined in May 1982.
(2) The Berne Convention on the Protection of Literary and Artistic Works joined in March 2004.
(3) The Convention for the Safeguarding of the Intangible Cultural Heritage joined in April 2008.
(4) The Protocol to the Convention for the Protection of Cultural Property in the Event of Armed Conflict joined in February 2008.
(5) The Second Protocol to the Hague Convention of 1954 for the Protection of Cultural Property in the Event of Armed Conflict joined in February 2008.
(6) The Universal Copyright Convention as revised on 24 July 1971, with Appendix Declaration relating to Article XVII and Resolution concerning Article XI, joined in July 1994.
(7) The Universal Copyright Convention of 6 September 1952, with Appendix Declaration relating to Article XVII and Resolution concerning Article XI, joined in July 1994.
(8) Convention concerning the Protection of the World Cultural and Natural Heritage (7 November 1978).
(9) Convention on the Means of Prohibiting and Preventing the Illicit Import, Export and Transfer of Ownership of Cultural Property (8 December 1976).
(10) Convention for the Protection of Cultural Property in the Event of Armed Conflict (20 April 1971).
(11) The Arab Agreement for the Protection of Authors' Rights, acceded to in 1986.
(12) Convention on the Protection of the Underwater Cultural Heritage, acceded to on 13 February 2016.

Before discussing in more detail the substantive requirements, subject matter and contents of the 2003 Saudi Copyright Royal Decree and its implementing regulations, it is noteworthy to make reference to the 2003 Saudi Copyright Royal Decree's scope of applicability. In this context, Article 18 of the 2003 Saudi Copyright Royal Decree states that the provisions of the law shall cover the following:

- First: Works of Saudi and non-Saudi authors published, produced, performed or displayed for the first time in the Kingdom of Saudi Arabia and works of Saudi authors published, produced, performed or displayed for the first time outside the Kingdom.

- Second: Works of broadcasting organizations and of producers of sound recordings and performers.[70]
- Third: Works copyrighted pursuant to international agreements or treaties for protection of copyright to which the Kingdom is a party.

§2. Subject Matter of Protection

I. Different Categories of Protected Works

11. Chapter 1 of the 2003 Saudi Copyright Royal Decree does not provide a definition of what may constitute a copyright but rather respectively sets out the main categories of copyright subject matter which would enjoy the legal protection in the country. In accordance with this, the 2003 Saudi Copyright Royal Decree states that:

> This Law shall protect the works created in the fields of literature, art and sciences, irrespective of their type, means of expression, importance or purpose of authorship.[71]

Accordingly, the 2003 Saudi Copyright Royal Decree adopts a non-exhaustive approach in dealing with what may constitute a copyrighted work provided that such works are permitted for circulation in the country.[72] Accordingly, Article 2 of the 2003 Saudi Copyright Royal Decree dwells more specifically on the scope of protection by providing examples of types of works which may be subject to legal protection and regardless of their value, type and means of expression or the purpose of their authorship (these are listed under twelve types of works). Based on this, the awarded legal protection shall include the following works in the Kingdom of Saudi Arabia:

(1) Written materials like books, booklets and others.

---

70. Performers are defined under Art. 1 of the 2003 Royal Decree as 'the person who acts, recites, sings or plays roles or participates in performing by any other means in literary or artistic works'. Furthermore, the 2004 Implementing Regulations defines performers as 'Actors, players of musical instruments, singers, dancers, reciters and others who perform an artistic activity of other literary or artistic works in one way or another.' The same article defines broadcasting as 'Transmission of a work, performance or an audio or visual recording to the public, using wires or wireless methods or any other means of transmission, to be received by the public, including transmission via satellite.' Producers are defined under Art. 1 of the 2004 Implementing Regulations as 'A natural or corporate person who undertakes to transform the artistic, audio or audiovisual work into a material means for the purpose of displaying it to the public under its financial responsibility.'

71. Article 1 of the 2003 Saudi Copyright Royal Decree defines a work as any literary, scientific or artistic work.

72. Article 32.1 of the Implementing Regulations states: '*All intellectual works of whatever type whether literary, scientific or artistic shall enjoy protection under the Law and these Regulations if they are permitted for circulation in the Kingdom.*'

(2) Works which are verbally delivered like lectures, speeches, poetry, songs and the like.
(3) Dramatic works, plays, shows and similar presentations which involve motion, sound or both.
(4) Works which are especially prepared for broadcasting or are presented through broadcasting.
(5) Drawings, works of plastic arts, architecture, decorative art and artistic embroidery and the like.
(6) Sound and audiovisual works.[73]
(7) Applied artworks, whether handcrafted or manufactured.
(8) Photographic works and the like.
(9) Illustrations, geographical maps, designs, plans, sketches and sculptured works related to geography, topography, architecture and science.
(10) Three-dimensional works of geography, topography, architecture or science.
(11) Computer programs.
(12) Protection shall include the title of a work, if it is of creative nature and not a common expression indicating the subject matter of the work.

12. In addition, the 2003 Saudi Copyright Royal Decree provides some additional categories which may be subject to copyright protection and are related to derivative works which are in line with the standards of the Berne Convention.[74] Therefore, Article 3 of the 2003 Saudi Copyright Royal Decree states that the following works shall enjoy the protection under this law:[75]

(1) Works of translation.
(2) Works of abridgement, modification, illustration, editing or any other forms of alteration.
(3) Encyclopaedias and anthologies which are deemed creative with respect to the selection of their content or arrangement, whether they are literary, artistic or scientific works.[76]
(4) Compilations of folkloric works and expressions and selections therefrom, if such compilations are creative as to selection or arrangement of their contents.

Notably, the same article further explains that copyright protection enjoyed by the authors of the works mentioned above shall in no way jeopardize the legal protection enjoyed by the authors of the original works.

---

73. Article 1 of the decree defines audio work as: '*Any audio fixation of a specific performance or sound, regardless of the means of fixation. Audio-Visual Work: Any work produced for simultaneous audio and visual use, consisting of a series of related images, accompanied by sound and recorded on an appropriate means and shown by suitable devices.*'
74. A derivative work is a work based on a pre-existing work.
75. Notably, the same article states that the protection, stipulated in the three previous paragraphs shall be without prejudice to any copyright subsisting in the underlying content.
76. Notably, Art. 1 of the 2004 Implementing Regulations defines literary works as 'Works which are expressed in words whatever their content may be, whether written or oral.'

Moreover, the 2004 Implementing Regulations also adds other types to the above works. In this regard, Article 2 of the 2004 Implementing Regulations states that the following shall be among the protected works:

(1) Dramatic works or musicals.
(2) Choreographic and mime works.
(3) Musical compositions with or without words.
(4) Cinematographic works or works expressed by a process analogous to cinematography.
(5) Sculpture, engraving and lithography.
(6) Photographic works or works expressed by a process analogous to photography.

Despite the inclusion of this detailed and wide list of categories, it is noteworthy to state that Article 2 of the 2003 Saudi Copyright Royal Decree contains the essential elements which determine the awarding of copyright legal protection. Accordingly, copyright protection is granted widely to 'works created in the fields of literature, art and sciences, irrespective of their type, means of expression, importance or purpose of authorship'.

From the above, it also appears that copyright legal protection in Saudi Arabia is extended to cover all types of works regardless if they were original and/or derivative ones. The nature, value, purpose, mode, form and importance of such works are irrelevant for the purpose of granting of legal protection in the country. However, in order to determine whether certain subject matter may be legally protected by copyright under the Saudi Legal regime, it is essential to evaluate the subject matter under the substantive requirements of the law in more detail.[77]

13. The Saudi jurisprudence and judiciary has repeatedly reaffirmed that these rights (including literary rights) are in fact personal rights and therefore shall only be attributed to the original author even after the assignment, disposal or sale of such works. Therefore, the original author shall be entitled to prevent and claim damages for any amendment, modification or alteration of the work and any other action which may distort the honour and reputation of the author.

II. Works Excluded of Protection

14. Article 4 of the 2003 Saudi Copyright Royal Decree explicitly excludes certain types of works from the scope of legal protection. Generally speaking and in line with established legal norms and principles, legal protection shall not cover mere ideas, procedures, working methods, mathematical concepts, principles, discoveries and data. In addition and more specifically under the Saudi legal regime, legal protection shall not be extended to cover the following:

(1) Laws and judicial judgments, decisions of administrative bodies, international agreements and all official documents, as well as the official translations thereof, subject to the provisions concerning the circulation of these documents.

77. Al Fuzan, *ibid.*

(2) What is published in newspapers, magazines and periodicals, or broadcasted in daily news or news-like events.
(3) Ideas, procedures, work methods, concepts of mathematical sciences, axioms and abstract facts.

Based on the above, it has been established under both court decisions and jurisprudence that copyright protection does not extend to ideas, but rather is awarded to the expression of the idea itself which is subject to the legal protection.[78] Additionally, it has been established for long by jurists that courts will not attempt to evaluate the financial value, artistic, or scientific merit of the work.

15. In general, the rationale behind excluding some of the above works – which as mentioned is common in most legal jurisdictions – is attributed to the perseveration of the state's sovereignty, social policy and public interest.[79] In addition, the need to ensure that a balance between the rights of holders and consumers is legally, administratively and institutionally preserved also forms part of such logic. However, it appears that Saudi Arabia opted for a more conservative and restricted approach with relation to the exceptions in comparison with other countries in the region which included more detailed grounds in the case of similar exceptions.[80]

III. Special Categories of Work

16. The 2003 Saudi Copyright Royal Decree contains reference to a number of specific works which may be protected under copyright law subject to the fulfilment of a number conditions and requirements.[81] However, the Saudi legal regime also extends the reach of legal protection to a number of specific works. The following may be mentioned in this regard.

A. Computer Software and Databases

17. Computer programs and databases are protected under the Saudi legal regime by virtue of Article 2 and the 2004 Implementing Regulations. Based on this, Article 10 of the 2004 Implementing Regulations provides that the original databases shall be protected by reason of the selection and arrangement of their contents as intellectual creations. This protection shall not extend to the data or the materials themselves.

Thereunder, the software per se is not patentable. However, it can be protected under the Saudi legal regime only in the case where the invention is a hardware accompanied with its operation software. Notably and despite various initiatives by

78. For a comparison of with the situation in other countries in the region *see* M. El Said, *IPRs in Jordan* (The Netherlands: Kluwer Law International, 2009) and M. El Said, *IPRs in Lebanon* (The Netherlands: Kluwer Law International, 2011).
79. For a discussion on public interest under Saudi law *see* Afida Mastura Muhammad Arif, 'An analysis of Copyright Protection in Saudi Arabia', *International Journal of Law and Management* 56, no. 1 (2014): 38–49.
80. El Said, *IPRs in Jordan* and *IPRs in Lebanon.*
81. *See* the discussion under ss I and II above.

the government in this field, software piracy remains a major problem in Saudi Arabia. Al Jabre explains, 'Between 2003 and 2006, losses due to piracy rose from $125 million to about $175 million. Software users acquired $449 million worth of unlicensed software in 2011. That number rose marginally from 2010 when the commercial value of unlicensed software totalled $414 million [4]. However, looking back to 2007 the value of unlicensed software was $170 million, which grew to $272 and $304 million in 2008 and 2009 respectively. The large disparity between 2007 and 2011 may be attributed to a number of factors including the rise in the market value of software, the increase in the number of computer users and the number of products available on the "black market".'[82]

B. Others

18. Different types of intellectual works have created specific legal issues, within the framework of copyright law, either because of their nature or as a result of changes in the economic value of such works. The following are of some relevance to Saudi Arabia that includes:

(1) Folklore. The 2003 Saudi Copyright Royal Decree defines folklore to mean all literary, artistic or scientific works which are assumed to have been created on Saudi territory and transmitted from one generation to the next and constitutes part of the traditional Saudi cultural and artistic heritage.[83] In addition, Article 7 of the 2003 Saudi Copyright Royal Decree states that folklore shall be the property of the state, and the Ministry of Culture and Information shall exercise the copyright pertaining thereto. In addition, the importation or distribution of copies of folkloric works, copies of their translations or others which are produced outside the Kingdom without a licence from the Ministry of Culture and Information shall be prohibited.
Moreover, Article 3 of the 2004 Implementing Regulations reiterates the above by stating that the Saudi Folklore shall be a public property of the state and no one may develop or amend it except with the prior approval of the Ministry of Culture and Information. In addition, the 2004 Saudi Implementing Regulations provides that any expression that reflects the traditional heritage which started or continued in the Kingdom of Saudi Arabia shall be deemed part of the Saudi national Folklore, especially if it includes any of the following expressions:

(a) Folk expressions, such as folk tales, riddles, puzzles, folk poems and other similar traditional expressions.
(b) Musical expressions, such as chants, songs, folk songs whether recited or accompanied by music.
(c) Expressions by movement, such as folk dances, artistic formations and those performed in festivals.

82. Abdulaziz Al Jabre, 'Understanding Software Piracy in Saudi Arabia and the Need for Change', *Journal of Emerging Trends in Computing and Information Sciences* 3, no. 11 (November 2012): 1517.
83. The 2003 Saudi Copyright Royal Decree, Art. 1.

(d) Plastic expressions, such as drawings by lines, colours, engraving and sculpture, pottery, products made from wood and iron and the like, or what is added to them of different figurations such as inscription and drawing, handcrafted bags, needle works, carpets and clothes and the like.

Moreover, the Regulations state that the importation of copies of Saudi Folklore works, copies of their translations or others, which are produced outside the Kingdom shall be prohibited except with the prior approval of the Ministry of Culture and Information.

(2) Adaptations. In cases where the adaptation is based on a protected copyrighted work, it is essential that the written consent or authorization of the owner of such copyright is granted. Thus, the scope of the adaptation shall be allowed to the extent granted under the awarded consent. If consent and authorization are granted, the co-author shall have the same legal rights as those awarded to the author.
(3) Authorization to translate. This act related to copyrighted works which shall be allowed where the prior consent or authorization of the owner is granted for such a purpose. Within this context the translation of the work into other languages, quoting or altering it and the redistribution of the sound or visual material shall be allowed.
(4) The right to convey and/or communicate the work to the public by any possible means including but not limited to public performance of the work, the communication to the public of the work and the broadcasting of the work or data transmission networks.
(5) Reproduction. The reproduction of the work in any format or manner available.
(6) Disposition. The disposition of the original or a copy of the work to the public through sale or other transfer of ownership.
(7) Rental rights. Rental of the original or a copy of the author's work embodied in sound recording, of his/her movie work, or computer program, for commercial purposes is covered under this activity.

§3. CONDITIONS OF PROTECTION

I. Formal Requirements

19. The general rule under the Saudi legal regime as in many other jurisdictions in the region is that copyright legal protection is granted by virtue of the creation of an original work, and thus there is no need for the work to be deposited or registered with any national authority or agency in order to be awarded legal protection. Accordingly, deposition under the Saudi Arabian legal regime – as in the case of other countries in the region such as Jordan, Oman, Lebanon and Egypt –[84] is only one method of proving the ownership and validity of the copyrighted work manifested in the legal protection for the work and its owner. This is established under the prevailing jurisprudence of

84. El Said, *IPRs in Jordan* and *IPRs in Lebanon.*

the country. However, in certain cases, non-compliance with deposition may result in penalties. Based on this, deposition may take place at the King Fahad National Library.[85]

II. Substantive Requirements

20. It has often been argued that 'Copyright is not about ideas, but about the way in which they are expressed'[86] Accordingly, the subject matter of copyright legal protection in Saudi Arabia as elsewhere is the manner of expression of an idea and not the idea itself. Thus if eligible for legal protection, an idea may be subject to legal protection under another type of intellectual property such as patents, utility models or industrial or layout-designs but not under copyright law.

Most legal doctrines and international treaties do not define what is precisely needed in order to award legal copyright protection to a certain work thus leaving considerable discretion for national courts and legislators to establish and implement such criteria. What is often needed under the majority of legal doctrines in this regard is the requirement of originality. This requirement dictates that the work must be new and created by the author himself/herself and not by someone else. However, the depth of such requirement will often depend on the type of the created work. In practice, the implications of the lack of unified criteria applicable to all creations also means that each type of creation shall have its own emphasis and will often be evaluated on a case-by-case basis.

In line with this, Article 1 of the 2004 Implementing Regulations defines innovation – as in creativity – as 'The personal style displayed by the author in his work, which makes the work distinctive and novel and presents the work through the elements of the concept displayed or the method employed to present the concept.' The difference between the requirement of originality and novelty (or the distinctiveness as referred to under the Saudi legal regime) is of some importance in this regard. While the latter is essential in the case of awarding a patent, it may not have such significance in the case of awarding legal protection to a copyrighted work particularly since an artist may create an engraving of something which already exists in nature.

The 2003 Saudi Copyright Royal Decree excludes several substantive requirements from the scope and ambit of legal protection. Accordingly, the value, type, way of expression or purpose of the work are all irrelevant to define copyright protection as long as the work is original and contains an element of creativity. Based on this, courts and other administrative authorities do not have the right to evaluate the financial, monetary, social, purpose and value of the produced work. What they may end up doing is determining the amount of damage suffered as a result of infringement, and not the value of the work itself.

85. For more *see* http://www.kfnl.gov.sa/En/About/Pages/Standards.aspx. For more specific legal requirements *see* Law of King Fahd National Library (promulgated by Royal Decree No. M/9 of 13/5/1410H (12 Dec. 1989), as amended by Royal Decree No. M/2 of 24/3/1417 (9 Aug. 1996).

86. P. Torremans, *Holyoak and Torremans Intellectual Property Law* (New York: Oxford University Press, 2005), 171.

In addition, the medium or manner by which the work is expressed is also irrelevant to grant legal protection. If the nature of the work permits it, a given work may be expressed in various manners and ways such as orally, in writing, electronically, pictorially, or even by public or private performance. Thus, all of these expressions shall receive some form of legal copyright protection in the country.

Finally, there is no limitation as to the types of intellectual work which may be protected under copyright law. In accordance with this, 2003 Saudi Copyright Royal Decree provides that a work shall include 'literary, scientific or artistic production irrespective of its type, importance, form of expression or purpose'. As long as works are created in the areas identified above, then legal protection shall be awarded without having the need to create them in a special manner, shape or format. Consequently, if in the future technological advances allow for the development of new types of works, then such works may be awarded copyright legal protection in accordance with the requirements and stipulations of the law.

It must be highlighted that – as it is the case in other legal jurisdictions in the region – the Saudi Arabian courts and case law has not been heavily involved nor tested with relation to debating issues arising from the various substantive requirements of copyright legal protection.[87]

§4. Ownership

I. The Author

21. As a general rule, the author of any work is the original owner of the copyright on such work. In pursuant to Article 1 of the 2004 Implementing Regulations, the author is defined as 'Every person who innovates by his own effort, any of the literary, artistic or scientific works such as the man of letters, the poet, the painter or the musician or any other artist, according to the form of expression.' In addition, the 2003 Saudi Copyright Royal Decree explicitly defines the author as the 'person who creates the work'.[88] Based on this, the provided definitions cover widely all types of owners.

Since ownership of an authored work necessitates an intellectual creation arising from a certain human activity, it has been stated that only individual persons may be the original owners of copyrights.[89] This is supported by the fact that the duration of copyright protection under the 2003 Saudi Copyright Royal Decree is calculated on the basis of the life of the author plus fifty years following his/her death.[90]

Before explaining in more details where ownership rests under various works in accordance with the 2003 Saudi Copyright Royal Decree, it is noteworthy to explain that there are some exceptional cases where ownership may be conferred to corporations or other legal entities instead of individuals under the 2003 Saudi Copyright Royal Decree framework. An example of this lies in the case of joint and collective works

87. For more *see* Al Fuzan, *ibid.*
88. The 2003 Saudi Copyright Royal Decree.
89. *See* G. Cabanellas, *IPRs in Argentina* (The Hague: Kluwer Law International, 1997).
90. *See* the 2003 Saudi Copyright Royal Decree, Art. 19.

whereby a group of natural individuals/persons participates in the creation of the work under the direction and/or organization of the collective work of a corporate person.[91]

It is noteworthy to explain that according to the 2003 Saudi Copyright Royal Decree, copyright protection enjoyed by the authors of the derivative works shall in no way jeopardize the protection enjoyed by the authors of the original works.[92]

Moreover, the 2003 Saudi Copyright Royal Decree provides that in the case of an audio or audiovisual works, the person(s) who participated in the creation of the work shall be treated as the author(s) of the work such as the following:[93]

(1) Author of text.
(2) Scenarist.
(3) Dialogue writer.
(4) Director.
(5) Composer.

Article 5.2 of the 2003 Saudi Copyright Royal Decree also provides that in the case of anonymous and pseudonymous works, the publisher whose name appears on the work shall be considered as the representative of the author, if the work is published under a pseudonym or anonymously.

The authorities granted generally to the author's heirs are not absolute in this regard but rather subject to the applicable general rules and principles and or any limitations stipulated by the author. Accordingly, the heirs of the author of any work shall only have the exclusive right of exercising the monetary exploitation rights of that work. Thus, if the author was party to a written contract with a third party during his or her lifetime granting that party the right to exploit the work, then this contract should be carried out as agreed. If more than one author contributed in the creation of the work and one of them passed away without leaving any heir, then his/her share in the work shall pass to the rest of the contributors in the creation equally provided that no written agreement states otherwise.

II. Joint Works: Works Created by Several Persons

22. The 2003 Saudi copyright legal regime contains a number of provisions differentiating between several scenarios in this regard. However, to start with, a joint work is defined under Article 1 of the 2003 Saudi Copyright Royal Decree as any work composed by two or more natural or corporate persons whether the contribution of each is separable or not.

Accordingly, Article 6 of the 2003 Saudi Copyright Royal Decree provides that when two or more persons participate in the authorship of a work in such a way that the contribution of each in the work cannot be separated, they shall all be considered equal partners in the ownership of the work, and none of them may independently exercise the author's rights prescribed by the law, unless otherwise agreed in writing.

91. *Ibid.*, Art. 6.3.
92. *Ibid.*, Art. 3.
93. *Ibid.*, 5.3.

Each of the participants in the authorship shall have the right to protective and summary procedures upon infringement on the work and shall have the right to claim for compensation for his/her share, against the damage he/she has incurred as a result of such infringement.

The 2003 Saudi Copyright Royal Decree further provides that when two or more persons collectively participate in the authorship of a work in such a manner that their contributions to the collective work can be separated, each party shall have the right to individually exploit his/her part, provided that no damage is caused to the exploitation of the collective work, unless otherwise agreed.[94]

Article 6.3 of the 2003 Saudi Copyright Royal Decree provides that a natural or corporate person who directed or organized the creation of such a collective work shall be treated as the owner of the moral and economic rights of the work and hence exercise the copyright accordingly.

More importantly, the protection period for such joint works shall continue for a period of fifty years starting from the date of the death of the last surviving author.[95]

Moreover, Article 8 of the 2004 Implementing Regulations states that a co-author of any work may individually request taking precautionary measures whenever there is an infringement of copyright and may individually claim his/her share of the compensation for harm incurred by him/her. In addition, a co-author may object to any development or modification desired by the majority of partners in the work.

III. Works Made for Hire

23. The 2003 Saudi Copyright Royal Decree does contain specific provisions which states that copyrights created by natural persons working under a work contract for a natural person or legal entity in the course of performing their duties or professional obligations are owned by the employer.[96] Those employers who wish to retain such rights must ensure that assignment agreements are signed by the individuals creating the work to ensure the transfer of copyright to the employer. The assignment should be in writing and explicitly specify the place and duration of the assignment.

---

94. The 2003 Saudi Copyright Royal Decree, Art. 1 defines collective work as: '*The work collectively composed by a group at the instruction of a person, natural or corporate, who undertakes its publication under his name or administration, where the work of the contributors is integrated in the general objective sought by that natural or corporate person, so that no contribution of any of the participants may be separated or singled out.*'
95. *Ibid.*, Art. 19.2.
96. Unlike other jurisdictions in the region including the Omani law. For more *see* M. El Said, *IPRs in Oman* (The Netherlands: Kluwer Law International, 2013).

§5. TRANSFER

I. Assignment of Copyright

24. In general, the Saudi Arabian legal regime grants the author or his/her successor(s) the right to fully or partially assign his/her financial and economic rights in the work to third parties.

In accordance with this, Article 11.1 of the 2003 Saudi Copyright Royal Decree states that copyrights provided for in the Royal Decree shall be transferable, in whole or in part, either through inheritance or by lawful disposal, which shall be recorded in writing and shall limit the scope of the transferred right in terms of both time and place.

Moreover, the Royal Decree includes a number of provisions dedicated to dealing with inheritance of the rights affiliated with the copyright. To start with, Article 11.2 of the 2003 Saudi Royal Decree states that the rights provided for in the Royal Decree shall be passed to the author's heirs, with the exception of performing any amendment to or deletion from the work. Moreover, if the author instructed in his/her will that the publication of his/her work be barred or if he/she specified a date for such publication, his/her will shall be carried out within its limits.[97]

Article 11.4 of the 2003 Saudi Copyright Royal Decree states that if the work is produced by an individual and its author passes away, or it is a joint work and one of the authors passes away with no heirs, his/her share shall be passed to those entitled to it according to the provisions of the Islamic *Shariah.*

Notably, Article 6 of the 2004 Implementing Regulations states that authors of original plastic art and of original musical manuscripts shall have the right to share by a percentage in the returns of any sale transaction of these works, even if they have assigned the ownership of the original copy of their works. Notably, this shall not apply to works of architecture nor to works of applied art.

Moreover, the 2003 Saudi Copyright Royal Decree states that the author is authorized to do so in whatever manner he/she chooses thus giving the author full discretion in this regard. However, the law prohibits others from exercising the copyright without obtaining the written consent of the author or his/her successor(s). As explained elsewhere, it must also be stated that the rights assigned in this regard are the economic and not the moral rights of the author.

Moreover, disposal or assignment by the author of all or part of his/her future works shall be completely null and void in accordance with Article 12 of the 2003 Saudi Copyright Royal Decree.

Finally, Article 14 of the 2003 Saudi Copyright Royal Decree emphasizes the principle of continuity of contracts. Based on this and as expressed earlier, the article provides that the author's heirs are obligated to abide by the contracts concluded by their testator during his/her lifetime, including the rights and obligations of third parties.

97. For the sake of clarity, Art. 1 of the 2004 Implementing Regulations defines publication as 'Transmittance or communication of the work directly or indirectly to the public or making copies or photo copies of it or of any part of it which may be read, viewed, listened to or performed.'

II. Licences

25. The 2003 Saudi Copyright Royal Decree does not include a set of general provisions applicable to copyright licensing. This field is thus governed by two very different types of rules: specific copyright provisions applicable to particular types of licences, and general contract law rules applicable to all types of contracts and therefore also to copyright licences.

Notably, Article 13 of the 2003 Saudi Copyright Royal Decree provides that the rights' owners shall make arrangements for their relations and their rights with the establishments of production, printing, publishing and distribution, broadcasting organizations and other entities licensed to perform their activities, pursuant to certified contracts that specify all rights and obligations of the parties concerned. Establishments of production, printing, publishing and distribution as well as broadcasting organizations and others shall not engage in any activity related to copyright except after concluding a contract with the copyright's owners or their attorney-in-fact, where the rights and obligations of each party shall be specified.[98]

In general, any contract for the exploitation or assignment of economic rights shall be made in writing. The contract shall also stipulate the details of the rights covered by the contract and indicate the duration and location of the licence. In addition, legal capacity is needed for contracts to be valid. Based on this, a contract shall be valid if the parties to the contract were above the age of 18 years old unless otherwise dictated by a legal reason/justification.

§6. Scope of Exclusive Rights

I. Moral Rights

26. Moral rights are considered an important element of copyright protection under any legal framework in any country. The same applies to Saudi Arabia. As often been observed in many other legal jurisdictions, moral rights occupy the first place of any of the rights granted to authors.[99]

Article 8 of the 2003 Saudi Copyright Royal Decree explicitly recognizes protection of moral rights by stating that the author shall enjoy a number of permanent moral rights. According to Article 8.1 of the 2003 Saudi Copyright Royal Decree, moral rights consist of the following four exclusive rights:

(1) Attributing the work to himself or publishing it under a pseudonym or anonymously.
(2) Objecting to any infringement on his/her work and preventing any deletion, change, addition, distortion, corruption or any other form of tampering with the work itself.
(3) Making any amendment to or deletion from his/her work, at his/her discretion.
(4) Withdrawing his/her work from circulation.

98. *See* generally Al Fuzan, *ibid.*
99. *See* Torremans, *Holyoak and Torremans Intellectual Property Law*, 215.

It important to state that these rights are rights which are independent from the author's economic rights and shall be vested with him/her even in case of transfer of such rights takes place.[100]

In addition, Article 5 of the 2004 Implementing Regulations provides that authors of dramatic works, musicals and musical works or their representatives shall have the right to authorize the following:

(1) Acting their works or performing them publicly by all methods or means.
(2) Fixation or transmission of acting and performance of their works to the public by all means.
(3) Translation of their works.

The Saudi Arabian legal framework explicitly provides that these rights are permanent rights of the author and are not subject to waiver or lapse by prescription. Moreover, these rights shall be retained by their owner and shall not be forfeited by granting the right of exploiting the work in any manner.[101]

Moreover, the author's general successor shall enjoy these rights, and the Ministry of Culture and Information shall succeed to these rights in the absence of any heirs or successors to the author.

II. Exploitation Rights

27. There are several exploitation rights with an economic effect (financial rights) stated under the 2003 Saudi Copyright Royal Decree. Accordingly, Article 9 of the 2003 Saudi Copyright Royal Decree provides that the following rights are granted to the author or whoever he/she delegates.

A. Reproduction Right

28. The reproduction (believed to cover the copying and/or printing) right of the author is one of the most universally established legal rights under copyright law. While this generally applies to all types of works, the scope of the right varies from one type of work to another depending on the subject matter of each work.

According to Article 1 of the 2003 Saudi Copyright Royal Decree, copying is 'Producing a copy or more of one of the literary, artistic or scientific works on a material means, including any sound or visual recording.'[102]

Under the 2003 Saudi Copyright Royal Decree, the copyright author shall have the right to printing and publishing the work in a reading format. In addition, the author will have the right to recording it on audio or visual tapes, compact disks or electronic memory or any other means of dissemination.

100. Afida Mastura Muhammad Arif, 'An Analysis of Copyright Protection in Saudi Arabia', *International Journal of Law and Management* 56, no. 1 (2014): 38–49, at 42.
101. The 2003 Saudi Copyright Royal Decree, Art. 8.2-3.
102. In addition, Art. 1 of the 2003 Saudi Copyright Royal Decree defines a copy as the 'the product of any copying, recording, printing, or photocopying of the original work'.

Consequently, no copying or reproduction of the work is legally valid without obtaining the consent and authorization of the copyright owner. Such an authorization is often based on a contractual relationship between the parties. In this regard, infringement takes place whether the copying or reproduction is permanent, transient, or temporary, or not and regardless if the reproduction is undertaken for a commercial or non-commercial purpose.

B. The Alternation, Quotation and Adaptation Right

29. The 2003 Saudi Copyright Royal Decree grants the author of the work the right of adaptation, quotation or alteration to his/her work. This may either be undertaken by the author himself or through authorizing a third party to do so, subject to the copyright owner's consent, in the case of the latter.

C. The Translation Right

30. Article 9 of the 2003 Saudi Copyright Royal Decree gives the author of the work the exclusive right to translate it into another language(s).

D. The Disposition Right

31. The Saudi Arabia legal regime grants the owner of all copyrighted works the right to dispose the original work or issue copies of the work to the public. This gives the owner the right to distribute the work by either selling, communicating and/or distributing it.

E. The Rental Rights

32. Article 9 of the 2003 Saudi Copyright Royal Decree explicitly grants the author the exclusive right to rent the original or copy of the work to the public through sale or other types of transfer of ownership.

In addition and more specifically, Article 9 of the 2004 Implementing Regulations states that copyright owners may rent them in the Kingdom in coordination with the Ministry of Culture and Information, upon obtaining its prior approval and by taking the necessary precautions, such as:

(1) ensuring that there is nothing to prevent renting them;
(2) submitting a list of works to be rented, including an indication of types of rentals for approval;
(3) determining the probable problems and infringements which may result from renting to consider the possibility of avoiding them;
(4) explaining to the targeted public the rental mechanism by the beneficiary;
(5) advertising, at the expense of the copyright owners, the necessary instructions to the targeted public; and
(6) fixing an effective date for the renting.

F. *Performance, Broadcasting and Communication Rights*

33. Article 9 of the 2003 Saudi Copyright Royal Decree grants the owner of the copyright the right to perform the work in public. Communicating the work to the public may take place via any possible means, such as displaying, acting, broadcasting or data transmission networks.

Further, the 2003 Saudi Copyright Royal Decree grants the author the right of communication of his/her work.

Accordingly, all works covered by copyright legal protection in the country may be the subject matter of such a right, within the limits set by the physical or intellectual nature of the work involved. Also, it is believed that all types and means of performance are included within the performing right which includes many rights including exhibitions of artistic works, either by means of the original or through films, television or other means, scenic performances of dramatic, musical, choreographic or theatrical works, in addition to readings and recitals of the works, radio and television transmissions or any other technologically possible way.

In addition, the author is granted the right of communication to the public of the work by any means whatsoever including by broadcasting or through data transmission networks.

In accordance with established principles, performing rights may be assigned or licensed to others. Such assignments or licences may be total or partial by referring to specific types of performances, or to performances directed to a specific public audience. However, compliance with recording requirements should be noted.

Finally, the 2003 Saudi Copyright Royal Decree provides the author with the right for all forms of material exploitation of the work. Based on this, the rights referred to in this section are mere examples and do not represent an exhaustive list.

§7. Limitations or Exemptions to the Scope of Copyright Protection

34. The 2003 Saudi Copyright Royal Decree contains reference to a number of limitations and exemptions to the general scope of copyright legal protection. Accordingly, the law contains a number of defences under which the copyrighted work will not be infringed upon if used thus rendering the allegedly infringing act a permitted one. These are referred to as 'lawful use' defences under the Saudi legal regime.

The rationale behind exempting these exceptions and defences from protection is clear. Thus, they are meant to restore the balance between the rights of copyright owners and the public by restricting the exclusive and monopolistic rights awarded to copyright holders and owners. These defences and exemptions are also recognized under international law and agreements including the TRIPS Agreement itself.[103]

Under Chapter 4, Article 15 of the 2003 Saudi Copyright Royal Decree contains several defences and exceptions which may be applied in this regard. However it must

103. TRIPS Agreement, Art. 13 states: 'Members shall confine limitations or exceptions to exclusive rights to certain special cases which do not conflict with a normal exploitation of the work and do not unreasonably prejudice the legitimate interests of the right holder.'

be explained that such works and productions are in fact works which are legitimately and legally protected under the copyright law; however, their use in the manner and in accordance with the conditions stipulated under the terms of the copyright law does not constitute infringement as such.

Notably, Article 15 of the 2003 Saudi Copyright Royal Decree lists twelve situations where the use of the copyrighted work, in its original language or in translation, shall be lawful without obtaining the permission of the copyright owner. Based on this, the following exceptions are explicitly mentioned under the 2003 Saudi Copyright Royal Decree.[104]

I. Private and Personal Use

35. Article 15.1 of the 2003 Saudi Copyright Royal Decree allows individuals to obtain copies of the work for the purposes of personal or private use only without the need to obtain the consent or authorization of the copyright owner and without any compensation. Some general points about what may constitute personal use may be found under Article 12 of the 2004 Implementing Regulations, which explains that it shall be deemed within the scope of personal use any use of intellectual works for personal use only, such as reproducing the work for the purpose of preserving the original copy, for writing on the reproduced copy, for translating some paragraphs or writing comments which expresses personal opinion.

Notably, the 2003 Saudi Copyright Royal Decree excludes computer software, software, audio and audiovisual works from the scope of this exemption. These do not fall under the scope of this exemption.

II. Educational Use Purposes

36. Article 15.3 of the 2003 Saudi Copyright Royal Decree permits to the extent justified by the purpose the use of the work by way of clarification for educational purposes, within the limits justified by the intended objective, or making a copy or two for public libraries or non-commercial documentation centres in accordance with the following conditions:

- The work shall not be for the purposes of commercial activities or for profit.
- The copying shall be restricted to the requirements of activities.
- The copying shall not impair the material benefit of the work.
- The work is out of print or is lost or damaged.

Moreover, Article 15.9 of the 2003 Saudi Copyright Royal Decree states that the copying of short quotations from published works, drawings, pictures, designs or maps in school books prepared for educational curricula or in books of history, literature

104. Article 15 of the 2003 Saudi Copyright Royal Decree states that the 2004 Implementing Regulations shall detail the circumstances required for these exceptions to apply.

and art, provided that copying is within the limits of necessity and that the title of the work and the name of the author are mentioned.

In addition, the citing parts of scientific articles and works by research institutions for their internal use or to fulfil the requirements of those who are conducting studies and research, provided that the source mentioned shall also be permissible.[105]

From the above, it becomes clear that the educational use exception stated under Article 20 of the 2003 Saudi Copyright Royal Decree is aimed towards wider usage of the work, with focus on the institutional dimension.

III. Computer Programs Reproduction

37. Article 15.12 of the 2003 Saudi Copyright Royal Decree provides that it shall be allowed to make one reserve copy of computer programs for the persons possessing the original copy for the purpose of protecting the original, while keeping the original with the user, to show upon request.

IV. Quotation Rights

38. The 2003 Saudi Copyright Royal Decree under Article 15.2 allows the work to be quoted by another. The article states in this regard that the quotation of passages from the work in another work shall be allowed provided that such quotation is consistent with the conventional practice and within the limits justified by the intended objective, and provided that the source and name of author shall be mentioned in the work where the quotation is cited. This shall also apply to journalistic summaries abstracted from newspapers and periodicals.

V. Speeches, Ceremonies and Public Performances

39. Article 15.6 of the 2003 Saudi Copyright Royal Decree also states that the copying of public speeches, lectures, judicial proceedings or any other similar works made in public, if such copying is made by the media, provided that the name of the author is clearly mentioned. The author shall retain the right to publish such works in the manner he sees fit.

In addition, music playing, acting, performing or showing any work, after publication, by government troupes or public corporate entities or school theatre shall be allowed, as long as such playing, performance or acting does not lead to direct or indirect financial gains.[106]

105. The 2003 Saudi Copyright Royal Decree, Art. 15.11.
106. The 2003 Saudi Copyright Royal Decree, Art. 15.8.

VI. News Reporting, Current News and Articles in Newspapers

40. Article 15 of the 2003 Saudi Copyright Royal Decree provides for a number of provisions dealing with the coverage of news and news reporting. Based on this, the following shall be allowed:

- The citing or copying articles published in newspapers or periodicals dealing with current subjects or broadcast works of similar nature, provided that the source and name of the author, if known, are clearly given.
- The copying of any broadcast work that may be viewed or listened to during presentation of current events by means of still or motion pictures, provided that copying remains within the intended objective with the source clearly given.

Moreover, the 2004 Implementing Regulations also explicitly provides that news reports and daily news facts are excluded from the copyright protection in the country.

VII. Broadcasting Rights

41. Article 15.7 of the 2003 Saudi Copyright Royal Decree provides that the production of temporary recordings by broadcasting organizations and through their own means – without impairing the author's copyright – in one copy or more for any protected work, for which they are licensed to broadcast and show shall be permissible, provided that all the copies be destroyed within a period not exceeding one year from the date of their preparation, or a longer period agreed to by the author. A copy of this recording may be kept with official archives, if the recording is a unique documentary work.

VIII. Photographs and Pictures

42. The 2003 Saudi Copyright Royal Decree states that the taking/capturing of new photographs of any previously photographed object or work and publishing these pictures, even if the new pictures have been taken from the same vantage point and under the same circumstances of said pictures shall be permissible and will not constitute any infringement of the copyrighted work.

IX. Prohibited Use of Certain Types of Works

43. Article 17 of the 2003 Saudi Copyright Royal Decree states that whoever produces pictures shall not publish, display or distribute the originals or copies thereof without permission of the individuals pictured or their heirs. This provision shall not apply if the pictures were published on the occasion of public events, if they are pictures of officials or public figures, or if publication is permitted by public authorities in the service of public interest. The person represented in the picture may give permission for its publication in newspapers, magazines and the like, even without the permission of photographer. Such provisions shall apply to the picture, regardless of the way the picture has been produced. Only the author shall have the right to publish his/her letters. However, this right shall not be exercised without the permission of the addressee, if publication may harm him/her.

The above exception is an interesting one as it appears to aim towards creating a balance between copyrights and privacy rights in the country.

Notably, the law neglected regulating copyright matters under some of the modern techniques in this regard such as the Internet.[107]

§8. Duration of Protection

44. Chapter 5 of the 2003 Saudi Copyright Royal Decree deals with the term and duration of protection of copyrights in the country. According to Article 19.1 of the 2003 Saudi Copyright Royal Decree, the duration of legal protection granted under the law to the economic rights of the author, shall be the life of the author plus fifty years following his/her death. Notably, this is in line with the protection term stipulated under the TRIPS Agreement.[108]

In the case of a joint authorship, the term of protection shall be the same period computed from the date of the death of last surviving joint author. Should one of the authors die without leaving heirs, his/her share shall pass to the co-authors or to their heirs, unless stated or agreed otherwise.[109]

Moreover, in the case of sound works, collective works, audiovisual works, films, computer programs, the term of protection shall be fifty years starting from the date of the first show or publication of the work, regardless of republication.[110]

In the case of corporate entity, Article 19.3 of 2003 Saudi Copyright Royal Decree states that the protection period for works where the author is a corporate entity, or if his/her name is unknown, shall be fifty years from the date of the first publication of the work. If the name of the author becomes known before the end of the fifty years, the duration of protection shall be the period specified in Article 19.1 of the 2003 Saudi Copyright Royal Decree.

However, the 2003 Saudi Copyright Royal Decree provides some special periods of protection for certain types of copyrighted works. An example of this is related to the case where the work consists of several parts or volumes, published separately or over a period of time, then the protection period for each part or volume shall be

107. *See* Mohammed Barak Al Fouzan, Netham Hemayet Hukok Al Mualef fi al Mamlaka al Arabia al Saudia, Al Kanon wa Al Ektsad Library, Riyadh, Saudi Arabia, first edition 2009, at 402.

108. The TRIPS Agreement, Art.12 states that: '*Whenever the term of protection of a work, other than a photographic work or a work of applied art, is calculated on a basis other than the life of a natural person, such term shall be no less than 50 years from the end of the calendar year of authorized publication, or, failing such authorized publication within 50 years from the making of the work, 50 years from the end of the calendar year of making.*'

109. The 2003 Saudi Copyright Royal Decree, Art. 19.2.

110. *Ibid.*, Art. 19.

considered an independent work for the purposes of the computation of its protection period.[111]

The 2003 Saudi Copyright Royal Decree also provides protection for some specific types of works. According to Article 19.5 of the 2003 Saudi Copyright Royal Decree, the protection period for sound works, audiovisual works, films, collective works and computer programs is fifty years from the date of the first show or publication of the work, regardless of republication.[112]

In addition, the 2003 Saudi Copyright Royal Decree contains reference to the protection of applied art and photographs. Accordingly, the protection period for applied art (either handcrafted or manufactured) and photographs shall be twenty-five years of the date of publication. Computation of the period starts in this case on the date of the first publication of the work, regardless of republication.

In addition, Article 19 of the 2003 Saudi Copyright Royal Decree provides that the protection period for broadcasting organizations shall be twenty years from the date of the first transmission of programmes or broadcast materials. Moreover, the protection period for the producers of sound recordings and performers shall be fifty years from the date of performance or its first recording, as the case may be.

In addition, the 2004 Implementing Regulations provides a number of cases related to the calculation of the term of protection. Article 33 of the Implementing Regulations states that musical and cinematographic works shall enjoy protection for fifty years effective from the first production of the work, and the period shall be calculated from the end of the Gregorian year in which it was produced. With relation to computer programs, the protection enjoyed shall be as literary works for a period not less than fifty years from the date of first production if the author is a corporate person or is anonymous. Finally, protection period of computer programs where the author is a natural person shall be in accordance with the protection specified for other literary works.

In relation to this, Article 1 of the 2003 Saudi Copyright Royal Decree defines publication as the 'making of copies of a work to meet the public need'.

The 2003 Saudi Copyright Royal Decree also deals with the duration of protection awarded to moral rights. Accordingly, Article 8 of the 2003 Saudi Copyright Royal Decree states that the moral rights provided for are permanent rights – perpetual in other words – of the author and are not subject to waiver or lapse by prescription.

111. *Ibid.*, Art. 19.4.

112. However, some variations and exceptions do exist. Art. 19.1(6) of The 2003 Saudi Copyright Royal Decree distinguishes between the main corpus of artistic works and photographs and works of applied arts. It extends to photographs and works of applied arts protection for a period of only of twenty-five years, which is actually consistent with the standards set by TRIPS Art. 12 and Berne Convention Art. 7.4. Other states do not bother to make the Saudi or TRIPS/Berne distinction between these and other literary or artistic works, thereby neatly avoiding the necessity of otherwise defining works of applied articles and distinguishing them from other works. For more *see* D. Price, 'Politics, Piracy and Punishment: Copyright Protection in the Arabian Gulf', *The Journal of World Intellectual Property* 14, no. 3–4 (2011): 276, at 282.

Also, the 2003 Saudi Copyright Royal Decree provides that the term of protection for the economic copyrights, shall be the life of the author and fifty years starting following the author's death.[113]

Before moving on to discuss the issue of neighbouring rights protection under the Saudi legal regime, it is noteworthy to mention that the 2003 Saudi Copyright Royal Decree verifies that literary, artistic and scientific works, acoustic recordings and broadcasting programmes published before the date whereby the 2003 Saudi Copyright Royal Decree becoming effective, pursuant to the periods specified in Article 19 of the 2003 Saudi Copyright Royal Decree, shall be protected, provided that the protection period under the previous law has not expired and that protection was not terminated in the countries of origin which are parties with the Kingdom of Saudi Arabia to international agreements or treaties for the protection of copyright.

§9. Neighbouring Rights

45. The 2003 Saudi Copyright Royal Decree protects neighbouring rights (some refer to these as moral rights). In short, neighbouring rights refer to these works created by entrepreneurs, such as sound recordings, broadcasts, cable programmes and/or the typographical format of published editions.[114]

Accordingly, Article 8 of the 2003 Saudi Copyright Royal Decree states that the author shall have the right to exercise any of the following:

(a) Attributing the work to himself/herself or publishing it under a pseudonym or anonymously.
(b) Objecting to any infringement on his work and preventing any deletion, change, addition, distortion, corruption or any other form of tampering with the work itself.
(c) Making any amendment to or deletion from his/her work, at his/her discretion.
(d) Withdrawing his work from circulation.

Furthermore, the 2003 Saudi Copyright Royal Decree provides that the moral rights provided for in the Decree are permanent rights of the author and are not subject to waiver or lapse by prescription.

In addition to the above, Article 8.3 of the 2003 Saudi Copyright Royal Decree provides that the moral rights shall be retained by their owner and shall not be forfeited by granting the right of exploiting the work in any manner. Notably, moral rights provided for under the 2003 Saudi Copyright Royal Decree shall pass to the Ministry of Culture and Information upon the death of the owner who has no heirs.

Article 9 of the 2003 Saudi Copyright Royal Decree further elaborates upon the financial and economic rights granted to performers under the Saudi legal framework. Based on this, the author, or whoever he/she delegates, shall enjoy the following (all or partial) exclusive economic rights:

113. *Ibid.*, Art. 19.
114. Lionel Bently & Brad Sherman, *Intellectual Property Law* (New York: Oxford University Press, 2004), 30.

(1) Printing and publishing the work in a reading format; recording it on audio or visual tapes, compact disks or electronic memory or any other means of dissemination.
(2) Translation of the work into other languages, quoting or altering it and the redistribution of the sound or visual material.
(3) Communicating the work to the public via any possible means, such as displaying, acting, broadcasting or data transmission networks.
(4) All forms of material exploitation of the work in general, including permissible commercial rental.

Notably, Article 9.2 of the 2003 Saudi Copyright Royal Decree explains that the authors of artistic and literary works, their performers, composers and producers of sound recordings and broadcasting organizations shall enjoy their financial rights, as prescribed by the 2004 Implementing Regulations. Based on this, Article 7 of the 2004 Implementing Regulations provides that performers and producers of sound recordings shall enjoy the exclusive right to authorize the following:

(1) Public performance of their works, including public recitation by all means or methods.
(2) Transmission and performance of their works to the public by all means.
(3) Fixation of their performance in material form.
(4) Permission to transmit all or part of their works through the Internet.
(5) Permission of audio fixation of their musical work and circulation thereof in specific countries. All copies imported from countries with an exclusive licence, or manufactured without permission from the author, shall be deemed in violation of copyrights and shall be subject to confiscation.
(6) Permission to distribute and rent their original works.
(7) Producers of sound recordings shall have the right to authorize or prohibit direct or indirect reproduction of their sound recordings.

Moreover, the same article provides that broadcasting organizations shall have the right to prohibit any of the following acts if undertaken without their prior explicit authorization:

(1) Fixation and reproduction of broadcasts.
(2) Retransmission by wireless means and communication of materials to the public.
(3) Determining the means of direct broadcast and reception or through receivers or by cable.
(4) Transmission to the public of radio broadcast in public places or through internal wire broadcasts of closed compounds.

Notably, Article 10 of the 2003 Saudi Copyright Royal Decree reaffirms the preservation of the rights of third parties. Within this context, the 2003 Saudi Copyright Royal Decree provides that the author shall refrain from performing such deeds that may prejudice exploitation of the authorized right of third parties. Nevertheless, the author may withdraw his/her work from circulation, amend, delete from or add to it, upon agreement with the party authorized to exercise said right. Should there be no agreement, the author shall be obligated to compensate the said person according to the decision of the committee.[115]

§10. Mandatory Licences

46. The 2003 Saudi Copyright Royal Decree makes reference to an important issue related to mandatory licences (or non-voluntary or statutory licences as some may refer to). Based on this, Article 16 states that the Minister of Culture and Information may grant a publication licence for the work after the lapse of a period to be specified by the 2004 Implementing Regulations for each case, if he/she sees that publication of this work serves public interest, in the following cases:

(1) If no copies of the published work in its original language are made available in the Kingdom by the copyright owner to satisfy the general needs of the public or school or university education, at a price comparable to the price of similar works in the Kingdom, upon the author's declining to make available copies of that work.
(2) If all editions of the original work or its Arabic translation are out of print, with the copyright owner's failure to make it available upon request.
(3) If no translation has been published for this work by the owner of the translation copyright or with his/her permission, provided that the purpose is to make use of this translation in educational curricula.
(4) If the heirs of the Saudi author or his/her successors decline to exercise the rights passed to them pursuant to Article 11 of the 2003 Saudi Copyright Royal Decree within a period of one year of the date of the request, if they have no valid excuse.

Notably, the mandatory licence shall be terminated and will expire upon publication of the work or the translation by the copyright owner, or with his/her authorization.

In general, the Minister of Culture and Information may specify the remuneration to be paid by the licensee to the copyright owners for every licence issued. The copyright owners will, however, have the right to appeal against the decision of the Minister of Culture and Information to the BoGs.[116]

Notably, Article 30 of the 2004 Implementing Regulations contains further details on this issue. Based on this, it states that the provisions regulating the procedures of issuing mandatory licences shall apply to works published for the first time in the Kingdom of Saudi Arabia, and licences shall not be granted before the expiration lapse of a period of three years from the publication date of the edition in question, in accordance with the following procedures:

(1) The Ministry of Culture and Information shall ensure that copies of the works in printed form or reproduced in any similar form are not displayed for sale in the Kingdom by the copyright owner or whoever acts on his/her behalf, or pursuant to permission from him/her, in response to the purposes referred to in Article 16

115. For more *see* Al Fuzan, *ibid.*
116. Article 16.2 and 3.

of the 2003 Saudi Copyright Royal Decree, unless such copies are displayed for sale within a continuous period of not less than six months.

(2) The applicant shall submit proof that he has requested a licence from the copyright owner but failed to obtain it, or that he was unable to find him after exerting necessary efforts.
(3) The applicant shall submit proof that he/she has made such a request to the publisher whose name appears on the work but has not received a response from him/her.
(4) No licence shall be granted unless it is proved that the author is unknown or impossible to contact, and the licence applicant submits the data proving such and submits the necessary guarantees to fulfil the rights of the copyright owner once he applies to claim his/her right, and the Ministry accepts these guarantees.
(5) The licence shall not be granted before the expiration of a period not less than six months from the applicant's attempts to obtain a licence from the author or the publisher.
(6) No licence shall be granted if the author or the publisher reprints his/her work during the six-month period.
(7) No permission shall be granted if the author has withdrawn from circulation all copies of the edition subject of the application.
(8) The permission shall not be granted if it is for pure commercial purposes.

As seen, the Saudi legal regime contains several conditions which should be met in order to issue such a mandatory licence. The stipulated requirements are in compliance with the provisions of the TRIPS Agreement in this regard.

§11. Infringement and Remedies

47. Under the Saudi legal regime, the unjustifiable and wilful infringement of a copyright shall result in a number of provisional, civil, punitive, criminal, border and/or administrative remedies, measures and penalties. According to Article 1 of the 2003 Saudi Copyright Royal Decree, infringement of copyright means any use of the work unauthorized by the copyright owner and conflicting with the instructions of usage determined by the copyright owner, or committing one or more of the violations provided for in the 2003 Saudi Copyright Royal Decree and its Implementing Regulations.

To start with, Article 21 of the 2003 Saudi Copyright Royal Decree contains a number of activities which represent and identifies infringement under the Saudi legal regime. These include the following:

(1) Publishing a work not owned by the publisher, publishing it under the pretence of its ownership or without obtaining a written authorization or a contract with the author of the work, his/her heirs or their representatives.
(2) Amending the contents of a work, its nature, subject or title without the knowledge of the author and his/her prior written consent thereof, whether the amendment is made by the publisher, the producer, distributor or anyone else.

(3) Reprinting the work by the producer, the publisher or the printer without obtaining prior written consent of the copyright owner, or having the documents authorizing the reprint.
(4) Removing any written or electronic information that may lead to forfeiting the owner's copyrights.
(5) Removing and cracking any protective electronic code that guarantees the use of the original copies of the work, such as coding or data recorded by the use of laser or other means.
(6) Using intellectual works commercially through deception, which is not permitted by the owners of the copyright, such as using copied software or receiving coded broadcasting programmes through illegal means.
(7) Manufacturing or importing tools – for the purpose of sale or rental – of any means which facilitate receiving or exploiting works through means other than those determined by owner of the rights.
(8) Copying or photographing parts of a book or a collection of books or parts of any work, with or without compensation, without obtaining the written consent of the copyright owners and the competent authorities of the Ministry, with the exception of cases of lawful copying specified in Article 15 of the 2003 Saudi Copyright Royal Decree.
(9) Import of counterfeit, imitated or copied works.
(10) Keeping non-original works at the commercial establishment, its warehouse or any other facility owned by it, whether directly or indirectly and under any pretence.
(11) Infringement on any of the protected rights specified in 2003 Saudi Copyright Royal Decree or violation of any of its provisions.

In addition to the above, the 2004 Implementing Regulations include a number of provisions related to infringement of copyright as well.[117] In accordance with this, the following activities shall also lead to the infringement of the copyright in the country thus leading to liability as a result:

- Any person who obtains an original copy of any intellectual work and exploits it by means of renting, adaptation or permitting others to copy or reproduce it or any other acts which affect or obstruct the author from exercising his/her rights shall be deemed to have infringed the copyright.
- Firms shall be deemed liable for any violations committed by an employee against any intellectual work if their knowledge or negligence is established, such as keeping forged or copied computer programs, audio or visual tapes, or conducting maintenance on an electronic equipment loaded with forged programs, decoded or similar works.
- Anyone who reproduces, sells, imports, exports, transports, publishes or rents protected works with knowledge of the violation shall be deemed to be committing an infringement of copyright and in violation of the provisions of 2003 Saudi Copyright Royal Decree and the 204 Implementing Regulations.

117. *See* the 2004 Implementing Regulations, Art. 11.

More specifically, the 2004 Implementing Regulations provide some specific provisions applicable in case of exceeding the personal use of literary works which also leads to the infringement of the copyright. In accordance with Article 12 of the 2004 Implementing Regulations, the following shall apply:

(a) Any use beyond the scope of personal use shall be deemed an infringement, such as the following:[118]
- Using and reproducing the work or exploiting it to perform job duties.
- Using the work for commercial or profit-making purposes.
- Using the work in ways not authorized by the author.
- Renting, reproducing or authorizing others to reproduce or adapt the work under the pretext of owning an original copy.
- Any act that hinders the author from exercising his moral or financial right.

Article 12.3 of the 2004 Implementing Regulations further explains that, as understood from Article 9.2 of the 2003 Saudi Copyright Royal Decree, the right of reproduction in any manner or form such as digital reproduction is included.

The 2004 Implementing Regulations further states that reproducing the work to make copies available for commercial exploitation or for selling them to students, to educational institutions or to others shall be deemed an infringement of the copyright in the country.

Moreover, Article 13 of the 2004 Implementing Regulations further includes specific provisions related to infringement of audio, visual and broadcasting works. In line with this, the article states that any use beyond that specified by the owner of audio, visual and broadcasting works shall be deemed an infringement of copyright, such as the following:

(1) Communicating the work to the public without obtaining a prior licence from the owners of the copyright, such as use of radio, music, video or satellite transmission in shops, restaurants, hotels, clubs, hospitals and other similar places where there are frequent visitors or gatherings.
(2) Breaking of protective barriers for the purpose of presenting broadcasting materials through illegal means.
(3) Reproducing broadcast materials for the purpose of presentation, rental or sale.
(4) Adding or removing electronic chips of display equipment for the purpose of making it exceed its manufactured limits in order to infringe the rights of others.

Article 14 of the 2004 Implementing Regulations further includes specific provisions related to infringement of the rights of performance. Based on this, it shall be an infringement of performance rights if the work is performed in school theatres or the like unless the performer of the work obtains the prior approval of the owner(s). Exceptionally, it shall be deemed lawful use in accordance with the substance of Article 15.8 of the 2003 Saudi Copyright Royal Decree if the performance of the work is in

118. Moreover, an employer's ownership of the original copy of the work does not grant him/her the right to reproduce and distribute it among his/her employees, under the pretext of personal use under the Saudi legal regime.

the classroom for the purpose of education. In addition, it shall be deemed an infringement of copyright any reproduction of the work during its performance, such as photographing or recording it for the purpose of exploitation or presentation to the public without the approval of the owner(s) of the right.

Article 15 of the 2004 Implementing Regulations contains reference to decoding activities. In line with this, the article states that it shall be an infringement of copyright law any act resulting in removal of the original precautionary information from the electronic equipment produced by the manufacturer, and any person who facilitates this is deemed to be committing an act of infringement, such as:

(1) Removing or adding electronic or non-electronic devices of display and receiving equipment for the purpose of exceeding the limits designed by the manufacturer.
(2) Cancelling the original programme that operates the display and receiving equipment and loading them with forged programmes for the purpose of exceeding the limits and capabilities for which the equipment is designed.

Infringement against computer programs and games also receives special attention under the 2004 Implementing Regulations. In line with this, Article 16 treats computer programs and games as literary rights and states that it will enjoy protection whether in the source code or in the object code. In addition, it shall be deemed an infringement of copyright any use of the programs different from that specified by the owner of the right, such as:

(1) Reproducing software and game programs.
(2) Renting the software or game programs or licensing their collective use in the absence of documents authorizing the renting person to exercise this right upon obtaining the approval of the Ministry.
(3) Loading the local networks or the equipment with reproduced software.

The 2004 Implementing Regulations include a dedicated article to the liability of maintenance centres in this field as well. Based on this, Article 17 of the 2004 Implementing Regulations provides that the liability of maintenance centres and workshops that provide maintenance service for display and receiving electronic equipment are deemed liable for and in infringement of the copyright if detected to have in their possession decoded equipment or equipment loaded with forged programs, or to use forged programs in carrying out their maintenance works.

Interestingly, the 2004 Implementing Regulations include a dedicated section to the procedures related to the detection and investigation of copyright violations. In accordance with this, Article 18 of the 2004 Implementing Regulations explains that the detection of violations of provisions of the 2003 Copyright Royal Decree and the 2004 Implementing Regulations shall be carried out in any of the following cases:

(1) Pursuant to a complaint or written notice filed by owners of the right or their representatives.
(2) Routine or sudden field visits by the inspectors of the Ministry to public firms and shops that use in their activities any of the intellectual works.

Furthermore, Article 19 of the 2004 Implementing Regulations explains that when performing detection and inspection, detecting officers shall follow a number of procedures as follows:

(1) Entering sites of firms which produce, display, distribute, sell, use or provide maintenance services to any of the protected works, including annexes and affiliates of those sites.
(2) Seizing copies of works and equipment strongly believed to be subject of infringement and of the relevant documents, when necessary, and recording such in the detection record.
(3) Prompt questioning of the violator and those working in the firm, if considered fit, after confronting them with the violation of which they are accused. In all cases, the violator shall be permitted to submit his/her defence(s) in writing or record them, and enclose the same along with the documents submitted with the detection record, after recording the violator's name, nationality, capacity and identification number as well as other evidentiary information.
(4) Notifying the accused of the violation of his/her obligation to appear before the competent authority within a period not exceeding three days, along with documents relevant to the matter detected.
(5) In case the person accused of the violation or his/her representative does not appear within a period of three working days from the date of the violation detection, he/she shall be summoned again to appear before the competent investigating officer within a period not exceeding five days. In case he/she fails to appear, the matter shall be reported to the police to summon him/her in order to complete the procedures of investigation, or the store shall be closed until he/she responds.

Article 20 of the 2004 Implementing Regulations further explains the tasks and activities of detection under the Saudi legal regime. Based on this, the officials of the General Department of Copyright in Riyadh and its branches in the Kingdom's provinces or the departments and offices of printed materials in provinces where there are no branches for the Department shall be responsible for the task of detecting violations and securing the evidence proving the existence of an infringement of copyright, such as equipment, works or commodities. In addition, a record for detecting the violation shall be drafted and signed by the drafter, and it shall contain the following information:

(1) Name, address of the store and identification of its owner.
(2) Place where the violation was detected and time by hour, day and month.
(3) Names of workers in the site when the violation was detected.
(4) Title, nature of the work subject of the violation, number and specification of copies detected.
(5) Type, facts, reasons and circumstances of the violation.

Analysis of evidence is undertaken in accordance with Article 21 of the 2004 Implementing Regulations. Accordingly, the General Department of Copyright or the competent branch shall, immediately upon receiving the evidence, take the following procedures:

- Conducting an external examination and inspection of equipment or works detected with regard to their external condition and number.
- Inspecting and analysing the content of evidence detected in order to ensure whether or not they contain evidence of copyright infringement and preparing a written inspection report indicating the condition of the materials detected.
- The complainant (plaintiff) may be permitted to conduct a brief inspection of the equipment with the participation of the analyst in the Department in order to prove the complaint, if the analysis proves the absence of infringement.
- The analyst shall submit his/her recommendation and report on the complaint to the Department, showing the extent to which the complaint is proved or not.

Moreover, the competent department which detected the works whose copyright is proved to be infringed shall prepare a report containing the following detailed information:

(1) Detailed description of the work.
(2) Number of copies of the works detected and their sale price for the public at the time of detection.
(3) Violations and infringements in the work.
(4) Method and form of infringement and whether committed inside or outside the Kingdom.
(5) Method of detecting the violation, whether pursuant to a complaint, a tip or a field visit.
(6) Method and form of displaying the violating works to the public.
(7) Any information or other technical facts about the work and the method of infringement, in order to confront the violator therewith.

The 2004 Implementing Regulations states out in detail the process of investigating violations. Based on this, Article 23 of the 2004 Implementing Regulations states that in case of violations in the works or detected equipment, the competent investigating officer shall initiate a record to enter the statements of the person or persons accused of the violation or whoever acts on their behalf and their defences, in relation to the information recorded in the report by the analyst, and to the complaint made against them. The investigation record shall contain the following data:

(1) Hour, day, date and place of the investigation.
(2) Name of the investigating officer and his/her capacity.
(3) Name of the person accused of the violation, his/her identification number and contact addresses.
(4) Confronting him/her with the violations of which he/she is specifically accused.
(5) Complete answers of the person accused of the violation to the questions addressed to him/her, including his/her defences and the statements of witnesses, if any.

In general, the violator(s) shall be questioned about the time period in which he/she infringed on the work and the financial returns he/she has reaped consequently as a result of the activity. However, the investigator(s) may, if necessary, summon anyone whose testimony he/she deems indispensable regarding the violation, and enter the same in the record. The General Department of Copyright may also seek the assistance of experts to reveal violations in accordance with the administrative procedures governing this. The person(s) testifying shall sign at the end of every answer they give, and each page of the record shall be signed by the investigator and those who have been interrogated, in addition to the witnesses. The pages shall be drafted in a consecutive serial order without cancellation or amendment. The investigator shall conclude the investigation record with the results he/she has reached, attaching therewith the documents, evidences and proofs submitted, along with the time of its completion. Departments and branches of the General Department of Copyright and printed material offices in the provinces where there are no branches for the General Department of Copyright shall refer the record of investigation along with all documents relevant to the infringement to the General Director of the Department. The General Department shall review all procedures and investigations, determine the violations committed, the articles governing these violations in the 2003 Saudi Copyright Royal Decree and the 2004 Implementing Regulations, and the views of the Department. The information related to the case shall be entered in a special register in order to make entries thereof. The General Department of Copyright shall refer the cases and violations along with all relevant documents to the violation review committee for consideration.

As seen, the Saudi copyright legal regime adopts a different approach in terms of dealing with infringements than some other jurisdictions in the region. The law starts with detailing what situations would give rise to infringement in extensive details, the process and procedures followed in identifying such cases, and then subsequently, sets the limits for the applicable penalty on any of the discussed acts.

In accordance with this, Article 22 of the 2003 Saudi Copyright Royal Decree sets out the various types of penalties to be applied against the above referred to infringements and violations.

A number of criminal penalties are included under the Saudi legal regime to that effect. Accordingly, any person who violates a provision of the 2003 Saudi Copyright Royal Decree shall be subject to one or more of the following penalties:[119]

(1) Warning.
(2) A fine not exceeding SAR 250,000 (approx. USD 66,000).

119. Notably, Price states that: '*Saudi Arabia's copyright law, at Article 22, has provision for penalties up to an impressive US$ 67,000 and a maximum 1-year term of imprisonment. This is a striking 30-fold increase on the maximum fine of US$2,700 (without any imprisonment provision) available under its former law of 1989. The harsher penalties illustrate the impact of the greater degree of critical scrutiny and pressure that Saudi Arabia received from the United States and from international business and intellectual property watchdog organizations (such as the USTR and the Business Software Alliance [BSA]) as part of its drive for WTO membership and the consequent necessity to demonstrate its commitment to TRIPS minimum standards.*' For more *see* D. Price, 'Politics, Piracy and Punishment: Copyright Protection in the Arabian Gulf', *The Journal of World Intellectual Property* 14, no. 3–4 (2011): 290.

(3) Closing the violating establishment or the one which participated in the violation of the copyright, for a period not exceeding two months.
(4) Confiscation of all copies of the work along with the materials used or intended for use in the infringement on the copyrights.
(5) Imprisonment for a period not exceeding a period of six months.

Notably, the above penalties shall be strengthened in the case of the repetition of the infringement regardless if the repetition was directed towards the same work or any other work. Accordingly, the maximum limit of penalty, fine and closure may be doubled in such a case.[120]

However, in order to review the above cases and decide the applicable penalties, the 2003 Saudi Copyright Royal Decree makes reference to a special committee in this regard. Based on this, there shall be a competent Committee (the Committee) formed to review violations resulting from the implementation of the provisions of the 2003 Saudi Copyright Royal Decree. Article 22.3 of the 2003 Saudi Copyright Royal Decree states that if the Committee sees that the violation entails imprisonment or a fine exceeding SAR 100,000 (approx. USD 26,000) or cancellation of the licence, the case shall be submitted to the Minister of Culture and Information for referral to the BoGs.

In addition to the above penalties and remedies, the 2003 Saudi Copyright Royal Decree grants the Committee the right to award damages. Based on this, the Committee may decide on financial compensation for the benefit of the owner whose right has been infringed upon and who files the complaint. Compensation shall be consistent with the size and severity of the infringement and the damage incurred.[121] Not only this, in fact the Committee may include in its decision the punishment of defamation against the person who commits the infringement. Publication of such shall be at his/her expense and by the method the Committee deems appropriate.[122]

In addition, the 2004 Implementing Regulations further elaborates on this issue and the mechanism of calculating the compensation. Based on this, Article 24 of the 2004 Implementing Regulations provides that the copyright owner or his/her representative is entitled to claim compensation for damages incurred as the result of the infringement of any of his/her rights protected by law, and shall submit a written memorandum to the competent department, if he/she desires, in which he/she explains in detail the damages incurred as a result of this infringement and how they occurred, as well as the estimated amount of compensation claimed by him/her and the basis for such estimation. In all cases, the copyright owner shall present the evidence and documents supporting his/her statements. The officer investigating the violation shall cross-examine such evidence and documents and check the gravity of the violation, and inform the defendant of what is brought against him/her, and grant him/her the ability to present his/her views and answers in this respect, and then refer the claim to the violation review committee for decision.

Additional powers are also granted to the Committee under the Saudi legal regime. Accordingly, Article 22.6 of the 2003 Saudi Copyright Royal Decree states

120. The 2004 Implementing Regulations, Art. 22.2.
121. *Ibid.*, Art. 22.4.
122. *Ibid.*, Art. 22 .5.

that the Committee may include in its decision suspension of participation of the infringing establishment in the activities, occasions or exhibitions, if the infringement was discovered during a commercial event, provided that the period of suspension shall not exceed a period of two years.

The committee shall also have the right to impose a number of administrative measures where needed. Based on this, the Committee may issue an injunction against the printing of the work infringed upon, its production, publication or distribution, in addition to protective impounding of the copies, materials and pictures made from it. It may take any temporary measure it finds necessary to protect the copyright until a final decision is reached regarding the complaint or grievance.[123]

Notably, Article 25 of the 2004 Implementing Regulations explains the procedures and rules related to the operation of the violations committee. Based on this, the committee shall exercise its jurisdiction in reviewing all violations of the provisions of the 2003 Saudi Copyright Royal Decree and the 2004 Implementing Regulations and shall determine the punishments according to what is stipulated in Article 22 of the 2003 Saudi Copyright Royal Decree in proportion to the gravity of infringement and the number of violations recorded with the committee against the violating party, and compensate owners of copyrights for the damage incurred by them as a result of the infringing activity, subject to the following guidelines:

(1) The chairman of the committee shall supervise its technical and administrative work, and shall determine the dates of sessions to review the cases brought before the committee in coordination with the members.
(2) The committee may convene its meetings if attended by not less than two-thirds of the members, provided that the legal and *Shariah* counsellors are present.
(3) The committee, as necessary, may seek the assistance of experts to obtain their opinions on some of the violations brought before it.
(4) The committee may summon any party to the violation to hear his/her statements, the inspector who detected the violation, the information analyst or the investigator or any other person whose statements the committee deems necessary to hear.
(5) The committee may return the violation papers to the investigation authority in order to request additional information or to complete whatever it deems necessary regarding the investigations.
(6) Decisions of the committee shall be issued by majority vote and shall be referred by the chairman of the committee to the Minister, and said decisions shall not be effective unless approved by the Minister.
(7) If the committee finds the violation committed grave and punishable with imprisonment or a fine exceeding SAR 100,000 (approx. USD 26,000), or closing the store permanently and cancelling the licence, the matter shall be referred to the Minister for his approval to forward this violation to the BoGs for review and to determine the appropriate punishment against the infringer.
(8) The committee shall inform the General Department of Copyright of the approved decisions in order to notify the relevant department to carry out the prescribed punishments.

123. *Ibid.*, Art. 22.7.

Article 26 of the 2004 Implementing Regulations provides a number of restrictions applicable to the execution of punishments. Accordingly, in case of a grievance regarding the decision issued by the committee before the BoGs, the punishments stated in the decision shall be suspended until a final judgment in relation thereto is rendered by the Board. However, punishments within the jurisdiction of the BoGs shall be carried out after a final judgment in connection therewith is rendered by the Board. Notably, when punishments are carried out, the following shall be taken into consideration:

(1) The competent department shall notify the person against whom the punishment is issued or his/her representative of the decision issued against him/her by an official letter stating the number of the decision issued, its date and punishments prescribed therein, and it shall be delivered to him/her or his representative or the person found in the firm after signing a copy of the letter, showing date of notification, name of the person who delivered the notification, his/her capacity, signature and identification number.
(2) In the case where the violator is notified of the decision by official mail, he/she shall be considered notified after a period of two weeks from the date of mailing the letter by registered or official mail.
(3) Upon payment of the fine prescribed in the decision by the violator, the Department shall complete the execution of the other punishments, such as provisional closure, suspension of participation of the firm in occasions or exhibitions, collection of compensation and the like.
(4) If a judgment is rendered by the BoGs to cancel the licence, the Ministry shall notify the government body that issued the licence to cancel it and follow up the execution of the judgment.
(5) The fine shall be paid to the treasury of the Ministry against an official receipt to be delivered to the Department in charge of execution of the punishment or by a certified cheque payable to the Saudi Arabian Monetary Agency and delivered to the Department concerned.
(6) The Department concerned shall refer the cheque to the competent authority at the Ministry to collect the fine, and a copy of which shall be kept in the file of the infringing firm.
(7) If the violator fails to pay the fine within a period not exceeding fifteen days from the date of the execution of the punishment, the police shall be addressed to compel him/her to pay, and the Ministry may close his/her store until he/she pays the amount.
(8) The Ministry shall prepare a summary of the content of the judgment rendered against the violator if the decision provides for the punishment of publicizing the conviction in accordance with Article 22.5 of the 2003 Saudi Copyright Royal Decree, and shall be published at the expense of the violator in a distinct place in one or two daily newspapers of wide circulation, one of which is published in the area where the head office of the violator is located, according to the gravity of the violation.

Moreover, the 2003 Saudi Copyright Royal Decree includes an appeal procedure against the Committee's decisions. Based on this, Article 23 of the 2003 Saudi Copyright

Royal Decree provides that anyone against whom a decision was made by the Committee shall have the right to file a grievance with the BoGs within a period of sixty days from the date of notification of the decision. Following such a grievance, the officers concerned at the Ministry of Culture and Information shall investigate the violation and visit media and commercial facilities, warehouses and public institutions and private establishments that use intellectual works in their activities and investigate them. They shall have the power of judicial investigation and protection of evidentiary proofs.[124]

Article 25 of the 2003 Saudi Copyright Royal Decree calls for the establishment of a specialized violations review committee. Based on this, a Committee to review the violation shall be formed by the Minister of Culture and Information's decision, with a minimum of three members, provided that one of them is a legal advisor and the other a *Shariah* advisor. The decisions of the Committee shall be made by majority vote, which shall be endorsed by the Minister of Culture and Information.

There are no specialized courts for copyrights in Saudi Arabia. The competent courts are the regular courts (civil, criminal and administrative).

In addition, Article 27 of the 2004 Implementing Regulations contains reference to various provisional measures. Based on this, the committee has the authority to take immediate provisional measures in order to prevent infringement of any copyright and to prevent imported works that contain infringement of copyright from reaching commercial outlets. Moreover, the committee has the authority to take provisional measures without the knowledge of the other party, if it is likely that a delay would result in harming him/her or it is likely to damage the evidence. In addition, the committee may request the plaintiff to undertake the following:

(1) Submit any evidence in his/her possession affirming that he/she is the owner of the right.
(2) Submit preliminary evidence proving that his/her right is being infringed or is about to be infringed.
(3) Submit a financial guarantee sufficient to protect the defendant and prevent abuse of rights or exercise thereof.
(4) The committee may request the plaintiff to submit any evidence necessary in order to determine the extent of the legitimacy of the lawsuit.

The committee may also, after taking the protective seizure measures, notify the affected parties to submit their viewpoint and defences within a provisional period not exceeding thirty-one days from the date of initiating the protective measures in order to consider whether to amend, cancel or confirm such measures. The committee may cancel the measures taken in accordance with paragraphs (1) and (2) Article 27 of the 2003 Saudi Copyright Royal Decree pursuant to a request by the defendant, or suspend said measures if the plaintiff does not submit documents required from him/her within a time period determined by the committee and not exceeding thirty-one days. Upon the cancellation of provisional measures or expiry of their effectiveness period as a result of the plaintiff's negligence, or upon becoming evident later that there was no infringement upon the works or commodities, the committee may, upon request of the

124. *Ibid.*, Art. 24.

defendant, order the plaintiff to pay appropriate compensations for any damage incurred by the defendant as a result of such measures.

Border measures are also included under the 2004 Implementing Regulations and under a specialized border measures regulation. Based on this, Article 28 of the 2004 Implementing Regulations provides that a copyright owner, who has legitimate reasons to suspect that works infringing his/her rights are intended for importation or exportation, may submit a written request to the committee in order to stop and seize works imported or intended for importation or exportation, upon reaching the borders. The committee may request the plaintiff to submit a financial guarantee sufficient to protect the defendant and prevent abuse of rights. The plaintiff shall submit to the committee, within a period not exceeding ten working days, the complaint and the supporting evidence that determine the infringements he/she has incurred, provided that the period of seizure does not exceed thirty-one days, after which amendment, cancellation or confirmation of such measures shall be considered. The committee may decide that the plaintiff pay to the importer or exporter an appropriate compensation for damages incurred by them as a result of wrongful seizure of works. The committee may grant the owner of the right (the plaintiff) sufficient opportunity to inspect the works in order to prove his/her allegations. The importer is entitled to an equal opportunity to inspect any of these commodities. The committee, in case the infringement is proved, is authorized to notify the owner of the right of the names and addresses of the sender and addressee of the works as well as their quantities.

In addition, precautionary measures are available under the 2004 Implementing Regulations. Article 29 states that the Ministry's office at the point of entry at the border may stop the procedure for release of works upon having prima facie evidence proving existence of copyright infringement, after coordination with the customs department at the point of entry. The office shall immediately notify the General Department of Copyright to take the necessary measures, in coordination with the committee.

In addition to these provisions, there are additional provisions applicable under the Regulations of Border Procedures for Protection of Intellectual Property Rights of Trademarks and Copyrights, 3 July 2004 (hereinafter 'the 2004 Saudi Border Measures Regulation').[125] Based on this, the Provisions of these Regulations shall apply to IPRs with regard to trademarks and copyrights.

In line with this, Article 5 of the 2004 Saudi Border Measures Regulation states that upon having legitimate reasons for suspending the clearance of infringing works, the copyright owner may, at any time, even prior to filing a civil or criminal lawsuit, submit a request in writing to the Ministry of Culture and Information for the issuance of a decision to suspend the clearance of said works, in accordance with the procedures specified by the 2004 Implementing Regulations. Furthermore, Article 7 of 2004 Saudi Border Measures Regulation provides that consequently, Customs shall, pursuant to a preventive seizure order by the BoGs or a decision by the Ministry of Culture and Information, suspend the clearance of infringing goods or works. However, it should be noted that without prejudice to the execution of the seizure, the party against whom the preventive seizure has been issued may, within a period of ten days from the date of notification of the seizure, file a request either with the circuit handling the case at

125. Ministerial Decision No. (1277) 15 *Jumada I* 1425H – 3 Jul. 2004.

the BoGs or the competent department at the Ministry of Culture and Information to reconsider it by revoking the same or staying its execution.[126]

Article 9 of the 2004 Saudi Border Measures Regulation states that the seizure order issued by the BoGs or the preventive seizure decision issued by the Ministry of Culture and Information shall be deemed null and void unless the right holder follows it by filing a civil or criminal lawsuit against whom such an order has been issued, within a period of ten days from the date of its issuance. In case where the right holder does not submit to the Customs Authorities, within the period of ten days from his/her notification of the preventive seizure order or decision, proof of his filing a civil or criminal lawsuit with the BoGs or with the competent committee at the Ministry of Culture and Information, the Customs Authorities shall clear the goods and works subject of seizure, if other conditions of import and export have been complied with.[127]

Moreover, Article 11 of 2004 Saudi Border Measures Regulation provides that the Customs Authorities shall be entrusted with the execution of judgments and decisions issued by the competent bodies for the confiscation or destruction of infringing goods and works, and they shall have the power to dispose of the same through non-commercial outlets, unless otherwise adjudicated by the judicial authority or as directed by the competent administrative authority.

Article 13 of the 2004 Saudi Border Measures Regulation states that the parties concerned may challenge the decisions issued by the Customs Authority, in respect of the application of the of the 2004 Saudi Border Measures Regulation, before the BoGs within a period not exceeding sixty days of notification in writing or through publication, if notification is not possible.

According to media sources, the General Department of Copyright has received more than 850 complaints between the period of January and September 2010 related to copyright infringement by which 250 penalties were issued as a result of established infringements.[128] The judiciary also started issuing criminal penalties against infringement, where in 2012 it was reported that imprisonment penalty was issued for the first time in the country against copyright infringement in accordance with Article 22.5 of the 2003 Saudi Copyright Royal Decree.[129] In one of the highly publicized cases, a Saudi court in 2012 issued its decision ordering a Saudi cleric to pay damages equal to SAR 330,000 (approx. USD 90,000) and confiscation of his book from the market as a result of his infringement of copyright through plagiarism.[130]

---

126. The 2004 Saudi Border Measures Regulation, Art. 8.
127. *Ibid.*, Art. 10.
128. For more on coverage of the case *see* Al Sharq Al Awsat, 5 Dec. 2010, issue 11695, at http://archive.aawsat.com/details.asp?section=19&article=598144&issueno=11695#.VaVdgfmqqko, visited 14 Jul. 2015.
129. For more *see* http://www.okaz.com.sa/new/Issues/20120229/Con20120229482183.htm. Last visited 11 Dec. 2015.
130. For more *see* http://www.alarabiya.net/articles/2012/01/23/190083.html. Last visited 22 Sept. 2015.

§12. Overlapping and Relations to Other Intellectual Property Law

48. A number of basic principles have been established under the Saudi copyright protection regime to assess copyright subject matter and the limits of protection. In particular, the notion that copyright protection is granted to the expression of ideas, and not the ideas themselves.[131] Also the law allows in accordance with several public order considerations some exceptions and exemptions against the use of copyright in addition to the issuance of compulsory licences.

There has been some influence of other laws upon the copyright protection regime in the country. For example, there are a number of laws and regulations pertaining anti-piracy measures and copyright enforcement in Saudi Arabia such as the Penal Law on Dissemination and Disclosure of Classified Information and Documents (promulgated by Royal Decree No. M/35 of 8/5/1432H (12 April 2011) and the Law of Printed Materials and Publication (promulgated by Royal Decree No. M/32 dated 03/09/1421H (29 November 2000) and the Regulations of Border Procedures for Protection of Intellectual Property Rights of Trademarks and Copyrights, (3 July 2004) and the Anti-Cybercrime Law (promulgated by Royal Decree No. M/17 in 8 Rabi'I 1428 (26 March 2007). Other general principles of litigation are also covered by the Law of Criminal Procedures (promulgated by Royal Decree No. M/39 of 28 Rajab 1422 (16 October 2001)).

131. However, the practical application of ideas is protected by patents. *See* Al Fuzan, *ibid.*

Chapter 2. Patents

§1. Sources: Legislation

49. The modern foundations of the legal framework of the Saudi patent protection regime dates back to 1989 whereby the first patent law was inaugurated in the country by virtue of the Royal Decree No. (M/38) dated 10/6/1409 H (18/1/1989 AD). The 1989 Royal Decree aimed to provide protection for inventions and patents in Saudi Arabia,[132] and it was modified in 19/7/1425 H (4/9/2004 AD) by the Law of Patents, Layout Designs of Integrated Circuits, Plant Varieties, and Industrial Designs (hereinafter 'the 2004 Saudi Patent Law')[133] thus paving the way towards the country's accession to the WTO. The 2004 Saudi Patent Law remains in force as we speak.[134] The 2004 Saudi Royal Decree was supplemented by the 2004 Implementing Regulations of the Law of Patents, Layout Designs of Integrated Circuits, Plant Varieties and Industrial Designs (hereinafter 'the 2004 Implementing Regulations').

Both the 2004 Saudi Patent Law and 2004 Implementing Regulations provide a comprehensive legal protection regime for patents, layout-designs of integrated circuits, plant varieties, in addition to the protection of industrial designs in Saudi Arabia.

Before the introduction of the 2004 Saudi Patent Law, legal patent protection was also available through the GCC unified patent registration system which was approved by the GCC Supreme Council in September 1992. The GCC Patent Office started its operations in 1998.[135]

The Saudi Patent Office is the national authority concerned with granting patents in the country. It is based in the KACST. It grants protection documents for inventions,[136] layout-designs of integrated circuits, plant varieties and industrial designs.[137] Notably,

132. Notably, the previous Saudi Patent Law conferred a term of protection of fifteen years with the possibility of a five-year extension.
133. Issued by the Royal Decree No. (M/27) dated 17/7/2004 and was published in the Official Gazette (Om Alqura) in 7/8/2004, and became effective as of 5/9/2004.
134. Article 64 of the 2004 Saudi Patent Law provides that the 2004 Patent Law shall replace the Patent Law issued by the Royal Decree No. (M/38) dated 10/6/1409H, and its provisions shall govern the patent applications and the patents in force, and shall supersede all provisions that are inconsistent therewith.
135. For more *see* the website of the Patent Office of the Cooperation Council for the Arab States of the Gulf, at http://www.gccpo.org/DefaultEn.aspx.
136. Protection document is defined as 'The document granted by the City for one of the subject matters of protection. It may either be a patent, a certificate of layout design, a plant patent, or a certificate of an industrial design.' *See* Art. 1 of the 2004 Saudi Patent Law.
137. *See* http://www.kacst.edu.sa/en/innovation/patents/Pages/Home.aspx.

the City shall have the authority to apply the provisions of the 2004 Saudi Patent Law and its 2004 Implementing Regulations.[138]

50. In 1982, KACST was notified of the Royal Decree approving the accession of Saudi Arabia to the WIPO. Accordingly, patents have been assigned to KACST since intellectual property is essentially about patents and technology transfer, and KACST is the scientific body qualified for this mission. According to Saudi Patent Office 2013 figures, there were 928 filed applications, 233 were granted patents (against 217 in 2012) while 361 were rejected and 344 lapsed.[139]

As mentioned, the 2004 Saudi Patent Law adopts a comprehensive and holistic approach in relation to industrial property protection by containing parts dealing with the protection of patents, utility models, industrial designs, geographical indications (GIs), in addition to enforcement provisions. Notably, the introduction of the 2004 Saudi Patent Law was influenced by country's desire to join the WTO.

The 2004 Saudi Patent Law comprises of six chapters each containing a number of articles (sixty-five articles). The chapters are divided into a number of parts in the following order:

(1) Chapter 1: General Provisions.
(2) Chapter 2: Special Provisions Governing Patents.
(3) Chapter 3: Provisions Governing Layout Designs of Integrated Circuits.
(4) Chapter 4: Provisions Governing the Protection of New Plant Varieties.
(5) Chapter 5: Special Provisions Governing Industrial Designs.
(6) Chapter 6: Concluding Provisions.

There is a general absence and scarcity of valid court and judicial precedents under contemporary Saudi patent law and legal regime. Court decisions are rare. This follows a similar pattern with the experience of other countries in the region.[140]

Saudi Arabia signed and ratified several regional and international agreements which are applicable to patent protection. The most important regional agreement is the GCC unified patent registration system which was approved by the GCC Supreme Council in September 1992. Based on this, the 2002 Patent Law of the Cooperation Council for the Arab States of the Gulf is also implemented in the country (hereinafter 'the 2002 GCC Patent Law').[141] Notably, Saudi Arabia has implemented national legislation ratifying the 2002 GCC Patent Law. However, this legislation does not deal with the enforcement of GCC patents in Saudi Arabia, despite the 2002 GCC Patent Law providing that enforcement issues are a matter for national legislation.[142]

---

138. The 2004 Saudi Patent Law, Art. 3. Furthermore, Art. 63 of the law further provides that: '*the President of the City shall issue the Implementing Regulations for the 2004 Saudi Patent Law, within the period of one hundred eighty days from the date of its coming into effect. They shall be published in the Official Gazette. He shall also issue the necessary decisions for implementing the provisions of this Law.*'
139. For more *see* http://www.kacst.edu.sa/en/innovation/patents/pages/statistics.aspx.
140. *See* generally M. El Said, *IPRs in Jordan* and *IPRs in Lebanon*.
141. For more *see* http://www.gccpo.org/conven/PatentRegulation.pdf.
142. Rob deans, at http://www.clydeco.com/uploads/Files/CC007038_MENA_IP_newsletter_March_2015_09-03-15.pdf.

Saudi Arabia is also a member of several international agreements focusing on the protection of patents. Accordingly, Saudi Arabia is a member of:

(1) The Paris Convention for the Protection of Industrial Property, joined on 11 March 2004.
(2) The Patent Cooperation Treaty (PCT), joined on 3 August 2013.[143]
(3) The Patent Law Treaty (PLT), joined on 3 August 2013.
(4) Convention Establishing the WIPO (22 May 1982).

These treaties and agreements are directly applicable nationally as part of Saudi's legal system.

§2. Patentable Subject Matter

51. The 2004 Saudi Patent Law was drafted in a manner which primarily meets the country's obligations towards accession to the TRIPS Agreement.[144]

To start with, Article 2 of the 2004 Saudi Patent Law defines an invention as 'An idea developed by the inventor that results in a solution of a certain problem in the field of technology.' Furthermore, Article 43 of the 2004 Saudi Patent Law explains that the invention may be a product, a process or relates to either. Based on this patent protection may be granted for any type of invention regardless if it is a process or a product.

Moreover, Article 43 of the 2004 Saudi Patent Law specifies the criteria of granting patent protection which includes three main elements: novelty, creativity and industrial applicability. These will be explained in the subsequent sections of this chapter.

Furthermore, Article 45 of the 2004 Saudi Patent Law explicitly excludes from the concept of invention several types of subject matter namely:

(1) Discoveries, scientific theories and mathematical methods.
(2) Schemes, rules and methods of conducting commercial activities, exercising pure mental activities or playing a game.
(3) Plants, animals and processes – which are mostly biological – used for the production of plants or animals, with the exception of microorganisms, non-biological and microbiology processes.
(4) Methods of surgical or therapeutic treatment of human or animal body and methods of diagnosis applied to human or animal bodies, with the exception of products used in any of these methods.

143. Article 1 of the 2004 Saudi Patent Law explains that 'Patent Cooperation Treaty' means the Patent Cooperation Treaty, done at Washington on 19 Jun. 1970, amended on 28 Sept. 1979, modified on 3 Feb. 1984 and 3 Oct. 2001.

144. Notably, Art. 1 of the 2004 Saudi Patent Law defines subject matter as 'Either an invention, a layout design of integrated circuits, a plant variety or an industrial design'.

In addition, Article 4 of the 2004 Saudi Patent Law provides that protection shall not be granted if its commercial exploitation violates the *Shariah* and if the commercial exploitation of the patent is harmful to life, to human, animal or plant health, or is substantially harmful to the environment.

Notably, the exclusion of inventions which are harmful to human life, to human, animal or plant health, or is substantially harmful to the environment are well-founded principle in many intellectual property legislations and is also recognized under the TRIPS Agreement.[145] Although often referred to patents and other types of intellectual property as 'private properties', the interest of society is also well preserved and in certain cases even paramount to that of private parties. This is the founding principle of this and other exclusions as provided under the majority of patent laws around the world.

From the above, it appears that the Saudi legislator took a moderate approach by listing the above referred to exclusions from the ambit of patentability under the national law.[146]

Generally, computer programs are not patentable under the Saudi legal regime. However, it can be protected under the Copyright Law. Only in the case where the invention is a hardware accompanied with its operation software, it can be patentable under the Saudi legal regime.

§3. CONDITIONS OF PATENTABILITY

52. Article 43 of the 2004 Saudi Patent Law states that an invention is patentable if it is new, involves an inventive step and is industrially applicable. This criterion is in line with the requirements of Article 27.1 of the TRIPS Agreement.[147] The 2004 Saudi Patent Law defines each of these accordingly.

The 2004 Saudi Patent Law further defines how the invention could be new. Based on this, Article 44 of the 2004 Saudi Patent Law states that an invention is new if it is not anticipated by prior art. In this respect, prior art means all that is disclosed to the public anywhere by means of written or oral disclosure, by use or by any other way through which knowledge of the invention is realized. This has to be prior to the filing date of the patent application or the priority application. The disclosure of the invention to the public shall not count if it takes place during the priority period. The

145. The TRIPS Agreement, Art. 27.2.

146. *See* TRIPS Agreement, Art.27.2 which states that: '*Members may exclude from patentability inventions, the prevention within their territory of the commercial exploitation of which is necessary to protect* ordre public *or morality,* including to protect human, animal or plant life or health *or to avoid serious prejudice to the environment, provided that such exclusion is not made merely because the exploitation is prohibited by their law*'. (emphasis added).'

147. 27.1 of the TRIPS Agreement states that: '*Subject to the provisions of paragraphs 2 and 3, patents shall be available for any inventions, whether products or processes, in all fields of technology, provided that they are new, involve an inventive step and are capable of industrial application. Subject to paragraph 4 of Article 65, paragraph 8 of Article 70 and paragraph 3 of this Article, patents shall be available and patent rights enjoyable without discrimination as to the place of invention, the field of technology and whether products are imported or locally produced.*'

2004 Implementing Regulations shall specify other cases of invention disclosure which do not fall within the meaning of prior art and the provisions governing temporary protection of inventions. Absolute novelty is what is adopted by the Saudi legal regime in this regard.[148]

In relation to inventiveness, Article 44.b of the 2004 Saudi Patent Law states that an invention shall be considered as involving an inventive step if, with regard to prior art related to the patent application, it is not obvious to a person with ordinary skills in the art.

Finally, paragraph (c) of Article 44 of the 2004 Saudi Patent Law defines industrial applicability by stating that an invention is deemed industrially applicable if it can be manufactured or used in any type of industry or agriculture, including handicrafts, fishing and services.

As in the case of many definitions under intellectual property law in general and patent law in particular, it is unlikely that the patent law would provide an exhaustive or decisive definition for the courts having to deal with this aspect of patentability.[149] The same could also be said in the case of the examination undertaken under the national patent office. Acknowledging this particular issue, the TRIPS Agreement grants Member States the discretion to define such criteria under the national patent law in accordance with each country's level of development.

§4. Formalities

53. The procedure for the grant of patents under the 2004 Saudi Patent Law is based on the registration of the patent with an administrative governmental body (the General Directorate of Patents at King Abdulaziz City for Science and Technology – hereinafter 'the Directorate'). Notably, a patent may also be granted by the GCC Patent Office if an application is made to that effect in Riyadh as will be discussed in this chapter as well.[150]

Article 2 of the Implementing Regulations explains the functions of the Directorate. Based on this, the Directorate is responsible for implementing the provisions of the 2004 Saudi Patent Law and the Implementing Regulations. It may especially perform the following:

(1) Receive protection applications, follow up their processing and prepare the protection documents.

148. Notable, the 2004 Saudi Patent Law provides that for the purposes of subs. (2)(b), disclosure to the public of the invention shall not be taken into consideration if it occurred within twelve months preceding the filing date or, where applicable, the priority date of the application, and if it was by reason or in consequence of acts committed by the applicant or his/her predecessor in title or of an abuse committed by a third party with regard to the applicant or his/her predecessor in title. It shall be understood that disclosure derived from the applicant or his/her predecessor in title is comprised by this paragraph.

149. Although some countries have attempted to introduce a strict definition,, *see* for instance the 2005 Indian Patent Law, s. 3 (d).

150. *See* GCC Patent Office at http://www.gccpo.org/.

(2) Propose issuance and amendment of the necessary forms to carry out its duties.
(3) Recommend the granting and issuance of protection documents and publish information regarding the same.
(4) Utilize information technology in dealing with protection applications and documents.
(5) Propose the necessary amendments to the provisions of the Law and the Regulations.
(6) Propose licensing regulations for attorneys-in-fact and lawyers to practise their profession before the Directorate.

The 2004 Implementing Regulations contains several clauses dedicated to the rules of engagement with the Directorate. Accordingly, correspondence with the Directorate shall be addressed to the 'Director General of the General Directorate of Patents' at King Abdulaziz City for Science and Technology in accordance with the mailing address determined by the Directorate or by any other means acceptable to it. Correspondence with the Directorate shall be in writing. The appearance in person of the applicant or the agent is not necessary. Procedures taken by the Directorate shall be based on what is presented to it in writing, without any regard to verbal promises and understandings.[151]

Article 4 of the Implementing Regulations states that the Directorate shall prepare records for different protection documents applications and registers for protection documents, where the main data of the applications and protection documents and any amendments thereof shall be recorded. Published files of forfeited applications for protection documents shall be available for review by the public. Applications for protection documents which are published or forfeited before publication shall be made available for review by the public too. Copies of the applications mentioned may be obtained upon payment of a certain fee. Applications for unpublished protection documents shall remain confidential. However, information may be given regarding whether the application is still pending or is forfeited or a patent has been granted and whether the application has been published. The Directorate may provide this information electronically only. The Directorate shall keep the originals of the applications or copies thereof for a period of five years from the date of withdrawal, rejection of the application or forfeiture of the right to the protection document or expiration of its term.

Article 6 of the 2004 Implementing Regulations states the Directorate shall publish a periodical gazette in Arabic containing all that is required by law to be

151. The 2004 Implementing Regulations, Art. 3 provides that:– Correspondence with the Directorate in connection with the applications shall refer to the application's number. Any non-complying correspondence shall be returned to the sender at the address mentioned therein; – The applications for granting protection documents and any relevant documents or correspondence shall be delivered to the Directorate by hand or by mail. It may decide to accept delivery thereof electronically;– Notices and correspondence relating to the applications for protection and protection documents shall be delivered by the Directorate by hand or by registered mail, and all correspondence from the Directorate shall be sent to the applicant or the agent at the address recorded with the Directorate and all such notices shall be deemed legally binding;– Any period expiring on weekends or official holidays of the country shall be extended to the first working day following these holidays;– The Directorate shall stamp the date of receipt on all correspondence it receives in connection with the application for protection documents.

published. The Gazette may also contain all that relates to the subjects and laws of protection, such as amendments, notices and news. If necessary, it may contain a translation of some information into English. The Gazette shall be issued in serial numbers, carrying both the Hijri and Gregorian calendar dates, and the Directorate shall make it available electronically on the Internet and shall keep a number of copies. Subscription may be by payment of specified subscription fees or according to the exchange system, whether inside or outside the country. The Directorate may publish the following in paper or electronic forms:

- Protection documents applications and protection documents containing the specification.
- Decisions issued by the Committee.

The Directorate may exchange these publications with others and with other patent offices where necessary. The Directorate shall provide public libraries with a copy of the applications for protection and the granted protection documents in paper or electronic form.

The registration procedure is explained under the 2004 Saudi Patent Law and the relevant provisions under the 2004 Implementing Regulations. The process begins by the filing of the application with the Directorate at the King Abdulaziz City for Science and Technology which shall be available to public view in accordance with the procedures set forth under the Patent Law and its 2004 Implementing Regulations. The Saudi regime adopts a first to file system, hence if several persons individually make or reach the same invention, the right to the patent shall be entitled to the first applicant.[152]

According to the 2004 Saudi Patent Law, the application for granting protection document shall be submitted to the Directorate in the prescribed form. The 2004 Implementing Regulations further specifies the information and documents required to be enclosed with the application. According to Article 8 of the 2004 Implementing Regulations, applications for granting protection documents and forms shall be submitted in paper form typed on computer in Arabic (in Simplified Arabic, size fourteen font and shall be bold, clear and distinct). A copy on an electronic medium shall be provided in accordance with the conditions stated in the chapters of Part Two of the 2004 Implementing Regulations. The forms shall contain all the information required and answers to all the queries. The Directorate shall determine as a date of filing, the date of receipt of the application for protection satisfying all the requirements stipulated in Articles 9–27 of the Implementing Regulations according to each subject matter of protection. Furthermore, Article 9 of the 2004 Implementing Regulations provides the conditions for the filing of the patent application. In accordance with this, the application shall include form titled ‘Application for Patent’, the specification of the invention and any relevant enclosures.

The 2004 Implementing Regulations further demands that the denomination of the invention shall comply with the specified conditions for filling the application form and shall not be different from the denomination mentioned in the specification of the

152. The applicant is the person requesting the protection document as registered in the Directorate records.

invention.[153] The documents submitted shall be original copies or certified by the competent authorities. Payment of the filing fees at the time of submission of the application shall also be made. The applicant shall satisfy all the requirements of the Directorate related to the application.

The Implementing Regulations specify the needed information to be included in the 'Application for a Patent'. Accordingly, Article 10 of the 2004 Implementing Regulations provides that the form shall be filled clearly and shall contain the name of the invention,[154] the name of the applicant,[155] the address, place of residence and place of work, the name of the inventor[156] and his/her address and the name of the agent,[157] if any, and his/her address, as well as information regarding priority and disclosure.

If the applicant is not the party which developed the subject matter of protection, then his/her name must be stated and the document proving the transfer of title of the patented subject matter to him/her must be enclosed, and the Directorate may, in this case, send a copy of these documents to the party which developed the subject matter of protection. After satisfying the requirements and payment of the specified fee, the application shall be registered. Notably, the applicant may introduce the amendments he deems fit in the application, provided that these amendments shall introduce no change to what was disclosed in the original application.[158]

Priority is also granted under the 2004 Saudi Patent Law and its Implementing Regulations. Based on this, the applicant may benefit from the priority given to a previous application filed during the priority period specified for each of the subject

153. The 2004 Implementing Regulations, Art. 9.2.
154. The name of the invention shall be brief and specific, preferably of not more than seven words. General statements such as 'A Chemical Process', 'An Electronic Equipment', 'An Electric Machine' and 'An Organic Compound of New Characteristics' shall not be considered as names of an invention. In order to shorten the name of the invention some statements shall not be used, such as 'New Method of ... ', 'Improvements in ... ', 'Development in ... '. An example would be: 'Improvements on a Building Structure Made of Ready Made Elements for Easy Installation'.
155. For individuals, the name shall be identical to what is in the identification document and in the following order: First name, father's name, grandfather's name, family name. As to corporations and companies, it shall be identical to the official name. If there are more than one applicant, the information relating to the first applicant shall be recorded in this part and the information relating to the remaining applicants shall be recorded in the special form for that purpose. Correspondence between the Directorate and the applicants shall be made through the first applicant if there is no agent. If the applicant is not the inventor, the document showing the transfer of the right to him shall be attached.
156. The name of the inventor shall be identical to what is stated in the identification document and in the following order: First name, father's name, grandfather's name, family name. If there is more than one inventor who actually participated in the invention, the information relating to the first inventor shall be recorded in this part, and the information relating to the remaining inventors shall be recorded in the special form for that purpose.
157. The name of the agent shall be stated, and he shall be authorized by a power of attorney issued by a notary public, if the principal is in the country. If the principal is outside the country, it is necessary to have a power of attorney approved by the competent authorities and certified by the country's embassies abroad, and the agent shall attach proof that he/she is licensed to practise such a profession in the country.
158. The 2004 Saudi Patent Law, Art. 9.

matters of protection, from the filing date of the previous application, provided that it is accompanied by a written declaration stating the date and number of the previous application and the place where it was filed by him/her or his/her predecessor. The applicant shall also submit a copy of the previous application approved by the authority where the protection application was submitted, within a period of ninety days from the date of filing the application with the Directorate.[159]

The priority period for patents shall be twelve months. If the invention was previously disclosed, the documents showing the date of disclosure and the reasons for that shall be attached. If the applicant is a national of one of the States of the Paris Union or a resident in one of them and desires to claim priority of an application previously filed in one of the states of the Union, the information relating to the priority claim (the state, the number of the application and the date of filing) and the number of the patent and its date, if any, shall be stated. In case there are multiple priorities, the information relating to the first priority shall be stated in addition to the information of the subsequent priority and an approved copy of the previous application and a translation thereof shall be attached within a period of three months. The information regarding other previous filings shall also be mentioned in the designated form.[160]

More is explained with relation to priority period under the 2004 Implementing Regulations. In accordance with this, Article 29 of the 2004 Implementing Regulations states that the periods of priority shall start from the date of filing the first application. The day of filing shall not be included in the period. However, if the last day of the priority period is an official holiday or a day in which the Directorate is not open for receiving applications, the period shall be extended until the first following working day. The applicant claiming the privilege of priority may defer providing the Directorate with the number of the previous application and the classification code of the application for the patent for a grace period not exceeding three months from the date of filing the application. If an applicant claiming the privilege of priority fails to submit a certified copy of the previous application and a translation thereof within the prescribed grace period, his/her right of priority shall be forfeited, and this shall be recorded in the registers of the Directorate. In addition, if the applicant does not pay within the specified period, the application and publication thereof shall be rejected, and this shall be recorded in the Register and published in the Gazette.[161]

In addition, Article 30 of the 2004 Implementing Regulations further clarifies the disclosure requirements. Cases of disclosure of inventions and industrial designs which are not considered as part of the previous state of technology shall be as follows:

(1) If the disclosure occurred in the last six months preceding the date of filing the application or the date of the priority claim due to arbitrary acts against the applicant or his predecessor.
(2) If the disclosure occurred as a result of displaying it in an officially recognized international exhibition in one of the countries of the Paris Union during the year preceding the filing of the application for the patent, or the six months preceding the date of filing the application for a certificate of an industrial design.

159. *Ibid.*, Art. 10.a.
160. The 2004 Implementing Regulations, Art. 10.4.
161. *Ibid.*, Art. 35.1.

If the applicant desires to have a provisional protection for an invention or an industrial design relating to products he wishes to display in any official exhibition, he/she shall apply to the Directorate expressing his/her desire to display, enclosing a brief statement describing the subject matter of protection, the illustrations and a list of the products relating to it. The Directorate may require the applicant to submit any other data it deems necessary. As for products displayed outside the country, a certificate authenticated by an official authority specifying the displayed product, its data and date of display shall be provided. It shall be noted that the periods referred to shall not entail extending the period of the right of priority provided for under Article 10 of the 2004 Saudi Patent Law.

Moreover, the specifications should include various details as highlighted under the 2004 Implementing Regulations. Article 11 of the Implementing Regulations provides that the Specification shall include the following contents and in the following order: 'Summary', 'Full Description', 'Elements of Protection' and 'Illustrations'. The beginning of each type of content shall be the beginning of a new page, and the name of each type of content shall be given in the centre of the line at the top of the page and shall be underlined. The specification papers (other than the drawings) shall be numbered consecutively; with the page number in the centre under the top margin (but not within it). The summary and the full description shall begin with the name of the invention. The specification shall be submitted in one original and two identical copies which can be directly duplicated by all means of duplication. The papers shall be clean, with no scratches, amendments, cancellation or any carbon stains. The summary, the full description and the elements of protection may include names, symbols, formulae, mathematical and chemical equations, scientific terms and others in Latin letters and none of them shall contain illustrations. As for tables, if any, they shall be included in the full description of the specification.[162]

Moreover, the 2004 Implementing Regulations contains a number of provisions related to application translated into Arabic language.[163] Specific conditions may also be found with relation to the summary and full description and elements of protection and illustration under Articles 13–16 of the 2004 Implementing Regulations accordingly.

162. Article 11 of the 2004 Implementing Regulations further provides that measurements shall be in the metric system and the temperature degrees in centigrade. The other units may be subsequently mentioned between parentheses. It is necessary to attach drawings and illustrations if that leads to full and clear understanding of the invention.

163. Accordingly, in such a case, the scientific term shall be given in its original language with the Arabic synonym, when used for the first time. Subsequently, the Arabic name only is given, except for the elements of protection where the term shall be repeated in both languages. In case of use of abbreviated names in a foreign language, the full name in both Arabic and English shall be mentioned when used for the first time in the text. Subsequently, the abbreviation only shall be given. The same Arabic term for a Latin word shall be used when the Latin term recurs in the text. Symbols, units, names and basic physical constants approved by the International Union for Pure and Applied Physics (IUPAP) – the SUNAMCO Committee – published in the Union Document No. 25 shall be adopted. 5. Latin letters shall be used in accordance with the IUPAC* System for writing structural figures and chemical formulae, symbols of chemical elements, compounds and names. If the chemical name appears in the title it shall be written in both Arabic and Latin. References, research papers, articles and scientific books shall be written in their original language. *See* Art. 12 of the 2004 Implementing Regulations.

Article 17 of the 2004 Implementing Regulations provides that the applicant shall provide the Directorate with a copy of the examination and research reports together with copies of applications previously filed or patents already granted by other offices for the same invention.

The Saudi Patent regime includes a number of provisions related to the amendment of the application. Based on this, amendments or additions to the application for protection, made by the applicant for the application or at the Directorate's request, may not exceed what was disclosed in the application at the time of filing, provided that the prescribed fees are paid. Further, amendments to any figure included in an application for a certificate of an industrial design entails that the date of amendment be deemed the date of filing. Nevertheless, the applicant for a patent may cancel or add any element of protection, provided that this does not lead to any change in the concept of the integrity of the invention. An applicant for protection may, free of charge, correct writing or calculation mistakes in the application, or request the introduction of changes to the data given in the application.[164]

If an applicant for a patent divides the application to several divisional applications, either on his/her own or in response to a request by the Directorate, as a result of the substantial examination which shows that the application includes more than one invention, the applicant shall specify the invention included in the original application. The applicant may also file the other inventions which are separated as independent applications governed by the provisions for a new application.[165] They shall keep the original application filing date and enjoy the right of priority, if any.[166] An applicant for protection may withdraw the application unless it has been finally decided upon.[167] However, such withdrawal shall not give the right to recover the fees paid or any other expense. The request for withdrawal shall be final and unconditional. If the application for protection is submitted by several persons, a request for withdrawal may not be accepted unless signed by them all.

Following the submission of an application, the Directorate shall publish applications for patents on invention and plant varieties within a period not exceeding eighteen months from the date of filing the application, after paying the specified fee.[168]

The Directorate shall examine the registered applications in terms of formalities. If it appears, from the examination, that some of the legally prescribed conditions are not satisfied it may instruct the applicant to satisfy them within a maximum period of ninety days from the date of notification. If the applicant did not fulfil what was

164. *Ibid.*, Art. 32.

165. Under Saudi law, the patent application should relate to a single invention or to a group of integrated parts that form a single inventive concept. The applicant, before a decision to grant a patent is made, may divide the application into more than one, provided that none of them shall deviate from what was disclosed in the original application. The date of filing the original application or the date of priority shall be deemed to be the date of filing of these applications. The 2004 Saudi Patent Law, Art. 46.

166. The 2004 Implementing Regulations, Art. 33.

167. The 2004 Saudi Patent Law, Art. 15.

168. The 2004 Implementing Regulations, Art. 11.

requested within the said period, the application would be considered as if it had never been filed.[169]

In addition, the 2004 Saudi Patent Law provides that once the application for patent or plant patent has been examined in terms of formalities, it shall be examined in terms of substance, in accordance with what is stated under the 2004 Implementing Regulations.[170]

In case where the Directorate finds that the application has satisfied the stipulated conditions, it shall issue a decision granting the protection document. The said decision shall be published in sequence as regard to its issuance by the Directorate. If the Directorate finds that the applicant does not qualify for the protection document, it shall issue a decision stating the reasons for the rejection, and the applicant shall be notified thereof.[171]

The registration procedures itself is highlighted under Part Five of the Implementing Regulations. Based on this, Article 34 of the Implementing Regulations states that registered applications shall be examined to ensure that they satisfy the formal conditions provided for in Articles 8 and 10 of the 2004 Saudi Patent Law and the articles of Part Two of the Implementing Regulations for each subject of protection. If it is found from the formal examination that some of the prescribed conditions are not satisfied, the applicant shall be requested to satisfy them within a period not exceeding ninety days from the date of notifying him thereof. If he/she fails to perform what is requested from him/her within the said period, his/her application shall be deemed null and void.

The Directorate shall assess the necessary expenses for the examination of the substance of the application for a patent or a plant patent. The assessments shall be in accordance with the actual cost of examination, and the applicant shall be required to pay it within three months from the date of his/her notification thereof. If the applicant fails to pay, the application shall be rejected and this shall be recorded in the Register and published in the Gazette. Upon payment of the costs assessed above, the Directorate shall examine the substance of the application.[172]

Actual substantive examination may take place in order to ensure that the application satisfies the conditions provided for in Articles 4, 43, 44, 45 and 46 of the 2004 Saudi Patent Law and the provisions stipulated in these Regulations. For that purpose, it may perform the following:

- Classify the application in accordance with the International Classification of Patents.
- Examine the protection elements, the description and the illustrations.
- Search the databases at the Directorate, or on the Internet or at other patent offices.
- Compare available documents with the invention.

The Directorate shall prepare the report of the substantial examination which shall include its opinion as to whether the application satisfies the conditions provided for

169. *Ibid.*, Art. 12.
170. *Ibid.*, Art. 13.
171. *Ibid.*, Art. 14.
172. *Ibid.*, Art. 35.2-3.

and the required explanations and amendments.[173] More specifically, Article 41 of the Implementing Regulations provides that the Directorate may, in the course of examining the substance of the applications submitted to it, make use of research reports, substantial examination reports and protection documents issued by patent offices and offices of plant variety protection of other countries. The Committee may request the Directorate to expedite the examination of an application for a protection document at the request of the applicant that there is an infringement or imminent infringement of the subject matter of protection.[174] The applicant shall provide the Committee with whatever supports his request to expedite the examination and whatever the Committee requires from him to prove that his claim is genuine.

Once completed, the Directorate shall notify the applicant of the result of the substantial examination, including the report of the first substantial examination. The applicant shall submit to the Directorate amendments to the application that are in line with the report. If he disagrees with any item in the report he shall give justification. If the Directorate is satisfied with the amendments or the justifications submitted by the applicant it shall proceed to complete the grant procedures. If the Directorate finds out the contrary, it shall notify the applicant of the report of the second substantial examination, and the applicant shall submit to the Directorate amendments to the application that are in give justification. If the Directorate is satisfied with the amendments or the justifications given by the applicant, it shall proceed to complete the grant procedures, but if it finds out the contrary, it shall issue a decision rejecting the application. The applicant shall respond to the notices addressed to him by the Directorate within three months from their date. This period may be extended for one month, if necessary, by a reasoned application submitted prior to the expiration of the grace period. In the absence of a response within the specified period, the application shall be rejected.[175]

Following the examination, and upon ascertaining that the application for protection has satisfied the prescribed conditions, the Directorate shall notify the applicant thereof and require him to pay the grant and publication fees within a period of three months. Upon payment, the Directorate shall issue the protection document and publish that in the Gazette. If he does not pay within the specified period, the application shall be rejected.[176] If it appears to the Directorate that the application for the protection document does not satisfy the prescribed conditions, it shall issue a reasoned decision rejecting the application and this shall be notified to the applicant and published in the Gazette.[177]

Notably, the filing of the patent application shall not be accepted unless the applicant pays the designated fee. The following table includes the applicable fees for registration and renewal of patents in Saudi Arabia.

---

173. *Ibid.*, Art. 36.
174. The Committee referred to is the committee stipulated under Art. 35 of the 2004 Saudi Patents Law.
175. The 2004 Implementing Regulations, Art. 42.
176. *Ibid.*, Art. 44.
177. *Ibid.*

No.	*Fees*	*Individuals* (SAR)	*Corporations* (SAR)
(1)	Registration Application	400	800
(2)	Change or Transfer of Ownership	200	400
(3)	Amendment or Addition to the Application	100	200
(4)	Obtaining a Copy of the Application or Certificate	50	100
(5)	Registration of Licence Contracts	400	800
(6)	Grant of Compulsory Licence	4,000	8,000
(7)	Grant and Publication	500	1,000
(8)	**Annual fees**		
(8/1)	1st Year	250	500
	2nd Year	500	1,000
	3rd Year	750	1,500
	4th Year	1,000	2,000
	5th Year	1,250	2,500
	6th Year	1,500	3,000
	7th Year	1,750	3,500
	8th Year	2,000	4,000
	9th Year	2,250	4,500
	10th Year	2,500	5,000
	11th Year	2,750	5,500
	12th Year	3,000	6,000
	13th Year	3,250	6,500
	14th Year	3,500	7,000
	15th Year	3,750	7,500
	16th Year	4,000	8,000
	17th Year	4,250	8,500
	18th Year	4,500	8,500
	19th Year	4,750	9,000
	20th Year	5,000	9,500

According to the available statistics realized by the Saudi Patent Office, 787 patent applications were filed in 2014, 561 patents were granted, 698 applications were rejected and 341 patents lapsed in 2014.[178]

178. For more details *see* http://www.kacst.edu.sa/en/innovation/patents/pages/statistics.aspx.

§5. Filing of Applications Through the GCC Patent Office

54. As mentioned, Saudi Arabia is a party to the GCC PCT. Therefore, interested applicants may file for patent protection in all GCC Member States through making an application to the GCC Patent office based in the Saudi Capital, Riyadh.

For patentability requirements, Article 2 of the 2002 GCC Patent Law requires that the invention must be new, involves an inventive step, industrially applicable and is not contrary to the laws of Islamic *Shariah*, public order or to morality observed in any of the GCC states. Moreover, Article 2 of the GCC Patent Law states that these inventions shall be 'pertaining to new products, industrial processes, or to manufacturing methods'.

Moreover, the 2002 GCC Patent Law includes a number of exceptions from patentability. These include the following:

(1) Discoveries, scientific theories, mathematical methods and computer programs.
(2) Schemes, rules, methods for doing business, performing purely mental acts or playing games.
(3) Plant varieties and species of animals and biological processes used to produce plants or animals with the exception of microbiological processes and the products thereof.
(4) Methods of surgical or therapeutic treatment of the human or animal body and methods of diagnoses applied to the human or animal body with the exception of products used in any of these methods.
(5) This regulation shall not protect varieties of plants or species of animals.[179]

More importantly, the 2002 GCC Patent Law grants the GCC Ministerial Council the right to exclude from patentability some inventions whenever necessary to safeguard public order or morality, including the protection of human or animal or plantation life and health, or to avoid serious damage to the environment.[180]

In addition, the 2002 GCC Patent Law and in line with the objectives set in its Preamble, exempts the following from patent protection:

> Acts carried particularly for scientific research purposes.
>
> The use of patent articles on means of transportation temporarily or accidentally entering the territories of the Council States, whether such articles were used in the body, apparatus, devices, equipment, or any other accessories of the said means, provided use of such articles is limited to their necessities.[181]

The 2002 GCC Patent Law awards patent protection for a period of twenty years from the filing date. This is the same term of protection also provided under the 2004 Saudi Patent Law.

179. GCC Patent Law, Art. 3.
180. GCC Patent Law, Art. 4.
181. GCC Patent Law, Art. 14 (1-2).

The GCC Patent Regulation Implementing Bylaws state that upon the satisfaction of the requirements for the granting of a patent, an objection/opposition against the patent application must be made within a period of three months from the date of announcing the acceptance of the patent application. If no objection was made during that period, the patent shall be officially registered and the patent certificate shall be delivered to the applicant.[182]

Patent examination process is undertaken through the GCC Patent Office in Riyadh. Following the establishment of the GCC back in 1981, the GCC Member States approved the creation of the GCC Patent Office as a regional office by the Supreme Council of the GCC states at its summit meeting held in Abu Dhabi, on 21 September 1992.

In addition, although some patent applications are available online through the GCC Patent Office website,[183] these remain limited to certain periods of time and do not cover all patent applications and registrations made throughout the years. Following are in brief the steps of patent registration under the GCC Patent Office.

First, the application to file a patent must be filled with all the relevant and requested details and documents provided attached to it. The patent request must include the following details: the title of the invention, the applicant's name, the investor's name, the authorized agent's name, enclosures, any additional information and finally the signing of the ratification section by the applicant.

Applicants domiciled outside the territory of the Member States must be represented by an intellectual property attorney or agent. According to Article 6 of the 2002 GCC Patent Law, if the patent applicant is not resident in any GCC state, he/she shall then appoint a registered agent who is a GCC resident to represent him in carrying out the various activities needed on his behalf.[184]

If an applicant elected to file a GCC patent application with the GCC Patent Office, he or his agent must as expressly provided for by the Implementing Regulations, should upon request by the Office, advise about 'the dates and numbers of any patent application he has filed with another office for the same invention, or for an invention that is identical to that applied for in the application submitted to the Director General of the Office'.[185] In the event, no application has been filed with any patent office of

182. The Implementing Bylaws of the GCC Patent Regulation, Art. 20 states: '*Should it be found from the substantive examination that the application meets the requirements stipulated in the Regulation and the Implementing Bylaws, the applicant shall be notified to pay the publication and grant fee, once the Office has approved the grant. Payment of the fee shall be made within three (3) months from the date of receipt of the notification. The decision shall be published, and the patent shall be delivered to the applicant after payment of the publication and grant fee. Otherwise, he shall be notified to pay within an additional period of three (3) months, after which the application shall be considered void. If any concerned individual submits no objection to the Committee within three (3) months from the proclamation date, the patent shall be entered in the register, and delivered to the applicant.*'

183. The country was the first in the region to allow for online filing in this regard. Available at www.gccpo.org.

184. GCC Patent Law, Art. 6 states: '*If the applicant is a non-GCC resident, he shall appoint a registered agent who is a GCC resident to represent him in carrying out activities entrusted to him by the Patent Office.*'

185. GCC Patent Implementing Bylaws, Art. 31.1.

any Member State, the applicant or his agent is required to sign an undertaking in the prescribed form not to file a patent application with any patent office of any Member State.

The application and the fees shall then be submitted to the GCC Patent Office which in turn will study the application from a formal aspect, checking that all relevant documents are available and that the file is ready.

Article 8 of the 2002 GCC Patent Law gives the applicant the right to withdraw the application anytime as long as no final decision has been taken against the application. The application withdrawal shall not entail the withdrawal of documents or the refunding of any fees or costs.

Once the application satisfies the terms and requirements, the GCC Patent Office shall register the application filing date and formally examine it. The 2002 GCC Patent Law provides that the Substantive Examination of the patent will either be undertaken by the Patent Office itself or referred to one of the approved examination authorities after payment of the Substantive Examination fee.[186]

If it was found during the examination that some of the terms prescribed by the law were missing, the Patent Office may request that the applicant completes the application requirements within three months at most from the date of notification. If the applicant failed to do so during that period, then the application will lapse.[187]

However, should the application meet and satisfy the requirements, the GCC Patent Office shall make a decision to grant, register and publish the patent. The Letters of Patent shall be delivered to the owner three months from the publication date as long as no party submits any objection to the Grievance Committee.[188]

On the other hand, if the Examination finds that the applicant is not eligible for a patent, the Patent Office shall make a decision to reject the application with reference to the reasons of such a rejection. A copy shall be delivered to the applicant and the rejection shall be published.[189]

The fees for filing a patent are SAR 2,000 (approx. USD 600) for Individuals and SAR 4,000 (approximately USD 1,200) for Companies.[190]

§6. Filing of International Applications

55. On 3 May 2013, Saudi Arabia deposited its instrument of accession to the PCT, thus becoming the 147th Contracting State of the PCT, and became on 3 August 2013 bound by the PCT. As a result of joining the PCT in 2001, it is now possible to file international patent and utility model applications in Saudi Arabia. This is done

186. An evaluation will be made to estimate whether substantive examination is required. In the event it is required, the applicant will be notified as such, provided the applicant shall pay the prescribed fee within three months from the date of notification. Substantive examination shall be carried out by the office, or referred to one of the approved examination authorities. *See* the 2002 GCC Patent Law, Art. 9.
187. GCC Patent Law, Art. 10.
188. GCC Patent Law, Art. 11.
189. GCC Patent Law, Art. 11.
190. Full list of fees is available at GCC Patent Office website, at www.gccpo.org.

through the Saudi Patent Office by using the forms designated to that purpose accompanies by the requested documents and the prescribed fees.[191] It was reported that the Saudi Patent Office has accepted its first PCT national stage entry on 3 February 2015, eighteen months after its accession to the PCT system.[192]

With relation to this, it was reported that the country has just published recently new Implementing Regulations of the Patent Law to include provisions concerning the national stage entry of PCT patent applications and that these regulations entered into force starting 19 December 2015.[193] Saba also reported that the new Implementing Regulations include the possibility of requesting extensions of time during prosecution, and the possibility to restore abandoned or cancelled patent applications. In addition, the international filing date will be the filing date of a PCT national entry and the base year for calculating annuities.[194]

Generally, the application may be submitted by the inventor, his/her successor or by an attorney. In the event the application is signed by an agent, the document appointing him/her shall be attached and shall observe the model established by the International Bureau.

The rules further provide that an international application filed with the Intellectual Property Department as receiving Office may be filed in Arabic or in English and the prescribed transmittal fee shall be paid to the Directorate. In any case, any application must comply with the requirements of the PCT and the Regulations thereunder. The Directorate states that a discount will be applied in the case of electronic filing.

Once received, the Saudi Patent Office shall stamp the date of receipt of the application on the application. If the application does not comply with the requirements

---

191. For the application form *see* http://www.kacst.edu.sa/ar/innovation/patents/Documents/Receiving-Office-information-for-filing-PCT-International.pdf, and for the fees *see* http://www.wipo.int/export/sites/www/pct/en/fees.pdf.

192. Notably, the Saudi Patent Office, in its capacity as a receiving Office, has notified the International Bureau that it is prepared to receive and process international applications in electronic form with effect from 1 Feb. 2015. *See* http://www.clydeco.com/uploads/Files/CC007038_MENA_IP_newsletter_March_2015_09-03-15.pdf. Last visited 4 Oct. 2015.

193. For more *see* Saba IP, available at http://www.sabaip.com/en/News/Saudi-Arabia-New-Regulations-for-Entering-PCT-National-Phase-.

194. *Ibid.*

of Article 11 of the PCT,[195] the Directorate shall give notice thereof to the applicant and shall establish the time period within which the necessary corrections must be submitted. For this purpose, the filing date of the international application is the date of the receipt of the application in compliance with Article 11 of the PCT or, in the event one or more corrections are necessary, the date of receipt of such correction or corrections. The Saudi Patent Office will follow the guidelines of the PCT accordingly.

§7. Ownership and Transfer

56. A patent awards its holder a number of legal rights. However, prior to obtaining such rights, it is important to determine the holder of such rights. The law in general have established a number of principles which would assist in determining the identity of the patent owner.

Article 5 of the 2004 Saudi Patent Law contains the rules applicable to patent ownership. Accordingly and as a general rule, the right to a patent shall belong to the inventor whose name was stated in the application.

The 2004 Saudi Patent Law also deals with the situation of joint ownership. Based on this, if two or more persons have jointly come up with an invention, the right to the patent shall belong to them equally unless they have agreed otherwise.[196] However, the 2004 Saudi Patent Law further elaborates that no one shall be deemed a partner unless he/she contributes to the subject matter of protection, and his/her efforts are only confined to assistance in its execution.[197]

Where the same invention was made by more than one person independently of each other, the person whose application has the earliest filing date or, if priority is claimed, the earliest validly claimed priority date shall have the right to the patent, as

195. Article 11 of the PCT states that the receiving Office shall accord as the international filing date the date of receipt of the international application, provided that the Office has found that, at the time of receipt: (1) The applicant does not obviously lack, for reasons of residence or nationality, the right to file an international application with the receiving Office, (2) The international application is in the prescribed language, (3) The international application contains at least the following elements: a. An indication that it is intended as an international application, b. The designation of at least one Contracting State, c. The name of the applicant, as prescribed, d. A part which on the face of it appears to be a description, e. A part which on the face of it appears to be a claim or claims.(4) (a) If the receiving Office finds that the international application did not, at the time of receipt, fulfil the requirements listed in para. (1), it shall, as provided in the Regulations, invite the applicant to file the required correction;(b) If the applicant complies with the invitation, as provided in the Regulations, the receiving Office shall accord as the international filing date the date of receipt of the required correction.(5) Subject to Art. 64(4), any international application fulfilling the requirements listed in items (i) to (iii) of para. (1) and accorded an international filing date shall have the effect of a regular national application in each designated State as of the international filing date, which date shall be considered to be the actual filing date in each designated State.(6) Any international application fulfilling the requirements listed in items (i) to (iii) of para. (1) shall be equivalent to a regular national filing within the meaning of the Paris Convention for the Protection of Industrial Property.

196. The 2004 Saudi Patent Law, Art. 5.b.

197. *Ibid.*, Art. 5.c.

long as the said application is not withdrawn, abandoned or rejected. In order to establish the right of preference, the Registrar shall take into account the matter claimed in the applications. Clearly, the Saudi legal regime adopts the 'first to file' approach in this regard.[198]

Regardless of the above, Article 5.e of the 2004 Saudi Patent Law provides that the person who develops the subject matter of protection shall have the right to state his/her name in that capacity in the protection document.

If the inventor is an employee the law provides several scenarios in this regard. To start with, as a general rule, the employer shall be the owner of the protection document, unless the work contract stipulates otherwise, where its subject matter results from the execution of a contract, or an obligation providing for exerting efforts to develop it, or if the employer proves that the employee would not have developed the subject matter of the protection had he/she not used facilities, means or data made available through his/her employment.[199] This however shall bc without prejudice to the employee's right to receive a special award to be agreed upon with the consent of both parties, or assessed by the Committee in light of the various circumstances of the contract of employment, and the economic importance of the subject matter of the protection. Any special agreement depriving the employee of this right shall be null and void.[200]

For the above purpose, the law further states that an application for a protection document filed by the employee within a period of two years from the date of termination of employment shall be deemed as if submitted during the employment.[201] These provisions will also apply to government employees.[202]

Notably, Article 6.e of the 2004 Saudi Patent Law contains some previsions related to the special case where the subject matter of protection developed relates to national security. In such a case, it shall be governed by the provisions stipulated in the 2004 Implementing Regulations.[203]

Article 7 of the 2004 Saudi Patent Law states that if the subject matter claimed in the application or in the protection document is derived from a subject matter owned by a person other than the applicant or the owner of the protection document, then this person may request the Committee to transfer the ownership of the application or protection document to him/her. The case for the transfer application shall not be heard after the elapse of a period of five years of granting the protection unless the applicant's bad faith is established.

Article 16 of the 2004 Patent Law deals with the issue of assignment of patents. Based on this, the law provides that any action resulting in the assignment of the protection application or the protection document itself must be in writing, signed by the two parties and approved by an authority acceptable to the Directorate. No transfer of title, relating either to the protection application or to the protection document itself

198. *Ibid.*, Art. 5.d.
199. *Ibid.*, Art. 6.a.
200. *Ibid.*, Art. 6.b.
201. *Ibid.*, Art. 6 c.
202. *Ibid.*, Art. 6 d.
203. *See* for more discussion Art. 40 of the 2004 Implementing Regulations.

shall be effective vis-à-vis a third party, except after filing the change application, paying the required fees and recording it in the Directorate registers.

If several parties participated in filing one protection application or in the ownership of one protection document, each one of them may assign his/her right in the application or the protection document to any of the partners, to all of them, or to a third party. The Directorate shall publish the transfer of title in the Gazette.

Moreover, if the protection document is disposed of to others in accordance with any act of disposition, or the right to exploit it is transferred to others for any reason, the owner of the protection document shall inform the party to whom the disposition is made or the party to whom the right of exploitation is officially transferred, of any legal measure taken in connection with the protection document, whether taken by him/her or by others against him/her.[204]

Moreover, Article 21 of the 2004 Saudi Patent Law deals with the situation of patent licensing. Based on this, the owner of the protection document may grant a contractual licence to others to perform all or some of the acts of exploitation stipulated in the special provisions, for each protected subject matter.[205] A licence contract shall not be valid vis-à-vis a third party unless the specified fee is paid and it is registered in the records of the Directorate. This licence shall not deprive the owner of the protection document from exploiting the subject matter himself or granting another licence for the same protected subject matter, unless the first licence contract states otherwise.[206]

Interestingly, the law grants the Directorate some role with relation to licensing. Based on this, the Directorate may instruct the parties to the licence contract to amend it in order to prevent abusing the right in the protection document or any other negative effect on competition or the acquisition of technology and its dissemination.[207]

The licence gives the licensee the right to perform all acts and enjoy all privileges assigned to the holder of the protection document related to the subject of protection throughout the country during the whole period of protection, unless it is otherwise stated in the licence contract. The licensee shall not assign the rights and privileges licensed to him by the owner of the protection document, unless it is expressly stated in the licence contract.[208]

§8. Scope of Exclusive Rights

57. Article 47 of the 2004 Saudi Patent Law provides the main rights exclusively derived from the legal protection of a patent. As a general rule, a patent shall confer on its owner the right to prevent third parties from exploiting the patented invention

204. The 2004 Saudi Patent Law, Art. 17.
205. Notably, Art. 1 of the 2004 Saudi Patent Law defines a contractual licence as 'A contract under which the owner of the protection document grants a third party some or all of his rights to exploit the protection document for a specified period against a specified fee.'
206. The 2004 Saudi Patent Law, Art. 21.
207. *Ibid.*, Art.22.
208. *Ibid.*, Art.23.

in the country. The right of the patent owner is defined by the submitted claims. In this regard, 'exploiting' a patented invention means any of the following acts:

(1) If it is a product: Its manufacture, sale, offering for sale, use, storage or its importation for any of these purposes.
(2) If it is a process: The use of the process, or performing any of the acts referred to in the previous paragraph, in relation to the product which is directly obtained by the use of this process.

Several types of activities are explicitly excluded from the effects of the patentee's exclusive rights under the 2004 Saudi Patent Law. As known, the majority of patent laws provide for exceptions to the exclusive rights granted by a patent; however, the scope and content of these provisions may vary from one country to another.[209] This confirms that patent rights are not absolute but rather subject to constraints and limitations. The purpose of these exceptions is to foster and promote the transfer of technology, prevention of abuse and anti-competitive intellectual property practices and the protection of public interest and health.

For example, Article 47 of the 2004 Saudi Patent Law states that:

(1) The owner of the protection document's right shall not preclude others from exploiting his/her invention in non-commercial activities relating to scientific research.

In addition, Article 47 of the 2004 Implementing Regulations states that the following acts related to government shall not be deemed infringement of a patent:

- The use of the means subject of the patent aboard ships of other countries of the Paris Union, whether in the body of the ship or its machines, equipment or in any part of it when such a ship temporarily or accidentally enters the country's territorial waters, provided that the use of all these means is limited to the needs of the ship.
- The use of equipment subject of the patent in the manufacture or operation of air or land vehicles or their spare parts belonging to another country of the Paris Union, when such vehicles enter the country temporarily or accidentally.

In relation to parallel importation, the 2004 Saudi Patent Law does not contain an explicit provision. However, it is believed the country adopts an international exhaustion regime in this regard. In brief, parallel importation allows for the importation of products when they are lawfully available in a foreign country at a lower price, thus enabling countries and consumers to buy cheaper products. This requires as a prerequisite that a country adopts an exhaustion regime suitable to its national needs and priorities.

209. *See* generally C. Garrison, 'Exceptions to Patent Rights in Developing Countries', paper submitted to the International Centre for Trade and Sustainable Development, ICTSD Project on IPRs and Sustainable Development, issue 17 (Geneva, August 2006). Also *see* C. Correa 'International Dimension of the Research Exception', SIPPI Project, AAAS (Washington, DC, 2005). Available at http://sippi.aaas.org/intlexemptionpaper.shtmli.

§9. Limitations and Exceptions to the Scope of Patent Protection: Compulsory Licences

58. The 2004 Saudi Patent Law includes some limitations on the rights derived from a patent. Article 24 of the 2004 Saudi Patent Law in compliance with Article 5 of the Paris Union Convention of 1883 (as subsequently amended) provides some guidance in relation to the issuance of compulsory licences in the country.[210] Based on this, the 2004 Saudi Patent Law states that a compulsory licence shall be issued without the consent of the owner based on the following conditions.

Article 24.a of the 2004 Saudi Patent Law explains the circumstances whereby a compulsory licence may be issued. Based on this, the City may grant a compulsory licence to a third party to exploit an invention covered by the patent upon an application submitted to it, according to the following:

(1) The application shall be submitted after the elapse of a period of four years from the date of filing the patent application or three years from the date of granting the patent, whichever expires later, without the owner of the protection document exploiting his/her invention or having exploited it in an inadequate fashion, unless he/she justifies that with a legitimate excuse.
(2) The applicant for the compulsory licence must prove that he/she has exerted – over a reasonable period of time – efforts in order to obtain a contractual licence on the basis of reasonable commercial conditions, and for a reasonable financial compensation. However, this provision and the provision of the preceding paragraph do not apply where the applicant is a government body or a person authorized by it, and the aim was to meet public interest – especially security, health, nutrition or the development other vital sectors of the national economy – or to meet a state of emergency or other very compelling circumstances, or where the aim thereof was public non-commercial purposes. In the latter case, and upon knowledge of the existence of a patent, their holder shall be promptly informed.[211]

Notably, the Saudi Law provides that the compulsory licence shall be granted to make the invention or design available in the local markets. But this provision does not apply where the aim of the licence is to prevent or restrict practices against which a decision or judgment is issued declaring them to be acts of unlawful competition.[212]

Notably, Article 24.a (5) of the 2004 Saudi Patent Law provides that the decision granting the licence shall specify the scope and term of the licence, according to the purpose for which it was granted. The licence shall be subject to termination if the

---

210. Article 1 of the 2004 Saudi Patent Law defines 'Compulsory License' as the permission given to others to exploit the subject matter of protection without the consent of the owner of the protection document, in accordance with the provisions of this law.
211. This is a situation applicable in the case of government use exception. With relation to this, Art. 48 of the 2004 Implementing Regulations states that: '*An application for a compulsory license submitted by any government agency to exploit the inventions shall include a statement of the public interest considerations requiring that. Such considerations shall be provided for in the decision permitting the exploitation.*'
212. The 2004 Saudi Patent Law, Art. 24.a (4).

conditions for which it was granted cease to exist and their recurrence is not likely, with due regards to the lawful interests of the licensee. The licence shall not be exclusive.

The City has the authority to decide on each application independently. However, the grant of the compulsory licence shall be subject to awarding the owner of the protection document a fair compensation. The Committee shall determine the amount of the compensation, and the licensee undertakes to pay it.[213]

Furthermore, if the compulsory licence is related to a patent of semi-conductor technology, the purpose of the licence shall be for public non-commercial purposes only or to control acts concerning which a decision or judgment is issued declaring them to be acts of unlawful competition.[214]

Another condition is stipulated under Article 24.c of the 2004 Saudi Patent Law related to the case of exploitation of another patent. Accordingly, if the patent involves a significant technological advance with a considerable economic value, which requires the exploitation of another patent, the City may grant the owner of the protection document a compulsory licence to exploit the other patent. In such a case the compulsory licence shall not be assigned unless the other patent is assigned. The owner of the other patent shall be entitled to a counter licence from the compulsory licence, in accordance with reasonable conditions.

Granted compulsory licences are non-assignable according to Article 26 of the 2004 Saudi Patent Law. Based on this, if a compulsory licence is granted for a patented subject matter the beneficiary of the compulsory licence may not assign it to others, unless the assignment includes all or part of the firm benefiting from the licence or its goodwill. The City's approval of the assignment is required; otherwise, it shall be null and void. If the City approves such assignment, the assignee becomes liable for the obligations assumed by the first beneficiary prior to the approval of the assignment. Nevertheless, the City may amend the decision to grant the compulsory licence if need arises. The owner of the protection document or the beneficiary of the compulsory licence may request the City to make this amendment if its prerequisites are fulfilled. The reasons for the decision of the City to amend the licence or to reject the request must be stated.[215]

Cancellation of the compulsory licence may take place under the following circumstances:[216]

(1) If the beneficiary of the licence fails to exploit it in a way that satisfies the country's needs, within a period not exceeding two years from the grant of the licence, renewable for an equal period, if it is proved that there is a legitimate cause.
(2) If the beneficiary of the compulsory licence fails to pay the due fees within a period of ninety days from the due date, including the compensations to which the owner of the protection document is entitled, as stipulated in the decision granting the licence.
(3) If the beneficiary of the compulsory licence fails to observe any condition necessary for granting of the licence.

213. *Ibid.*, Art. 24.a 7.
214. *Ibid.*, Art. 24.b.
215. *Ibid.*, Art. 27.
216. *Ibid.*, Art. 28.

The beneficiary of the compulsory licence may relinquish/terminate the licence by a written request to the City. However, the relinquishment/termination becomes effective from the date of approval of the City.[217] In addition, the relinquishment/termination of compulsory licence shall only be accepted with a written consent of the beneficiary of the licence, or the proof of the existence of compelling circumstances justifying this relinquishment/termination. Decisions of compulsory licence, its amendment, withdrawal, transference to others and relinquishment/termination shall be entered in the records of the Directorate, published in the Gazette and notified to the owner of the protection document accordingly.[218]

The relinquishment/termination shall be registered and published in the Gazette, and it shall not be effective against a third party except from the date of publication.[219]

Any party with interest may challenge the decision of granting of a protection document before the Committee, and seek total or partial revocation, relying upon the violation of the stipulated conditions for granting the protection document. The owner of the protection document shall include the beneficiary of the licence as a party to the lawsuit; otherwise, the latter may interfere on his/her own. The Committee may order to enter any party with interest, and the 2004 Implementing Regulations shall specify the grounds upon which the request for the revocation of any protection document shall be based.[220]

A judgment of total or partial invalidity of the decision granting the protection document renders the decision null and void from the date of issuance, within the scope of what is nullified. However, the decision to nullify the protection document shall not imply a refund of the sums paid for the licence to exploit it, unless the licensee proves that what he/she has gained, as a result of the licence, is not equal to what he/she has paid, in which case he may recover the amount exceeding the gain he/she received. The decision of annulment of granting the protection document shall be published after its issuance, and shall be effective vis-à-vis a third party from the date of publication.[221]

Any act of exploitation provided for in the special provisions governing each of the protection subject matters, performed by any person in the country without a written consent of the owner of the protection document recorded with the Directorate, shall be deemed an infringement on the subject matter of protection. At the request of the owner of the protection document, and any party with interest, the Committee shall grant an injunction to prevent the infringement in addition to the necessary damages, and it may impose a fine upon the infringer not exceeding SAR 130,000 (approx. USD 30,000). The maximum fine shall be doubled in case of repetition. If the Committee sees that the infringement calls for the punishment of imprisonment, the infringer shall be referred from the start to the BoGs. The Committee may take the necessary prompt measures it deems necessary to prevent the damages resulting from the infringement. The decision issued by the Committee in this case shall be published in the Official Gazette, the Gazette and two daily newspapers, at the expense of the party against

217. *Ibid.*, Art. 29.
218. *Ibid.*, Art. 30.
219. *Ibid.*, Art. 31.
220. *Ibid.*, Art. 32.
221. *Ibid.*, Art. 33.

whom the decision is issued. The provision of this article shall be applied, without prejudice, to any harsher punishment provided for in any other law or regulation in the country.[222]

A committee shall be formed of three law specialists and two technical experts whose grade shall not be lower than grade twelve.[223] The members shall be nominated by the President of the City. The formation of the Committee shall be pursuant to a resolution by the Council of Ministers for a term of three years renewable for one time only. The resolution shall appoint one of the law specialists as chairman of the Committee.[224]

The Committee shall have jurisdiction over the following:

(1) All disputes and appeals against decisions issued in connection with protection documents
(2) Penal lawsuits for violations of the provisions of the 2004 Saudi Patent Law and its 2004 Implementing Regulations.

The litigants shall be notified of the lawsuits filed with the Committee, in accordance with the Implementing Regulations.[225]

Decisions of the Committee shall be issued by majority vote, provided that the grounds for the decisions are stated, and their text is read in a public session. The Committee shall not refuse to issue a decision in the lawsuit on the ground that there is no provision to govern the dispute in the 2004 Saudi Patent Law or the 2004 Implementing Regulations. In that case the Committee shall refer to the general rules observed in the country. An appeal against any decision issued by the Committee may be brought before the BoGs within a period of sixty days from the date of notification of the decision.[226]

The Committee may contact the government bodies concerned and request any explanation and information it deems necessary. The City shall provide the Committee with all documents and papers relating to applications or subject matters of protection in dispute, whenever requested to do so by the Committee.[227]

The Committee may seek the assistance of different expert bodies for whatever it deems necessary of the technical matters referred to it, and it shall determine the litigants liable for the expenses incurred.[228] Reviewing of the protection documents and any related information registered with the Directorate may be allowed free of charge. Any person may obtain copies therefrom, upon payment of the required fees.[229]

Employees of the Directorate and members of the Committee shall not disclose technical information relating to the protection applications of which they become cognizant in their capacity to any person, unless such person is officially authorized

222. *Ibid.*, Art. 34.
223. In accordance with the Saudi administrative trading regime.
224. The 2004 Saudi Patent Law, Art. 35.
225. *Ibid.*, Art. 36.
226. *Ibid.*, Art. 37.
227. *Ibid.*, Art. 38.
228. *Ibid.*, Art. 39.
229. *Ibid.*, Art. 40.

to receive that information in accordance with the rules applicable in the country. They shall also not disclose such information to the public or use it in any way. This undertaking continues after the end of their service. Employees of the Directorate and members of the Committee may not obtain any of the protection documents or deal in any of the rights relating to them during their service and for a period of at least two years after the end of service.[230]

Finally, it is noteworthy to explain the 2004 Implementing Regulations contain several clauses specifically dedicated to security related applications. Based on this, Article 49 of the 2004 Implementing Regulations states that the procedures for security related applications shall be as follows:

- Each government employee, military or civilian, who invents a device or military ammunition within the scope of his duties, undertakes to assign his invention and all resulting benefits to the competent authority in the government upon its approval.
- Also, any person, other than the above mentioned, who invents a device or military ammunition, undertakes to assign his/she invention and all resulting benefits to the competent authority in the government upon its approval. This authority shall pay the person a fair compensation.
- Each person who assigns his/her invention to the competent authority in the government in accordance with the above two paragraphs and all others who are aware of the assignment undertake to keep secret the invention and the assignment, and shall not disclose the same except to authorized persons.
- The competent authority in the government, after obtaining the necessary assignment from the inventors, may apply to the Chairman of the City for a patent for all these inventions and enclose with the application a request to keep the application confidential. The City shall follow all usual procedures in connection with the application and undertake not to publish information about it.
- The application, specification, drawings, amendments, the patent and any copy thereof shall be kept in a sealed and stamped file, and it shall be at the disposal of the competent authority in the government throughout the term of the protection. It may be opened only by the competent authority or by its order.
- Contents of the sealed file may not be made available for publication or review by others under any circumstances.
- The sealed, stamped file shall be delivered at any time during the term of protection to any person to whom the competent authority in the government requests delivery, and it shall be resealed and stamped again immediately upon its return.
- The sealed, stamped file shall be sent to the competent government authority after the expiration of the protection period of the invention.
- An application to repeal a decision granting a patent in accordance with this article may not be accepted except with the approval of the competent government authority.
- Initiation of an action for infringement in connection with these inventions may not be permitted.

230. *Ibid.*, Art. 41.

- Communications with the competent government authority in connection with an invention that includes the development of weapons or ammunitions for the purpose of examination and study of the invention shall not be considered disclosure or use. Nor shall actions, not deemed to affect the entitlement to the patent, taken by the competent government authority for the purpose of studying and examining the invention.
- The Chairman of the City may order that the application and invention be dealt with as if licensed to the competent government authority, if he/she determines that a given invention in the field of weaponry and ammunitions, as described in the patent application, has not been assigned to the competent government authority, is security related and its publication is prohibited on national security grounds.

Although the 2004 Saudi Patent Law provides conditions for the issuance of compulsory and government use licences, it must be stated in this regard that there is still the need for more detailed regulations in this regard particularly those related to the process and procedures of issuing such licences. For example, there is no guidance for determining the 'fair compensation' that should be paid to the patent holder in the event that a compulsory or government use licence is issued.

As it is the case with the majority of other countries in the region, no compulsory or government use licence has ever been issued in the country. An explanation is the lack of awareness about the issue of compulsory licensing in general in addition to the lack of specific legislations designed to organize and simplify the processes and procedures related to the utilization and use of compulsory licensing in the country.

§10. Duration of Protection, Maintaining and Termination of Patent Protection

59. The duration of patent protection as set by Article 19.a of the 2004 Saudi Patent Law shall be for a period of twenty years commencing from the date of the filing of the application for the registration.

According to Article 46 of the Implementing Regulations, a patent may be invalidated for a number of reasons. The bases for invalidating a patent fully or partially are the violation of the provisions of Articles 4, 43, 44 and 45 of the 2004 Saudi Patent Law. Such an option is available to any interested person who may request the court to invalidate a patent. Invalidation actions are subject to no time limitations and any interested party can file an invalidation action at any time. Notably, the party initiating an infringement action must establish its personal interest in the action by proving its ownership of the patent or its rights of exploitation under a duly recorded licence.[231] In addition, patents shall be declared void and invalidated if it turns out that the protection document was issued to a person other than the person who developed the subject matter of protection. The Directorate shall be notified of any final decision

231. Notably, this is not required under an action for revocation.

relating to invalidation of any of the protection documents immediately upon issuance, and it shall register and publish it.[232]

Finally, Article 18 of the 2004 Saudi Patent Law provides that in order to maintain the patent or patent application, a progressively increasing annual fee shall be paid in advance to the Registrar for each year. Based on this, annual fees shall be due for the protection application or the protection document – in accordance with the table referred to earlier in this section – which shall be paid at the beginning of each year starting from the year following the application filing date. If the applicant or the owner of the protection document fails to pay it within a maximum period of three months from its due date, he shall be liable to pay double the amount. If he/she fails to pay after being warned during the three months following the expiration of the first three months, the application or the protection document shall cease to be valid, and this shall be recorded in the Register and published in the Gazette. Notably, Article 18.b of the 2008 Saudi Patent Law provides that where the applicant has paid the required fees for three years without being granted the protection document, he/she may postpone payment of the fees for the following years until the decision to grant the protection document is issued.

§11. Infringement and Remedies

60. The 2004 Saudi Patent Law and its 2004 Implementing Regulations provide both criminal and civil remedies in cases of infringement of patent rights. As will be explained subsequently, the Saudi patent protection regime also provides a number of other precautionary and border measures applicable in the case of patent infringement.

Before delving into more details about the applicable remedies and penalties available under the Saudi protection regime, it is worth noting that Saudi applies a flat system of penalties applicable to all acts of infringement in this area.

Article 61 of the 2004 Saudi Patent Law makes reference to penalties applicable in case of infringement. Based on this, the article states that without prejudice to what Article 34 of the 2004 Saudi Patent Law stipulates, any party that violates any of the provisions provided for in the law shall be punished with a fine not exceeding SAR 50,000 (approx. USD 15,000), and the maximum limit shall be doubled in case of repetition.

Article 34 of the 2004 Saudi Patent Law states that any act of exploitation provided for in the special provisions governing each of the protection subject matters, performed by any person in the country without a written consent of the owner of the protection document recorded with the Directorate, shall be deemed an infringement on the subject matter of protection. At the request of the owner of the protection document, and any party with interest, the Committee shall grant an injunction to prevent the infringement in addition to the necessary damages, and it may impose a fine upon the infringer not exceeding SAR 100,000 (approx. USD 30,000). The maximum fine shall be doubled in case of repetition.

If the Committee sees that the infringement calls for the punishment of imprisonment, the infringer shall be referred from the start to the BoGs. The Committee

232. The 2004 Implementing Regulations, Art. 46.

may take the necessary prompt measures it deems necessary to prevent the damages resulting from the infringement. Moreover, the decision issued by the Committee in this case shall be published in the Official Gazette, the Gazette and two daily newspapers, at the expense of the party against whom the decision is issued. The provision of this article shall be applied, without prejudice, to any harsher punishment provided for in any other law.

Actions related to the infringement may be initiated to the Committee. Based on this, Article 47 of the 2004 Saudi Patent Law states that the owner of the protection document may initiate an action before the Committee against any person who infringes his/her invention by exploiting it in the country without his/her consent.

It is noteworthy to highlight that various clauses regulating the activities of the Committee overseeing infringement of patent cases are stated under the 2004 Implementing Regulations. Based on this, Article 50 of the 2004 Implementing Regulations states that all communications with the Committee shall be addressed directly to its chairman at the address it determines. In addition, the actions shall be filed with the Committee through a petition of one original and a number of copies equal to the number of the litigants involved, and it shall be delivered to the Secretariat of the Committee provided that it includes the following data:[233]

(1) Full name of the plaintiff, his/her profession or position, place of residence, number, date and place of issue of his identification document and the same for his/her representative, if any.
(2) Full name of the defendant, his profession or position, place of residence and the address of the plaintiff and defendant, including the number of post office box, telephone, fax the commercial name and any other means through which he may be contacted.
(3) Statement of the subject matter of the action.
(4) Statement of data and supporting evidence.

The notice shall be delivered to the address of the defendant specified in the plaintiff's petition. The notice shall be in two identical copies, one original and one copy. If there are several defendants, the copies shall be equal to their number. The notice shall contain the following:[234]

(1) Subject matter and date of the notice, indicating the day, month and year.
(2) Full name of the plaintiff, his/her profession or position, place of residence and the full name of his/her representative, his/her profession or position and place of residence.
(3) Full name of the person to whom the notice is addressed, his/her profession or position and place of residence.

Article 53 of the 2004 Implementing Regulations states that the litigants shall be notified of the actions filed with the Committee as follows:

233. The 2004 Implementing Regulations, Art. 51.
234. The 2004 Implementing Regulations, Art. 52.

(1) A copy of the notice shall be delivered to the person to whom it is addressed at his place of residence or work, if any; otherwise, it shall be delivered to the person found at his place of residence who shares it with him. If none of them is available or the person found refused to accept delivery, then it shall be delivered to the *Umdah* of the district or to the police station, as the case may be.
(2) As for government authorities, it shall be delivered to the heads or deputies of said authorities.
(3) As for commercial companies and private establishments, the notices shall be delivered to one of the joint partners, the chairman of the board or their representative or to the owner of the private establishment or his representative.
(4) As for foreign companies which have a branch or an agent in the country, notices shall be delivered to the manager of the branch or the agent.
(5) As to those residing outside the country, they shall be notified through the Ministry of Foreign Affairs. In this case, it is sufficient to receive a reply proving delivery of the notice.
(6) As for military personnel and employees of military authorities, notices shall be delivered through their competent persons in charge.
(7) As for prisoners, notices shall be delivered to prison warden.

The notice shall be legal if it is delivered to the person to whom it is addressed even if in a place other than his/her place of residence or work. In all cases the notice may be delivered by registered mail, and such notification shall be legally effective.

Article 54 of the 2004 Implementing Regulations provides that the Committee shall notify the Directorate of all rulings and decisions issued regarding actions relating to protection documents. Moreover, the Committee may immediately order, upon filing a claim, the taking of precautionary and provisional measures against the defendant, provided that the plaintiff furnishes the guarantees determined by the Committee to protect the defendant's right if the claim is not proven. The Committee may rule that the defendant compensate for damages sustained by the plaintiff as a result of the exploitation, in addition to removing the infringement.[235]

If the Committee decides to seek the assistance of expertise agencies, it may order any of the litigants it thinks liable to deposit, within a certain period of time, a sum equal to the estimated expenses of the expertise by a check certified by an approved bank in the country. If he/she fails to deposit the sum within the time specified by the Committee, the other litigant may deposit this sum without prejudice to his right of recourse against his/her opponent if the case is decided in his/her favour.

Finally, protection of patents is included under the Law of Commercial Data Royal Decree No. M/5 14 Rabi' II 1423 / 25 June 2002 (hereinafter 'the 2002 Saudi Commercial Data Law'). Based on this, Article 1 of the law states that 'as regards the implementation of the provisions of this law, any clarification related, whether directly or indirectly, to the following shall be considered as commercial data:

(a) Number of goods, their quantity, size, volume, capacity, weight, production date or expiry date.
(b) Place or country where they were manufactured or produced.

235. *Ibid.*, Art. 55.

(c) Components of their composition.
(d) Name of producer or manufacturer or his attributes.
(e) Patents or other industrial proprietary rights or any concessions, rewards, or commercial or industrial features.
(f) Nomenclature or form by which some goods are normally defined or evaluated.

Moreover, Article 7 of the 2002 Saudi Commercial Data Law states that without prejudice to any harsher punishment, anyone violating the provisions of this law shall be punished with a fine not exceeding SAR 100,000 (approx. USD 30,000). In case of repeated violation, the punishment shall be doubled, and the place of business closed for a period not exceeding a year'.

The Competent officers of the Ministry of Commerce and Industry are entrusted with inspecting and recording violations to the provisions of the 2002 Saudi Commercial Data Law.[236] The Bureau of Investigation and Prosecution shall have the jurisdiction to investigate violations to the provisions of this law and to prosecute such violations before the competent juridical authority.[237] The BoGs shall have the jurisdiction to adjudicate violations and disputes arising from implementation of the provisions of the 2002 Saudi Commercial Data Law.[238] The BoGs may render a judgment to confiscate seized items and sell whatever is sellable and to deduct its value from the compensation and fines which may be imposed, and destroy the remaining or dispose of it in the manner it may deem appropriate. The Board may render a judgment to publish the decision of conviction, confiscation or destruction in one of the daily newspapers issued in the area of residence of the convicted at his expense.[239]

Without prejudice to the right of the parties concerned to claim compensation for damages arising from the use of untruthful data, they may at any time, even prior to filing any lawsuit, resort to the BoGs to take the necessary protective measures.[240]

§12. Overlapping and Relations to Other Intellectual Property Law

61. Patent protection has been strengthened in Saudi Arabia following the accession of the country to the WTO. The 2004 Saudi Patent Law adopts a holistic approach thus encompassing under its legal framework protection for several types of intellectual property branches including trademarks, plant varieties, trade secrets and confidential information, and semi-conductors protection. Notably, the legal regime for the protection of utility patents is currently under consideration in the country.

236. The 2002 Saudi Commercial Data Law, Art. 8.
237. *Ibid.*, Art. 9.
238. *Ibid.*, Art. 10.
239. *Ibid.*, Art. 11.
240. *Ibid.*, Art. 12.

Chapter 3. Utility Models

§1. Sources: Legislation

62. It should be highlighted that the 2004 Saudi Patent Law does not contain explicit provisions for the protection of utility models. However, it was recently reported that the Saudi Patent Office is planning to introduce new directives and regulations governing the protection of utility models or 'petty patents' as may be referred to. The new directives and regulations are expected to contain provisions on the granting requirements of utility models (including the novelty requirements), the protection term, the particular subject matters excluded from utility model protection, the compulsory licensing requirements, etc.[241]

241. For more *see* http://www.sabaip.com/en/News/Saudi-Arabia-Utility-Models-Protection-on-the-Way.

Chapter 4. Trademarks

§1. Sources: Legislation

63. The legal framework of trademark protection in Saudi Arabia dates back to the 1940s.[242] In fact (and in a similar fashion to other countries in the region), trademark protection was one of the first IPRs to receive dedicated legal protection in the country.[243] In preparation for its accession to the WTO in December 2005, Saudi Arabia reformed its intellectual property protection regime by revamping it in its entirety through the introduction of various laws related to the protection of copyright, trademarks and patents. This led to the inauguration of the 2002 Saudi Trademark Law in the country (hereby referred to as the 2002 Saudi Trademark Royal Decree).[244] The 2002 Saudi Trademark Royal Decree repealed the Saudi Trademarks Law issued by the Royal Decree No. M/5 dated 4/5/1404. Furthermore, the 2002 Saudi Trademark Royal Decree was supplemented by the issuance of the 2003 Implementing Regulations (hereinafter 'the 2003 Implementing Regulations').[245]

The major changes included under the 2002 Saudi Trademark Royal Decree are:

(1) Under Article 13, an applicant may file an appeal with the Ministry of Commerce and Investment (MOCI) within a period not exceeding sixty days from the date of receiving a refusal notice. If the appeal is rejected, the applicant may file an appeal with the BoGs, the Administrative Court, within a period not exceeding thirty days from the date of receiving a notification.
(2) According to Article 15, formerly Article 16 of the repealed law, interested parties may file their opposition against registration of marks with the BoGs within a period not exceeding ninety days from the publication date without the need to substantiate opposition.
(3) Article 23 gives the trademark owner a grace period of six months following the expiry of the protection period to file a renewal application.
(4) Pursuant to Article 54, formerly Article 60, the Investigation and Public Prosecution Commission shall be the authority to defend public rights in respect of penal actions.

242. *See* The Trademarks Law issued by Royal Decree No. 8762 dated 28.7.1358 (corresponding to year 1939) repealing the Saudi Trademark Act of 1934.
243. *See* Abdullah Al Fehaidi, Al Alamat Al Tejareyeh, First Edition. 2011 Dar Al Hadarah Lilnasher wa Al Tawzee, Saudi Arabia, at 85.
244. The Royal Decree No. M/21 28 *Jumada I* 1423/7 equivalent to August 2002. This law shall be published in the Official Gazette and shall come into effect after ninety days from its publication, and shall repeal the Trademarks Law issued by the Royal Decree No. M/5 dated 4.5.1404. The Royal Decree No. 38/2000 Promulgating the Law of Trademarks, Descriptions and Secrets and Protection from Unfair Competition.
245. The 2003 Implementing Regulations were issued on 4 Oct. 2002 by Ministerial Order Number 1723. The law repeals the Trademark Law and Implementing Regulations 1984.

As explained, the Saudi Arabian trademark protection regime has been subject to a major reform following the country's accession to the WTO in 2005.[246] As many other countries in the region, the Saudi Trademark Law has a rich history of court and judicial decisions.

Trademark protection is obtained through applications made at the Trademark Office based at the Ministry of Commerce and Industry in Riyadh.

Several international treaties with direct effect on the trademark protection regime have been ratified by Saudi Arabia. The following may be mentioned in this regard:

(1) The Paris Convention for the Protection of Industrial Property of 1883, in force in the country since 14 July 1999.
(2) The TRIPS Agreement of 1995, in force in the country since 2000.

In addition, Saudi Arabia is party to some Regional Free Trade Agreements (FTAs) which also have an impact on the trademark protection regime in the country. These include:

(1) GCC Trademark Law issued in 2006 but yet to be ratified by all GCC Member States (ratified by Saudi Arabia, Qatar, Bahrain and Kuwait).

Following is a discussion of the provisions of the 2002 Saudi Trademark Royal Decree and its Implementing Regulations with relation to the protection of trademarks in Saudi Arabia.

§2. Subject Matter of Protection

I. Signs Which May Serve as Trademarks

64. Article 1 of the 2002 Saudi Trademark Royal Decree states that in implementing the provisions of this 2002 Saudi Royal Decree, trademarks shall be names of distinct shapes, signatures, words, letters, numbers, drawings, symbols, stamps and protruding inscriptions or any other sign or combination thereof which can be recognized by sight and suitable to distinguish industrial, commercial, vocational or agricultural products or a project to exploit forests or natural resources or to indicate that the object upon which the trademark is placed upon belongs to the owner of the trademark on grounds of manufacture, selection, invention thereof or trading therewith or to indicate the rendering of a certain service.[247]

From the above, it appears that the Saudi legislator adopts a general and flexible approach in terms of what may be registered as trademark in the country extending it

246. *See* the WTO, the Working Party on the Accession of the Kingdom of Saudi Arabia, WT/ACC/SAU/61, 1 Nov. 2005.
247. The 2002 Saudi Trademark Royal Decree, Art. 1.

to also cover service marks too.[248] The main criterion for protecting a trademark in Saudi Arabia is the element of 'distinctiveness'.[249] This requirement – distinctiveness – is the defining one, since the fact that an element is not included in the list will not preclude trademark protection provided such element has the required distinctive feature. Notably, it should be highlighted that the definition of marks adopted by the Saudi legislator is restricted to visually perceptible trademarks. Sound, touch or smell marks or representations are not addressed – and therefore are not protected – unlike some other jurisdictions in the region.[250]

In line with consistent practices across the region, the Saudi legal regime provides that during the course of verifying if a trademark has a distinctive character or not, the Registrar or the court may, in the case of a trademark in actual use, take into consideration the extent to which such use has rendered the trademark in fact distinctive for the goods in respect of which it is registered or is intended to be registered.

Article 2 of the 2002 Saudi Trademark Royal Decree provides a list of signs which may not be eligible for registration as trademarks in the country. These include the following signs:

(1) Signs without any specific distinction and which are descriptions of characteristics or which are no more than common names which are by custom given to the products or services.
(2) Any expression or sign or drawing violating religion, or which is identical or similar to a symbol of religious nature.
(3) Any expression, sign or drawing inconsistent with public order or public morality.
(4) Public emblems, flags and other signs, names or denominations pertaining to the country or pertaining to one of the countries with which it has reciprocal treatment or pertaining to one of the countries being a member of a multilateral international treaty in which Saudi Arabia is a party or pertaining to an international or governmental organization and also any imitation to these emblems, flags, symbols, names and denominations unless permitted by such owner.
(5) Official signs and imprints of the country and the countries and organizations referred to in paragraph (4) of Article 2 of the 2002 Saudi Trademark Royal Decree, if these signs and imprints pertain to its control over the products or services or the guarantee thereof unless permitted by the owner thereof.[251]
(6) Geographical names if their use is liable to create confusion as to the source of the products or services or their origin or liable to monopolize notice of origin or name the source without rightful justification. The pictures of others or their personal or trade names unless they or their heirs agree to such use.
(7) Statements relating to honorary degrees.

---

248. For more *see* Abdullah Al Fehaidi, Al Alamat Al Tejareyeh, First Edition. 2011 Dar Al Hadarah Lilnasher wa Al Tawzee, Saudi Arabia.
249. Al Fehaidi, *Ibid.*
250. *See* El Said, *IPRS in Oman.*
251. Notably, the 2002 Saudi Trademark Royal Decree includes an exception to the above principle. Based on this, Art. 2 provides that the prohibition related to the above signs and emblems does not apply unless the trademark is intended to be put upon the products themselves or the services or upon similar products or services.

(8) Statements that are liable to mislead the public or contain false information as to the source of the products or services or other descriptions of the products or services as well as trademarks that contain a fictitious, imitated or forged trade name.
(9) Trademarks that are identical or similar to trademarks well known in the country even if they are not registered in it in connection with identical or similar goods or services and trademarks that are identical or similar to trademarks well known in the country and registered in it in connection with goods or services that are not identical or similar provided that this use causes injury to the owner of the well-known trademark.
(10) Trademarks owned by natural or juristic persons with whom dealing is prohibited in accordance with a decision issued by the competent authority.
(11) Signs identical or similar to trademarks already filed or registered by others in connection with identical or similar products or services as well as signs whose registration for certain products or services would reduce the value of products or services of others.

II. Different Categories of Trademarks

65. The 2002 Saudi Trademark Royal Decree and the judiciary over time have distinguished between different categories of trademarks. The following may be referred to in this regard:

(1) On the basis of the type of signs which constitute a trademark, a number of categories have been distinguished and are usually applied in legal practice: words (including personal names), designs, letters, colours or combinations of colours, numerals or the shape of goods or their packaging, holograms and GIs. Notably, signs which are not visually perceptible cannot be registered in Saudi Arabia. These include musical, scent or taste based signs.[252]
(2) Collective trademarks. The 2002 Saudi Trademark Royal Decree refers to collective marks as jointly owned marks as well.[253] Based on this, these are trademarks which are owned jointly by natural or juristic persons who control specific products, services or inspection thereof with respect to their origin, ingredients, method of manufacture, performance, descriptions or any other characteristic.[254]
(3) Well-known trademarks. A trademark is characterized as a well-known mark if it has a world renown reputation which surpassed the country of origin where it has been registered and acquired fame in the relevant sector among the consumer public in the country. The 2002 Saudi Trademark Royal Decree does not explicitly define what is meant by well-known mark with this context; however, the 2002 Saudi Trademark Royal Decree prohibits the registration of marks that are identical or similar to marks having 'an international reputation', which extends to also

252. *See* Al Fehaidi, *ibid.*
253. For more *see* Al Fuzan, *ibid.*, at 244.
254. *See* the 2002 Saudi Trademark Royal Decree, Art. 38.

include unregistered well-known trademarks.[255] To that end, unregistered well-known marks may be relied upon as relative grounds for initiating court proceedings in the country. The 2002 Saudi Trademark Royal Decree is silent on the issue of a time limit for establishing unregistered rights for well-known marks. However, it has been observed that litigants do carry a relatively heavy evidentiary/proof burden in their attempt to prove the fame of a trademark in Saudi Arabia.[256]

(4) National and foreign trademarks. This distinction is theoretical. The 2002 Saudi Trademark Royal Decree does not differentiate between national and foreign trademarks. If a trademark is registered in the country, the fact that it is also registered abroad does not alter the rights resulting from the local registration. Nationals of countries which treat the country on reciprocal basis will enjoy protection.[257]

(5) Service marks. The 2002 Saudi Trademark Royal Decree provides legal protection to service marks. Within this context, the 2002 Saudi Trademark Royal Decree explains that signs shall be registered if they are given to products or services.

(6) Domain name marks. The 2002 Saudi Trademark Royal Decree does not contain reference for the protection of domain names. However, the domain name registration authority in Saudi Arabia is called Saudi Network Information Center (SaudiNIC). It is responsible for administering domain name space(s) for the country's code (ccTLD) of Saudi Arabia (.SA). This includes the operation of the DNS root servers for .SA domains and the registration and maintenance of all third level .SA domain names. SaudiNIC is also a Local Internet Registry (LIR) responsible for allocating blocks of IP addresses to universities and local ISPs in Saudi Arabia. SaudiNIC has been managed and operated by King Abdul Aziz City for Science and Technology since 1995.[258]

(7) Trademarks in Exhibitions.[259] Article 32 of the 2003 Implementing Regulations provides that if the owner of a trademark desires to secure provisional protection to his/her trademark which is used on products or services displayed in national or international exhibitions held in the country or in any other country having reciprocal treatment with the country, the said owner shall notify the Trademarks Office at the Ministry of Commerce and Industry of such desire, not less than one month before the opening of said exhibition. The said notification shall be submitted on the form designated for that purpose including four reproductions of the trademark and proof of payment of the prescribed fee in accordance with Article 41 of the 2002 Saudi Trademark Royal Decree.

---

255. *Ibid.*, Art. 2.

256. For more *see* the http://www.kadasa.com.sa/services/intellectual-property-protection-country-saudi-arabia#C1.

257. *See* the 2002 Saudi Trademark Royal Decree, Art. 4.

258. For more *see* http://www.kadasa.com.sa/services/intellectual-property-protection-country-saudi-arabia#C.

259. The 2002 Saudi Trademark Royal Decree, Art. 55 states that: '*The Implementing Regulations shall include the procedures of temporary protection for any trademark used on the products or services on display at national or international exhibitions held in the Country or in any of the countries which treat the Country on reciprocal basis. Such exhibitions shall be specified by a decision of the Minister of Commerce.*'

§3. Conditions of Protection

66. As highlighted, the essential condition for full protection of a trademark in Saudi Arabia is its registration in the country. However, use of a trademark is not a prerequisite for protection, although lack of use may result in the lapsing of the trademark rights and protection after a period of five consecutive years if no justifiable or legitimate reason exists.[260]

In principle, the Saudi courts recognize the first-to-use principle. In appropriate circumstances, therefore, Saudi Arabia grants protection to unregistered marks where these are considered well known. However, the 2002 Saudi Trademark Royal Decree prohibits the registration of marks that are identical or similar to marks that enjoy an international reputation, which is therefore extended to include unregistered well-known marks. To that end, unregistered well-known marks may be relied on as relative grounds for initiating court proceedings in the country. As been observed, the 2002 Saudi Trademark Royal Decree is silent on the issue of a time limit for establishing unregistered rights for well-known marks. However, in practice, it is observed that usually litigants carry a relatively heavy evidentiary burden to prove the fame of a mark in Saudi Arabia.[261]

It should be highlighted that some restrictions do also apply to some products and services in Saudi Arabia. For instance, alcohol related trademark products and services cannot be protected in the country as highlighted in the discussion above.

§4. Formalities: Procedures for Protecting, Establishing and Maintaining Trademarks

67. Full and exclusive legal protection for trademarks is obtained under the 2002 Saudi Trademark Royal Decree through the registration of the trademark in the country.[262] Registration takes place under the specified classes of goods and services.[263] The classification table of goods and services as mentioned in the Saudi legal regime is basically based on the Nice International Agreement for Classification of Goods and Services.[264]

Article 3 of the 2002 Saudi Trademark Royal Decree provides that a register shall be set up at the competent department of the Ministry of Commerce and Industry to be called: 'Trademarks Register'. In which shall be recorded all registered trademarks and notices of assignment of ownership, transfer, mortgage, attachment or licence to use them and also their renewal and cancellation and all information provided for in the 2003 Implementing Regulations.

260. *Ibid.*, Art. 25.

261. For more *see* http://www.worldtrademarkreview.com/Intelligence/Yearbook/2014/Country-chapters/Saudi-Arabia.

262. The 2002 Saudi Trademark Royal Decree, Art. 36.1.

263. A full list of classes of goods and services are provided under Appendix 1 of the 2003 Implementing Regulations. According to this, there are 45 classes stated under the Appendix.

264. *See* Appendix 1 of the 2003 Implementing Regulations for the actual classification.

Moreover, the 2002 Saudi Trademark Royal Decree explains the categories which are given the right to register a trademark in the country. These include:[265]

(1) Natural or juristic persons of Saudi nationality.
(2) Persons regularly residing in the country and permitted to engage in any commercial or vocational activities.
(3) Nationals of countries which treat the country on reciprocal basis.
(4) Nationals of a country which is a member to an international multilateral treaty, in which the country is a party to or persons who reside in that country.
(5) Public agencies.

Article 5 of the 2002 Saudi Trademark Royal Decree states that a registration application for every trademark meeting the conditions provided for in Article 1 of the 2002 Saudi Trademark Royal Decree may be filed by the individual concerned if he/she is domiciled in Saudi Arabia or by an official agent domiciled in the country with the competent department at the Ministry of Commerce in accordance with the conditions and procedures specified in the 2003 Saudi Implementing Regulations.

Notably, the 2002 Saudi Trademark Royal Decree further provides that the application for registration of a trademark may be made for one or more categories of products or services, but a separate application shall be submitted for each such class in accordance with the conditions and procedures provided for in the 2003 Saudi Implementing Regulations. However, the law explains that one application may be filed to register a group of trademarks if they are identical as to their essential elements and differ only in ways that do not affect their character such as colour or the details of the products or services related thereto provided that these products or services belong to the same class.[266] It should be noted in this regard that the country applies a single class filing system.[267]

According to the 2003 Saudi Implementing Regulations, the application for registration of trademarks shall be filed in the form prepared for that purpose with the Trademarks Office at the Ministry of Commerce and Industry by the party concerned, if domiciled in the country, or by an official agent domiciled in the country. The application must be limited to the registration of a single trademark in one class. The number of applications shall be equal to the number of the classes of goods or services in respect of which registration is sought, which are listed in the Appendix attached to the 2003 Implementing Regulations, which is updated from time to time, pursuant to a Ministerial decision issued by the Trademarks Office, whenever necessary, in accordance with the Nice International Classification of Goods and Services.[268]

---

265. The 2002 Saudi Trademark Royal Decree, Art. 4.
266. *Ibid.*, Art. 7.
267. Jon Parker from Clyde & Co explains that 'The officials use an adapted version of the 10th Edition of the Nice Classification, but applicants are restricted to pre-approved terms only. This can pose significant issues as everyday terms such as "retail services" or "streaming services" are not included in the acceptable list.' *See* Clyde & Co Monthly Insights/Updates, March 2015 letter. Available at http://www.clydeco.com/insight/updates/view/trade-mark-protection.
268. The 2003 Implementing Regulations, Art. 1.

The application for the registration of the trademark itself shall include the following details and information:[269]

(1) A reproduction of the trademark sought to be registered, affixed to the application for registration in the space designated for that purpose.
(2) Applicant's name, surname, address, nationality and trade name, if any. If the applicant is a corporate person, its name, head office address and nationality shall be stated.
(3) If the application is filed by an agent, the agent's name, surname and address shall be stated.
(4) Description of the trademark sought to be registered.
(5) Goods or services in respect of which registration of the trademark is sought, and classes thereof.
(6) Signature of the applicant or his agent. If the applicant is a corporate person, the application must be signed by a person authorized to sign on behalf of such corporate person.

In addition to the above details, the application for registration shall be accompanied with:

(1) Ten reproductions of the trademark identical to the representation of the trademark shown on the application for registration.
(2) A copy of a power of attorney, together with the original thereof for verification purposes, where the application is filed by an agent.
(3) Proof of receipt of application fees as prescribed in Article 41 of the 2002 Saudi Trademark Royal Decree.[270]

However, if the trademark sought to be registered contains one word or more written in a foreign language, the applicant must submit a certified Arabic translation of such word(s) together with the phonetic transcription of the mark.[271]

The Saudi trademark legal regime includes several clauses related to priority claims.[272] Accordingly, Article 9 of the 2002 Saudi Trademark Royal Decree states that if an applicant for registration of a trademark or his/her successor desires to enjoy the right of priority on grounds of a previous application deposited with another country which is a member of an international multilateral treaty to which the country is a party or another country which treats the country reciprocally, he/she shall enclose

269. *Ibid.*, Art.2.
270. The 2002 Saudi Trademark Royal Decree, Art. 41.
271. *See* the 2003 Implementing Regulations, Art. 4.
272. Notably, Art. 8 of the 2002 Saudi Trademark Royal Decree states that: '*In case of two or more persons simultaneously apply to register the same trademark or similar trademarks that cause confusion for the same class of products or services and the applications are of the same date of depositing or same date of priority, the registration application shall be suspended until one of the applicants presents a written statement from the other(s) legally endorsed to the effect that they waive their application or until a final judgment is rendered by the Board of Grievances in favour of the registration of one of them.*'

with his/her application a statement wherein he/she mentions the date and number of the previous application and the state wherein he/she deposited the application. The applicant shall also deposit a copy of the previous application duly endorsed by the competent authority in the state wherein it was filed within a period of six months of the date on which he/she filed the registration application on account of which he claims the priority right, otherwise his/her right to the claim will be forfeited.[273]

A special register entitled 'Applications Filing Register' shall be maintained at the Trademarks Office in which the applications for registration shall be entered in serial numbers according to the filing dates of such applications. The said register shall include the following data:[274]

(1) Application number and date.
(2) Reproduction of the trademark.
(3) Applicant's name, address and nationality.
(4) Goods or services class.
(5) Agent's name, if any.

Once the application is made, the Trademarks Office shall examine the application for registration and compare the trademark sought to be registered with the other trademarks filed or registered on a prior date. It shall decide on the application, within a period of sixty days from the application filing date, either by accepting it, if it meets the conditions and procedures stipulated in the 2002 Saudi Trademark Royal Decree and the 2003 Implementing Regulations thereof, or by rejecting it, if it fails to meet such conditions and procedures. The Office shall notify the applicant of its decision in writing or require the applicant to meet the conditions or make the necessary amendments in order for the application to be accepted.[275]

If the competent department is of the opinion that the registration application is not in accordance with the provisions of the 2002 Saudi Trademark Royal Decree, it shall notify the applicant in writing to that effect, and may request the satisfaction of the conditions or incorporation of the amendments necessary for the approval of the registration application.[276] If the applicant fails to respond to the requests of the

273. Similarly, Art. 5 of the Implementing Regulations states that if the applicant for registration of a trademark, or his/her successor, wishes to enjoy the right of priority on account of a prior application filed in a country which is a member of a multilateral international treaty to which the country is a party, or a country which has reciprocal treatment with the country, he/she shall support his/her application with a statement showing the filing date of the prior application, its number and the country where it was filed. Further, the applicant shall file a copy of such prior application duly authenticated by the competent authority in the country of filing, and from the official authentication agencies, including the Saudi Ministry of Foreign Affairs, within a period not exceeding six months from the date of the prior application for which he/she claims right of priority, otherwise, he/she will lose his right for such claim.

274. *Ibid.*, Art. 6.

275. *Ibid.*, Art. 7. In addition, Art. 10 of the 2002 Saudi Trademark Royal Decree states that the competent department at the Ministry of Commerce and Industry shall, within a period of sixty days after submission of the application, decide on the application if it meets the conditions and procedures provided for in the Royal Decree and the 2003 Implementing Regulations.

276. The 2002 Saudi Trademark Royal Decree, Art. 11.

competent department to satisfy the conditions or incorporate the amendments within a period of ninety days from the date of his/her notification to this effect, his/her application shall be considered rejected from the date of expiration of this period.[277]

If a decision to reject the registration of a trademark is issued, the applicant may file a grievance against such decision with the Minister of Commerce within a period of sixty days from the date on which the applicant is notified of such decision, or from the expiry date specified in Article 12 of the 2002 Saudi Trademark Royal Decree.[278]

The appellant shall be notified of the Minister's decision in writing. If the grievance is rejected, the party concerned may file an appeal with the BoGs within a period of thirty-nine days from the date of receiving a notice thereof.[279]

The party concerned may file a grievance to the Minister of Commerce against the decision rejecting the application within a period of sixty days from the date of notification thereof, and if the grievance is rejected by a decision issued by the Minister, the party concerned shall have the right to appeal to the BoGs within a maximum period of thirty days from the day of notification thereof.[280]

Article 14 of the 2002 Saudi Trademark Royal Decree states that if registration of the trademark is accepted, the competent department shall publicize this registration in the manner and in accordance with the procedures specified in the 2003 Implementing Regulations and the applicant shall bear the cost of publicizing. In addition, if a trademark is accepted, the Trademarks Office shall prepare a notice of the trademark including the following data:

(1) Applicant's name, address and nationality.
(2) Reproduction and description of the trademark.
(3) Goods or services in respect of which registration of the trademark is sought, and their class.

The applicant shall receive the notice within a period of ninety days from the date of the decision accepting the registration or from the date of the Minister's decision accepting the appeal. The applicant shall publish the said notice in the Official Gazette at his/her own expense and shall, within a period not exceeding six months from date of receiving the said notice, provide the Office with a copy of the newspaper in which the said notice has been published, failing which the application shall be deemed as relinquished.[281]

277. *Ibid.*, Art.12.
278. The 2003 Implementing Regulations, Art. 8.
279. *Ibid.*, Art. 9.
280. The 2002 Saudi Trademark Royal Decree, Art. 13.
281. The 2003 Implementing Regulations, Art. 10.

The Saudi legal regime contains some opposition procedures which are to be filed before an administrative court (referred to as BoGs).[282] Based on this, Article 15 of the 2002 Saudi Trademark Royal Decree states that any interested party may object to the acceptance of registration of the trademark before the BoGs within a period of ninety days from the date of publicizing and a copy of the objection and evidence of submission shall be deposited with the competent department in the Ministry of Commerce and Industry. Moreover, Article 11 of the 2003 Implementing Regulations states that any party with interest may file with the BoGs an objection against acceptance of the registration of a trademark, within a maximum period of ninety days from the date of publication of the notice in the Official Gazette, provided that a notice thereof shall be filed with the Trademarks Office by the appellant, along with depositing a copy of such objection within the same period. The Office shall not take any further action, pending the issuance by the BoGs of the final decision determining said objection. As a party with interest, an applicant for registration shall be deemed, before the BoGs, a principal party to the objection action brought against the acceptance of the registration of a trademark and shall be confronted with said objection, and his arguments shall be heard.[283] As often the case, the opposition is filed against the Trademark Office rather than the applicant.[284]

Article 16 of the 2002 Saudi Trademark Royal Decree states that the competent department shall register the trademark in the register provided for in Article 3 of the Royal Decree after the decision accepting registration of the trademark becomes final or when a judgment to this effect is rendered by the BoGs. The registration shall be in accordance with the procedures and conditions specified in the 2003 Implementing Regulations.

Article 17 of the 2002 Saudi Trademark Royal Decree also explains that once the registration is completed, the owner of the trademark shall be given a certificate containing the information specified by the 2003 Implementing Regulations, and in particular:

(1) The serial number of the trademark's registration.

282. For more on procedures *see* http://www.kadasa.com.sa/services/intellectual-property-protection-kingdom-saudi-arabia. According to this, third parties may oppose acceptance of a trademark application at Court within a non-extendable period of ninety days term from the date of its publication on the trademark office's website. Whether the applicant files a counter-statement, or not, before issuing its judgment, the Court will hold multiple hearings to receive arguments and evidence from all the parties involved, including the trademark office as for the opposition grounds, the opponent may oppose the registration of a trademark on the basis that it is contradictory to the relevant provisions of the 2002 Saudi Trademark Royal Decree and could cause material or moral damage to the opponent's interests. An opponent may rely on any of the following grounds in an opposition: – relative grounds based on prior rights, such as a prior conflicting application or registration or rights in an unregistered well-known mark;– absolute grounds, such as lack of distinctiveness or a violation of religious principles or public morals;– bad faith, such as a false claim of ownership;– related rights, such as infringement of rights in a trademark.

283. The 2003 Implementing Regulations, Art. 12.

284. *See* Clyde and Co, MENA Intellectual Property Newsletter: March 2015, 9 Mar. 2015. At http://www.clydeco.com/insight/newsletters/view/intellectual-property-newsletter-2.

(2) The date of depositing the registration application and the date of registration and the date of priority, if any.
(3) The commercial name or the name of the trademark owner, his place of residence and nationality.
(4) A copy of the trademark.
(5) Details of the products or services and the class for which the trademark is registered.

Moreover, Article 13 of the 2003 Implementing Regulations provides that the applicant for registration must pay the trademark registration fees as prescribed in Article 41 of the 2002 Saudi Trademark Royal Decree within a period of ninety days from the date of issuance of the final decision accepting the registration of the trademark. The decision accepting registration shall be final upon the elapse of ninety days from the date of publication of the notice of the trademark in the Official Gazette without any objection against registration being filed or upon the issuance of a final judgment in this regard by the BoGs, failing which the application shall be considered null and void. Notably, the 2003 Implementing Regulations states that a register entitled 'Trademarks Register' shall be maintained at the Ministry of Commerce and Industry wherein shall be entered the following data:[285]

(1) Trademark registration number and date.
(2) Trademark owner's name, surname, nationality, address and trade name, if any. If the trademark owner is a corporate person, its name, address and nationality shall be stated.
(3) Goods or services in respect of which registration of the trademark is sought, and classes thereof.
(4) Reproduction and description of the trademark.
(5) Protection period starting and expiry dates.
(6) Priority date, if any.
(7) Recording the acts of disposing of the trademark, such as notices of assignment, transfer, licence to use the trademark, renewal or cancellation of the trademark registration.

It should be noted that the Trademarks Office shall register the trademark in the said Trademarks Register and shall give the trademark owner a certificate of registration which shall contain the following data:[286]

(1) Trademark registration number and date.
(2) Protection period starting and expiry dates.
(3) Priority date, if any.
(4) Trademark owner's name, surname, address, nationality and trade name, if any.
(5) Reproduction and description of the trademark.
(6) Goods or services in respect of which registration of the trademark is sought and their classes.

285. The 2003 Implementing Regulations, Art. 14.
286. *Ibid.*, Art.15.

The registration of a trademark shall be effective as from the application filing date as recorded in the 'Applications Filing Register' as stipulated in Article 6 of the 2003 Implementing Regulations.

Article 18 of the 2002 Saudi Trademark Royal Decree provides that the owner of a registered trademark may request the competent department to introduce any additions or modifications thereon provided that they do not substantially affect the character of the trademark. Such a request shall be subject to all conditions and procedures applicable to original applications for registration.

The 2002 Saudi Trademark Royal Decree further provides that any interested party may peruse the register provided for in Article 3 of the 2002 Saudi Trademark Royal Decree and request information or copies of the records.[287]

Notably, the 2002 Saudi Trademark Royal Decree explains the effect and impact of trademark registration in the country. In accordance with this, the law provides that the registration of a trademark shall be effective from the date of filing the application of registration.[288] Moreover, the person who has registered a trademark shall become its exclusive owner, and the use of a registered trademark by any person is subject to the consent of its owner. The owner of a registered trademark shall have the right to file a lawsuit to prevent others from using it or from using any other sign similar to it and liable to mislead the public as to the products or services for which the trademark is registered and as to similar products or services. The rights resulting from registration of the trademark do not include the fair use of the signs, statements and descriptive drawings which do not include the special characteristic of the registered trademark.[289] Based on this, ownership is determined by the use of the trademark in the country.[290] This view was contrary to the previous practise before the issuance of the new law by the Saudi judiciary.[291]

68. As mentioned earlier, the 2002 Saudi Trademark Royal Decree itself does not contain reference for the protection of domain names. However, legal protection is awarded to domain names in the country under a different legal regime. Based on this, the domain name registration authority in Saudi Arabia is called Saudi Network Information Center (SaudiNIC).[292] It is responsible for administering domain name space for the country code (ccTLD) of Saudi Arabia (.SA). This includes the operation of the DNS root servers for .SA domains and the registration and maintenance of all third level .SA domain names. SaudiNIC is also an LIR, responsible for allocating blocks of IP addresses to universities and local ISPs in Saudi Arabia. SaudiNIC has been managed and operated by King Abdul Aziz City for Science and Technology since 1995.[293]

287. The 2002 Saudi Trademark Royal Decree, Art. 19.
288. *Ibid.*, Art. 20. This date shall be determined in accordance with the provisions of the 2003 Implementing Regulations.
289. *Ibid.*, Art. 21.
290. Al Fehaidi, *ibid.*
291. *See* the Court Decision Number 118/t/4 for the Year 1990 stating that the rules ownership of a mark is established by its prior use and not by its registration.
292. For more *see* http://www.nic.sa/en/cat/rules.
293. For more *see* http://www.kadasa.com.sa/services/intellectual-property-protection-country-saudi-arabia#C4.

In general, the Saudi regime provides that a domain name is merely an electronic address used on the Internet. A registered domain name does not confer any legal right or ownership to that name even with the existence of a trademark or trade name. A registered domain name is not itself a property that can be trademarked or trade-named in Saudi Arabia.[294]

In accordance with this, there are specific regulations for the protection of Domain names in Saudi Arabia, namely the Saudi Domain Name Registration Regulation of 2011 (hereinafter 'the 2011 Regulations').[295] In this regard, Article 2.2 of the 2011 Regulations states that the registration services for domain names are provided only to the following categories:

(1) an entity physically located in Saudi Arabia;
(2) a natural person, not underage, with a Saudi national identification card or equivalent document issued by the Ministry of Interior of Saudi Arabia;
(3) an entity with a registration or licence issued by a pertinent authority in Saudi Arabia;
(4) an owner of a trademark or trade name that is registered in Saudi Arabia.

As for the actual application itself, Article 3.1 of the 2011 Regulations states that the registrant who wishes to obtain any registration services shall submit a service request in accordance with procedures established by the SaudiNIC. The service request should contain valid, accurate and up-to-date information. Notably, the 2011 Regulations emphasize the need for all registrants to comply with all CITC and SaudiNIC policies, rules and procedures with regard to service requests.[296] By submitting a service request, a registrant is deemed to be aware of the terms and conditions of the 2011 Regulation and to have accepted them without reservation. A registrant shall be responsible for any errors made in the service request.[297] By acting on the registrant behalf, the Administrative Contact certifies that it:

(1) is authorized to apply for SaudiNIC services on the registrant behalf;
(2) has notified the registrant of the terms and conditions of the 2011 Regulations; and
(3) will forward all communications and notices from SaudiNIC to the registrant and vice versa.

Article 5.1 of the 2011 Regulations further states that in addition to the information provided in the service request, SaudiNIC, at any time, may request additional information and documentations from the registrant. These additional information and documentations must be provided within the time period determined by SaudiNIC and according to the means of communication or format specified by SaudiNIC. A registrant failure to provide any of such information or documentations within the period specified

294. The 2011 Regulations, Art. 7.4.
295. *See* the Saudi Domain Name Registration Regulation Version 3.0 26/04/1432 H (31 Mar. 2011). Available at http://www.nic.sa/en/view/regulation.
296. The 2011 Regulations, Art. 3.2.
297. *Ibid.*, Art. 3.3.

by SaudiNIC and in accordance with the request by SaudiNIC format shall be grounds for rejection, suspension or deletion of the service request. In dealing with developments related to written evidence, Article 5.2 of the 2011 Regulations provides that electronic messages, documentations and correspondences exchanged between SaudiNIC and the registrant in connection with a service processing and any other records maintained by SaudiNIC shall be deemed to be evidence. Consequently, in the event of a dispute regarding the date or time of receipt or processing of a service request, the information on the SaudiNIC servers shall be definitive.[298]

Interestingly, the 2011 Regulations include a list of prohibited activities. Based on this, Article 6.1 states that the registrant may neither register, use or maintain a domain name nor submit any service request related to it as a mean to do or to support any of the following activities:

(1) Reselling or renting the domain name.
(2) Domain name warehousing.
(3) Cyber-squatting or phishing other websites and services.
(4) Acquiring fraudulently personal or confidential information or other means of identification.
(5) Spamming or sending malicious e-mails.
(6) Hosting or distributing malware.
(7) Hijacking domain names.
(8) Cracking systems and networks, or perform denial of service attacks.
(9) Activities or content against the Islamic religion or Saudi laws and regulations (e.g., pornography, illegal drugs, alcohol, gambling and intellectual property piracy).
(10) Activities classified as information crimes according to the pertinent regulations.
(11) Activities that are in violation of this regulation or any SaudiNIC regulations and procedures.

Following the approval of the CITC governor, SaudiNIC may add any additional prohibited activities to those mentioned under Article 6.1 of the 2011 Regulations.[299] In that case, it will be posted on SaudiNIC website.

Article 7.1 of the 2011 Regulations contains the main conditions needed for the registration of domain names in the country. Based on this the following conditions must be fulfilled for registering a Latin domain name:

(1) An ASCII Label should be at least two and not more than sixty-three characters. The first and last character should be a letter or number. Labels shall not include two consecutive dash (-) characters.
(2) Individuals may register personal names (using Latin characters), whether first or family name (e.g., Ahmad, Ali or Alfulani), under (.sa) or the (pub.sa) according to SaudiNIC terms and procedures.

298. *Ibid.*, Art. 5.3.
299. *Ibid.*, Art. 6.2.

The following conditions must be fulfilled for registering an Arabic domain name under the 2011 Regulations:[300]

(1) The Arabic Label should be at least two symbols.
(2) The Arabic Label should have a valid Corresponding ASCII Label.
(3) The Arabic Label should not start or end with a dash (-) and should not have two consecutive dashes.
(4) The symbols representing the Arabic Label should comply with terms and conditions specified by SaudiNIC which include permitted characters and symbols to be used in registering Arabic domain names.
(5) Individuals may register personal names (using Arabic characters), whether first or family name (e.g., Ahmad, Ali or Alfulani), according to SaudiNIC terms and procedures.

Moreover, the Saudi Legal regime requires that domain names should have some reasonable relationship/connection to the registrant. SaudiNIC, at any time, may request the registrant to prove it.[301]

The SaudiNIC will register domain names on first-come, first-served basis, unless otherwise provided by special rules issued by SaudiNIC.[302] Moreover, domain names must not contain words, phrases, abbreviations or references that are obscene, scandalous, indecent, abusive, racist or contrary to Saudi Arabian law or Islamic morality and/or *Shariah.* [303] The SaudiNIC may establish rules and procedures to resolve the problem of character variants within the Arabic language or with other Arabic based script languages (e.g., Persian, Urdu).[304]

In addition, the SaudiNIC has the authority to create and manage lists of domain names that are reserved or otherwise unavailable for registration, which may include but not limited to domain names that are numerical, geographical, names of religions, names containing words that are obscene, scandalous, indecent, abusive, racist, or contrary to Saudi Arabian law or Islamic morality, or names considered by SaudiNIC as undesirable or contrary to the public interest or otherwise unsuitable for registration.[305] The SaudiNIC may establish rules and procedures to govern the creation and management of the reserve list.[306] Notably, when a name is removed from the reserve list, it becomes available for registration according to procedures issued by SaudiNIC.[307]

The 2001 Regulations includes an objection/opposition procedure. Based on this, any objections or oppositions regarding SaudiNIC decision related to domain name registration shall be filed to CITC in accordance with its statutes. Objections will be handled according to CITC concerned statutes, including the Saudi Domain

300. *Ibid.*, Art. 7.2.
301. *Ibid.*, Art. 7.3.
302. *Ibid.*, Art. 7.6. Furthermore, Art. 7.5 states that reserved domain names will not be registered except to authorized entities based on roles and procedures issued by SaudiNIC.
303. *Ibid.*, Art. 7.7.
304. *Ibid.*, Art. 7.8.
305. *Ibid.*, Art. 8.1.
306. *Ibid.*, Art. 8.2.
307. *Ibid.*, Art. 8.3.

Names Objection Rules.[308] Article 9.2 of the 2011 Regulations provides that the SaudiNIC is not an arbiter of any disputes arising on the rights to register any domain name. Also SaudiNIC is not obliged to verify whether a service request or the use of a domain name constitutes an aggression against a third party.

Article 9.3 of the 2011 Regulations provides that neither the SaudiNIC nor CITC is liable for any interruption of business, any direct or indirect damages of any kind (including material or moral) or otherwise when they fulfil their duties.

In general, it is the registrant's sole obligation and responsibility – represented by the administrative contact – to update registration information through submitting a service request.[309] Moreover, the SaudiNIC may establish procedures to authenticate registrants for the purpose of providing online access to enable a registrant to modify its registration information. SaudiNIC may take additional measures to verify the validity of the information in a service request for modification.[310] The SaudiNIC may request from the registrant to update its information or to confirm its correctness.

The 2011 Regulations include several clauses related to transfer of domain name. Based on this, Article 11.1 states that although a domain name is not the property of a registrant, the SaudiNIC may permit the transfer of a domain name to a third party, provided both the registrant and transferee are in compliance with the terms and conditions of the 2011 Regulation or the other rules and procedures issued by SaudiNIC. Moreover, the SaudiNIC may request any relevant documents from both parties it deems necessary for the transfer of domain name registrations.[311] The SaudiNIC has the authority to reject a transfer request if the transfer seemed to be as a result of any of the prohibited practices mentioned in the 2011 Regulation, the necessary documents are not provided or if the approval from both parties is not obtained.[312] The SaudiNIC has the authority to issue any additional procedures to regulate the process of domain name transfer.[313]

The 2011 Regulations further states the procedures for the rejection, deletion and suspension of domain names. Based on this, Article 12.1 of the 2011 Regulations states that a registrant may submit a service request to delete or suspend a registered domain name. The SaudiNIC has the right to take additional measures to verify the validity of the service request. In addition, the SaudiNIC reserves the right to reject a service request, suspend or delete a domain name from the registry at any time in any of the following cases:[314]

(1) SaudiNIC finds any of the information supplied by the registrant to be incomplete, incorrect or inaccurate
(2) The registrant fails to provide any documentation requested by SaudiNIC.
(3) The domain name is not correctly hosted in the name servers.
(4) The registrant fails to pay fees or dues owed to SaudiNIC.

308. *Ibid.*, Art. 9.1.
309. *Ibid.*, Art. 10.1.
310. *Ibid.*, Art. 10.2.
311. *Ibid.*, Art. 11.2.
312. *Ibid.*, Art. 11.3.
313. *Ibid.*, Art. 11.4.
314. *Ibid.*, Art. 12.2.

(5) The registrant fails to renew a domain name registration.
(6) The registrant does not confirm the registration information when requested by SaudiNIC.
(7) Upon the acceptance by CITC of an objection regarding the domain or a service request.
(8) SaudiNIC receives an order from a pertinent Saudi authority, including any judicial authority.
(9) SaudiNIC receives notice from any natural person or a legal entity that the registration or use of a domain name breaches a law, or a regulation issued by any government or regulatory authority, and it has been confirmed.
(10) The registrant, domain name or service request violate any of the terms and conditions of this Regulation or any policies and statutes of CITC.
(11) SaudiNIC or CITC determines that rejection of a service request or suspension or deletion of a domain name is necessary to protect the public interest or any other rational reason.

In case of any rejection, suspension or deletion of any domain name, the SaudiNIC shall notify the registrant mentioning the reasons.[315] However, the SaudiNIC may reactivate a suspended domain name registration when the reasons for suspension become invalid or by a request from the registrant in case the suspension was done upon his/her request.[316] Suspended domain names are not available for registration and cannot be used for any electronic services. However, registration information should be available through WHOIS services during the suspension period.[317] A deleted domain name may become available for registration by other registrants in accordance with procedures established by SaudiNIC.[318]

Article 13.1 of the 2011 Regulations states that the SaudiNIC may collect information and documentation about registrants for the purpose of performing its duties and fulfilling its responsibilities. SaudiNIC may also collect other technical information, such as visitors log for SaudiNIC website. Moreover, the SaudiNIC may provide specific information about any domain name to the public through (WHOIS) or any other service.[319] The SaudiNIC may determine the information that will be available to the public and modify it, as necessary, provided that the information is published on SaudiNIC website.[320]

Article 13.4 of the 2011 Regulations further states that with the exception of the information available to the public, SaudiNIC will not reveal any documentations or information about any domain name except in the following cases:

(1) As a prerequisite for the implementation of the 2011 Regulation, or other regulations issued by SaudiNIC.

315. *Ibid.*, Art. 12.3.
316. *Ibid.*, Art. 12.4.
317. *Ibid.*, Art. 12.5.
318. *Ibid.*, Art. 12.6.
319. *Ibid.*, Art. 13.2.
320. *Ibid.*, Art. 13.3.

(2) Compliance with CITC regulations pertinent (Saudi Domain Names Objection Rules and Procedures).
(3) Compliance with an order from a pertinent Saudi authority including any judicial authority.

On the other hand, the registrant or any person may access the WHOIS service or any service offered by SaudiNIC provided that it is used for the following purposes only:[321]

(1) Checking the domain name availability.
(2) Obtaining registration information about a certain domain name.

In addition, information acquired from the 'WHOIS' service or any similar service shall not be used for any undesired activities, including, but are not limited to, any activities which are unsolicited such as sending any commercial or marketing advertisement or sending unsolicited e-mails (spam).[322] It is not permitted to utilize automated tools and/or electronic processes that send queries or data to the WHOIS service or any similar service provided by SaudiNIC that will negatively affect or interrupt the service.[323]

Article 14.1 of the 2001 Regulations states that the CITC may impose fees for registration services provided in connection with the registration and management of domain names. SaudiNIC shall issue procedures with respect to any fees established. The SaudiNIC may require registrants to renew their registrations of domain names periodically at a specified period of time. SaudiNIC shall issue procedures with respect to any renewal periods established.[324] SaudiNIC may authorize others (Registrars) to provide registration services on its behalf. SaudiNIC shall provide terms and conditions of the relationship between SaudiNIC, Registrars and registrants, as well as, rules and procedures appropriate for that.[325]

In addition, Article 17.1 of the 2001 Regulations states that SaudiNIC is not liable for any damage resulting directly or indirectly from any of the following conditions, regardless of the form of action performed by SaudiNIC:

(1) Not implementing a service request.
(2) Interruptions or stop of registrant business.
(3) Access delay or interruption to SaudiNIC services, including the delay or interruption caused by a failure in the Saudi ccTLD DNS servers.
(4) Inability to use or benefit from any domain name.
(5) Errors in processing any service request.
(6) Usage of any domain name.
(7) Force majeure.
(8) Applying any regulation, rule or procedure issued by SaudiNIC or CITC or any another governmental or regulatory authority.

321. *Ibid.*, Art. 13.5.
322. *Ibid.*, Art. 13.6.
323. *Ibid.*, Art. 13.7.
324. *Ibid.*, Art. 15.1.
325. *Ibid.*, Art. 16.1.

The 2011 Regulations states that the registrant is obligated to protect both CITC and SaudiNIC in case any claims or conflict arise related to registration or use of domain name or its sub-levels.[326]

Finally, Article 21.1 of the 2011 Regulations states that the Regulations and any of its terms and conditions herein are subject to change from time to time by CITC without any prior notice. Moreover, the SaudiNIC may issue separate (special) regulations and procedures as well as decisions in cases not provided for in the present Regulation.[327] Registrants shall be bound by any revised terms and conditions as well as any additional terms and conditions in the 2011 Regulations or any related regulations or procedures. These changes shall be applied after a period of thirty days from the date that a notification of such change is published on SaudiNIC or CITC websites.[328] A registrant's continued use of any domain name shall constitute that registrant's acceptance of the revised and new terms and conditions, in the 2011 Regulations or any related regulations or procedures. The registrant not willing to be bound by any of such changes shall submit a service request to SaudiNIC for cancellation of its domain name registration. The registrant acknowledges and agrees that cancellation will be its exclusive remedy whether it is from a request from the registrant or as a result of not willing to abide by any changes to the 2011 Regulations.[329]

§5. Ownership and Transfer

69. The 2002 Saudi Trademark Royal Decree adopts somehow a flexible approach with regard to the person(s) who may own or apply for the registration of a trademark. Accordingly, any person desiring to have the 'exclusive use of a trademark' for distinguishing his/her goods or services can apply for trademark protection in the country. This requirement has often been interpreted liberally by both the courts and the trademark Registrar.[330]

Moreover, the 2002 Saudi Trademark Royal Decree explains more specifically the categories which are given the right to register a trademark in Saudi Arabia. These include the following:[331]

(1) Natural or juristic persons of Saudi nationality.
(2) Persons regularly residing in the country and permitted to engage in any commercial or vocational activities.
(3) Nationals of countries which treat the country on reciprocal basis.
(4) Nationals of a country which is a member to an international multilateral treaty, in which the country is a party to or persons who reside in that country.
(5) Public agencies.

326. *Ibid.*, Art. 17.2.
327. *Ibid.*, Art. 21.2.
328. *Ibid.*, Art. 21.3.
329. *Ibid.*, Art. 21.4.
330. Al Fehaidi, *ibid.*
331. The 2002 Saudi Trademark Royal Decree, Art. 4.

Moreover, the person(s) who has registered a trademark shall become its exclusive owner, and the use of a registered trademark by any person is subject to the consent of its owner. The owner of a registered trademark shall have the right to file a lawsuit to prevent others from using it or from using any other sign similar to it and liable to mislead the public as to the products or services for which the trademark is registered and as to similar products or services. The rights resulting from registration of the trademark do not include the fair use of the signs, statements and descriptive drawings which do not include the special characteristic of the registered trademark.[332]

From the above, it could be seen that no restrictions are imposed on foreign ownership of trademarks in the country. Non-Saudi citizens are eligible to apply for a trademark registration in the country as long as they are residents or have an actual commercial or industrial business in Saudi, or come from a country which treats Saudi Arabia on reciprocal basis. However, applicants are required to designate a special domicile address in the country and to appoint a representative for procedural purposes.

Notably, the 2002 Saudi Trademark Royal Decree deals with cases of joint ownership of a trademark on exceptional cases (these are also called collective trademarks). Based on this, Article 38 of the 2002 Saudi Trademark Royal Decree provides that the Minister of Commerce may permit the registration of a trademark owned jointly by natural or juristic persons who control specific products, services or inspection thereof with respect to their origin, ingredients, method of manufacture, performance, descriptions or any other characteristic, in accordance with the procedures and conditions provided for in the 2003 Implementing Regulations. Notably, the 2002 Saudi Trademark Royal Decree further provides that a non-renewed jointly owned trademark may not be registered for the benefit of others with respect to identical or similar products or services.[333] It is worth to highlight that the provisions of the 2002 Saudi Trademark Royal Decree shall apply to the jointly owned trademarks provided that they are not inconsistent with their specific nature.[334]

The 2002 Saudi Trademark Royal Decree does not impose any restrictions with regard to the pledge, attach and transfer of the trademark. Generally, it is understood that it will be allowed to transfer, pledge or attach the trademark without the ownership transfer of the business concern using the mark in distinguishing its products or to assign the business concern itself.[335] In addition, the trademark may also be used as a subject to a security interest independently from the business concerned.

More specifically, Article 29 of the 2002 Saudi Trademark Royal Decree states that ownership of the trademark may be transferred to others by any event or action transferring ownership, provided it is in writing and not intended to mislead the public, especially with respect to the nature, origin, characteristics or performance of the products and services.[336]

---

332. *Ibid.*, Art. 21.
333. *Ibid.*, Art. 39.
334. *Ibid.*, Art. 40.
335. Al Fehaidi, *ibid.*, at 104.
336. The 2003 Implementing Regulations, Art. 18 states that a trademark may be disposed of by any act of ownership transfer, and it may be pledged in accordance with the rules established by law provided that such acts be publicized and recorded in the Register, pursuant to the procedures and situations stipulated in the following articles.

In addition, the 2002 Saudi Trademark Royal Decree verifies that if the ownership of the place of business or the project for which a trademark is used to distinguish its products or services is transferred without transfer of a trademark's ownership, the party who continues to own the trademark may still use it for products or services for which the same trademark was registered, unless otherwise agreed.[337]

As stated, a trademark may be pledged or attached with or without the place of business or the project for which the trademark is used to distinguish its products or services.[338]

The transfer of ownership, pledge or attachment of a trademark shall not take effect with respect to others except after its publicizing and its being entered in the Register provided for in Article 3 of the 2002 Saudi Trademark Royal Decree. In this regard, Article 19 of the 2003 Implementing Regulations states that trademark ownership transfer shall be recorded in the Trademarks Register based on an application filed with the Trademarks Office by the transferee, or the transferee's agent, accompanied with the original certificate of registration and the documents proving such transfer and including the following data:

(1) Trademark registration number.
(2) Transferor's name and surname.
(3) Transferee's name, surname, trade name (if any), nationality and address.
(4) Date of ownership transfer and the disposal act by virtue of which the transfer has been effected.
(5) The agent's name, surname and address, if said application is filed by an agent.

In line with the above, the Trademarks Office shall prepare a notice of the trademark ownership transfer including the following data:

(1) Description of trademark.
(2) Trademarks registration number and date.
(3) Transferor's name.
(4) Transferee's name, nationality and address.
(5) The applicant shall publish the said notice in the Official Gazette at his expense, and he shall provide the Office with a copy of the newspaper in which the said notice has been published.

The Trademark Office shall record the trademark ownership transfer in the Trademarks Register and on the original certificate of registration along with the name and address of the new owner, the reason for transfer and date of recording it.[339] In addition, the trademark pledge shall be recorded in the Register in accordance with the same procedures and situations pertaining to trademarks ownership transfer. The notice of pledge to be published shall include the same specifications stipulated in Article 19 hereof of the 2003 Implementing Regulations.[340] A trademark pledge shall be removed

337. *Ibid.*, Art. 30.
338. *Ibid.*, Art. 31.
339. The 2003 Implementing Regulations, Art. 21.
340. *Ibid.*, Art. 22.

from the Trademarks Register based on an application filed in the Trademarks Office by the owner of the trademark accompanied with the original certificate of registration and the documents proving that said pledge has been removed.[341]

The applicant shall publish the said removal in the Official Gazette at his/her expense in accordance with the notice prepared by the Office in this regard. The applicant shall provide the Office with a copy of the newspaper in which the said notice of removal has been published in order to record the said removal in the Register and on the original certificate.

In addition, Article 33 of the 2002 Saudi Trademark Royal Decree explains that the owner of a trademark may license any natural or juristic person to use it for all or some of the products or services for which it was registered. The trademark owner shall have the right to licence others to use it and shall have the right to use it himself/herself, unless agreed otherwise. The period of the licence may not exceed the protection period of the trademark.[342] Moreover, the law stipulates that the licence contract shall be in writing and the signatures, thumbprints or stamps of the contracting parties shall be officially authenticated in accordance with the provisions of the 2003 Implementing Regulations.[343] Following the signature, the licence contract shall be recorded in the register provided for in Article 3 of the 2002 Saudi Trademark Royal Decree. The licence shall not take effect towards others unless it is recorded in the register and publicized in accordance with the procedures and conditions provided for in the 2003 Implementing Regulations. For the trademark owner, the registration of a licence agreement helps in the process of relying on the use of the mark by its licensee to ensure that such trademark registration does not become vulnerable to attack for non-use. For the licensee, this can enable it to bring action in its own name directly against an infringer of the trademark.[344]

Accordingly, although the registration of a trademark licence with the Saudi Registrar can be seen as a formality requirement, the failure to register the agreement can have substantive consequences for both the trademark owner and the licensee. Commonly, the parties to trademark licences register summary agreements (known as registered user agreements) in order to simplify the registration process and to keep the commercial terms of the trademark licence off the register.[345]

In addition to licensing, the licensee may not assign the licence to others or grant sub-licences unless agreed otherwise.[346]

Article 37 of the 2002 Saudi Trademark Royal Decree states that the licence registration shall be cancelled from the register upon a request by the trademark owner or the licensee after presenting evidence of expiration or termination of the licence. The competent department shall notify the other party about the request to cancel the licence. In this case, the other party shall have the right to object to this before the BoGs, within a period not exceeding thirty days from the date on which he/she was notified of the request to cancel.

341. *Ibid.*, Art. 23.
342. Al Fehaidi, *ibid.*, at 109.
343. The 2002 Saudi Trademark Royal Decree, Art. 34.
344. *Ibid.*, Art. 35.
345. For more *see* Clyde & Co, *ibid.*
346. The 2002 Saudi Trademark Royal Decree, Art. 36.

On the other hand, Article 26 of the 2003 Implementing Regulations states that if the owner of a trademark grants a licence to any natural or corporate person to use the trademark for all or some of the goods or services in respect of which the trademark is registered, the licence contract shall be in writing and the signatures, finger prints or stamps of the contracting parties shall be authenticated by a notary public, as to license contracts concluded in the country, or by the official authentication bodies, including the Saudi Ministry of Foreign Affairs, in accordance with the relevant applicable rules as to license contracts concluded outside the country. The Office shall record the licence to use the trademark in the Register and on the original certificate of trademark registration. The licence contract shall be announced pursuant to a notice prepared by the Trademarks Office including the following data:[347]

(1) Reproduction of the trademark.
(2) Trademark registration number and date.
(3) Name, address and nationality of the owner of the trademark.
(4) Name, address and nationality of the licensee.

The applicant shall publish the said notice in the Official Gazette at his/her expense and provide the Office with a copy of the newspaper in which the said notice has been published.

The licence registration shall be cancelled based on a request filed with the Trademarks Office by the owner of the trademark or the licensee, accompanied with proof that said licence has been terminated or cancelled.[348] The Office shall notify the other party in writing of the request to cancel the registration. The said party may file an objection with the BoGs within a period of thirty days from the date on which he/she has been notified of the cancellation petition and shall deposit in the Trademarks Office a copy of the said objection, together with a proof that the same has been filed, whereupon the Office shall suspend the petition for cancellation pending an agreement by the two parties or a final judgment rendered by the BoGs regarding the said objection. In case there has been no objection to the cancellation of the licence or, in case a final decision pertaining to the objection has been issued by the BoGs, the Office shall prepare the necessary notice.[349]

The cancellation petitioner shall publish the said notice in the Official Gazette at his/her expense and shall provide the Office with a copy of the newspaper in which the notice has been published, in order for it to record the cancellation of the licence in the Register and on the original certificate.[350]

The trademark owner may license one or more persons, under a notarized contract to be filed with the Registrar, to use the mark for all or some of the goods. However, a change in ownership of the registration of a mark shall, however, be invalid if it is likely to deceive or cause confusion, particularly in regard to the nature, origin,

347. The 2003 Implementing Regulations, Art. 27.
348. *Ibid.*, Art. 28.
349. *Ibid.*, Art. 29.
350. The 2002 Saudi Trademark Royal Decree, Art. 32.

manufacturing process, characteristics, or suitability for their purpose, of the goods or services in relation to which the mark is intended to be used or is being used.[351]

§6. Scope of Exclusive Rights

70. In general, the trademark owner is granted an exclusive right to use the trademark in accordance with the stipulations of the law. The law in this regard determines the scope of the exclusive right to be exercised by the trademark owner.

Generally, the 2002 Saudi Trademark Royal Decree explains that a person who has registered a trademark shall become its exclusive owner, and the use of a registered trademark by any person is subject to the consent of its owner. The owner of a registered trademark shall have the right to file a lawsuit to prevent others from using it or from using any other sign similar to it and liable to mislead the public as to the products or services for which the trademark is registered and as to similar products or services. The rights resulting from registration of the trademark do not include the fair use of the signs, statements and descriptive drawings which do not include the special characteristic of the registered trademark.[352]

From the above, it appears that the exclusive rights of the trademark owner are not confined to those identical trademarks – which are easier to identify – but also extends to those trademarks which are confusingly similar – or misleading – with the registered trademark.

Notably, the Saudi courts established a number of principles to that effect. For example, in the case of the Decision Number 44/d/1 for the Year 1995, and subsequently confirmed by the Decision Number 143/t/ for the Year 1995, it was established that legal protection is awarded additionally against misleading the public through the use of a sign which is confusingly similar – not identical. More specific example, it was found that the trademark 'Bettol' was found confusingly similar to the trademark 'Dettol' related with some detergent products. The court's decision took into consideration the spelling of the word itself in addition to the similarity of the product used by the trademark as well.[353]

In general, it was established that the criteria for determining counterfeiting and/or imitation in the country is based on a number of elements including:

(1) The similarity and not the difference between the two marks under comparison.[354]

351. The 2008 Omani Decree, Art. 94. 3.

352. *Ibid.*, Art. 21. For more *see* Al Fuzan, *ibid.*

353. *See* Court Decision Number 206/t/4 for the Year 1991.

354. For example, it was decided that a decision cancelled the registration of the word 'Friendship الصداقة' because it is identical with the word 'Friendship' without the Arabic word. *See* the Decision Number 65/d/3 for the Year 2004 and supported by Decision Number 105/t/5 for the Year 2004. Also the cancelation of the registration of the word DEMO because of similarity with the word DEMA. *See* the Decision Number 44/d/3 for the Year 1422 supported by Decision Number 101/t/3 for the Year 2003.

(2) The general look/feel between the marks in question and not in the tiny details and differences.[355]
(3) The standard applicable in the comparison is that related to the normal (hypothetical) consumer and not the less aware.[356]
(4) Attempting to view each mark separately rather than collectively at the same time.
(5) The way a mark sounds (hearing) may be a determining factor in some specific cases.[357]

As highlighted, these are the principles which are developed in accordance with emerging case law in the country and may be subject to further additions in the future as a result of evolving case law.

§7. Limitations of the Scope of Trademark Protection

71. The Saudi legal regime includes various limitations against trademark use. In addition, limitations on the scope of trademark protection are also applied indirectly by means of other legal concepts. Generally, once a trademark is registered, it will grant exclusive rights to its owner with regard to certain goods and services. However, as described,[358] certain trademarks may not be registered and therefore lack effective legal protection, and subsequently the scope of the exclusive rights derived from registration will vary depending on aspects including the popularity and familiarity of a trademark. Accordingly and as highlighted, the fact that a trademark has not been used will not prevent the effectiveness of the full extent of its legal protection, provided it remains registered. However, lack of use will indirectly limit protection, since the trademark will not acquire the well-known status (or fame) and may therefore be characterized as defensive.

As it is the case with other legal regimes, the Saudi legal regime will not limit the scope of trademark protection due to deterioration or changes in the quality of the goods or services identified by the trademark. It is considered that the consequences of this deterioration or changes will bear directly on the commercial and financial value of the trademark and its owner as a result of the consumers' reaction. A similar reasoning is applied not to limit trademark protection in cases in which the trademark is licensed without exercising proper controls over the licensee. Tolerance or acceptance

355. *See* the Appeal against the similar trademark 'soft in' with 'Massimo Dotti soft' on the basis of too much similarity, however, the Appeal was revised and the marks were allowed to be registered. *See* Decision Number 68/d/ for the Year 2003 supported by Decision Number 236/t/ for the Year 2003.
356. *See* the decision refusing the registration of the mark 'Levitra' because of similarity with the mark 'Levitra'. The basis of the decision was due to the high level of similarity. *See* Decision Number 105/d/ for the Year 2003 and supported by Decision Number 117/t/ for the year 2003.
357. *See* the decision to refuse to register the marks REFCO due to similarity with RICO in spelling and hearing. *See* the Decision Number 58/di/ for the year 2003 supported by Decision Number 218/t for the Year 2003.
358. *See* Ch. 2.

of trademark violations will not limit the scope of trademark protection, except to the extent that the statute of limitations limits the legal actions that may be directed against such violations.

§8. Use Requirements

72. As a general rule, the Saudi legal regime provides that any person claiming to be the proprietor of a used or proposed to be used trademark who is desirous of registering such trademark shall apply in writing to the Registrar in the prescribed manner. For the purposes of the law, use may take place by the owner of the trademark or any another person who might be authorized to do so by the rights holder such an employee, agent, or a licensee.

In principle, the 2002 Saudi Trademark Royal Decree demands the use of a registered trademark in order to maintain its registration in the country. However, this is not a strictly use obligation, since no fines or other legal sanctions are imposed for failure to use the trademark within a specified period of time. A trademark registration may be cancelled due to non-use of the trademark for a period of three consecutive years as discussed in the previous section. Expiration of trademark registration has also been dealt with in the previous section.

This is often evaluated on a case-by-case situations in accordance with the facts of each case. In any case, the registration of a trademark may be cancelled for lack of use. Upon the expiry of the protection term, the effects of registration lapse immediately and automatically and no restoration shall be allowed.

§9. Duration of Protection: Renewal and Termination

73. Trademark protection in Saudi Arabia is awarded for a period of ten years from the date of its application for registration unless renewed for similar additional periods of time indefinitely.[359] As evident, the 2002 Saudi Trademark Royal Decree provides a longer term of protection than that provided under the TRIPS Agreement which requires a minimum period of seven years to be renewed indefinitely.[360]

Notably, the 2002 Saudi Trademark Royal Decree provides a different term for protection for the category of trademarks displayed in exhibitions. Article 34 of the 2003 Implementing Regulations provides that the Trademark Office shall issue the

359. *See* the 2002 Saudi Trademark Royal Decree, Art. 22. It should be noted that the Saudi follows the Hijri calendar whose year is eleven days shorter than the Gregorian year. This is important in case of renewal of trademark registrations.

360. *See* TRIPS Agreement, Art. 18 which states that 'Initial registration and each renewal of registration, of a trademark shall be for a term of no less than seven years. The registration of a trademark shall be renewable indefinitely.'

trademark a certificate of provisional protection for a period not exceeding six months from the opening date of the said exhibition.[361]

Registration may be cancelled for lack of use. Upon expiration of the protection term, the effects of registration lapse immediately and automatically and no restoration shall be allowed.

Trademark registration may be renewed for a period of ten-year periods indefinitely. For renewal to take place, an application must be made in this regard to the Registrar with the prescribed annual renewal fees. A period of grace of six months shall be allowed for the late payment of the renewal fee on payment of the prescribed surcharge, otherwise the registered mark shall lapse. There shall be no restoration of lapsed registered marks.

Renewal of trademark registration takes place upon the request from the trademark owner(s). Based on this, the owner of a trademark who desires to renew registration of his/her trademark may file with the Trademarks Office an application to that effect during the final year of the trademark protection period as well as during a period of six months following said protection period. The renewal application shall be accompanied with the original certificate of registration and a proof of payment of the renewal fees prescribed in Article 41 of the 2002 Saudi Trademark Royal Decree. Applications submitted after said deadline or without payment of said fees shall be disregarded.[362]

The following table includes the applicable fees for registration and renewal of trademarks in Saudi Arabia.

361. The 2002 Saudi Trademark Royal Decree, Art. 35. States that the certificate of provisional protection stipulated under Art. 34 may not be issued except for exhibitions in respect of which a decision has been issued by the Minister of Commerce.

362. The 2003 Implementing Regulations, Art. 16.

No.	*Fees*	*1,000 SAR for Each of Below*
(1)	(a) Application to register a trademark for one class. (b) Application to register a jointly owned trademark for one class. (c) Request to examine a jointly owned trademark for one class. (d) Review of the register with respect to one trademark for one class. (e) Every copy of what is recorded in the register with respect to one trademark ,for one class. (f) Request to enter the transfer or assignment of ownership for one trademark with respect to one class. (g) Request for a licence to use a trademark for one class, and to enter a trademark under pledge according to Articles 31, 32 and 33 of the 2002 Saudi Trademark Royal Decree. (h) For every modification or addition in a trademark for one class, according to Article 18 of this law. (i) Request to add or change any information for which no fee is specified, in connection with one trademark for one class. (j) Request to renew a registration of a trademark for one class during the six months that follow the period of its protection.	
		3,000 SAR for any of the following procedures:
(2)	(a) Application for a temporary protection of a trademark for one class. (b) Registration of a trademark for one class. (c) Registration of a jointly owned trademark for one class. (d) Renewal of registration of a trademark for one class. (e) Renewal of registration of a jointly owned trademark for one class.	

No.	*Fees*	*1,000 SAR for Each of Below*
(3)	- The official fee from first filing to registration in the normal course of action is SAR 7,000.00 (approx. EUR 1,400.00) per class. As from 14 January 2014, the e-publication fees of new trademarks are SAR 1,500 (EUR 290) for local companies and SAR 3,000 (EUR 590) for foreign companies.	

Renewal applications accepted in terms of form shall be approved without a re-examination. The Trademarks Office shall prepare a notice of renewal including the following data:

(1) Trademark description.
(2) Trademark registration number.
(3) Trademark owner's name, address and nationality.

The owner of a trademark shall publish the said notice of renewal in the Official Gazette at his/her own expense, and shall provide the Office with a copy of the newspaper in which the said notice of renewal has been published in order for it to record the renewal in the Register and on the original certificate of registration.[363]

Furthermore, Article 23 of the 2002 Saudi Trademark Royal Decree provides that an owner of a trademark may file an application for renewal of its registration during the last year of its period of protection and for a subsequent period of six months pursuant to the conditions and procedures provided for in the 2002 Saudi Trademark Royal Decree and its Implementing Regulations. The trademark shall be renewed without any new examination, and the renewal of registration shall be publicized in accordance with the conditions and procedures provided for in the Implementing Regulations.[364]

In addition, Article 25 of the 2002 Saudi Trademark Royal Decree provides that the competent department and every interested party may request cancellation of a trademark registration in the following cases:

(1) If the owner of a trademark does not use it for a period of five consecutive years without a legitimate excuse.
(2) If a trademark was registered in violation of public order or public morality.
(3) If a trademark was registered through fraud or false information.

The BoGs shall have the jurisdiction to decide on requests for cancellation of registration.

In addition, Article 26 of the 2002 Saudi Trademark Royal Decree provides that a trademark registration shall be cancelled by force of law in the following two cases:[365]

363. *Ibid.*, Art. 17.
364. The 2002 Saudi Trademark Royal Decree, Art. 24.
365. The 2003 Implementing Regulations, Art. 25 provides that apart from the situations stipulated in Art. 26 of the Royal Decree, the Board of Grievances shall have jurisdiction to determine all petitions for cancellation of registration.

(1) Trademarks whose registration was not renewed in accordance with 2002 Saudi Trademark Royal Decree and its 2003 Implementing Regulations.
(2) Trademarks owned by natural or juristic persons with whom dealing is prohibited pursuant to a decision issued by the competent authority.

In the case where a trademark is cancelled, it shall not be registered for the benefit of others for the same products, services, or for similar products or services except after the elapse of a period of three years from the date of cancellation, unless the decision of cancellation specified a shorter period.[366] The cancellation of a trademark registration shall be publicized in accordance with the procedures and conditions provided for in the 2003 Implementing Regulations. The cancellation shall be effective from the date of a judgment by the BoGs, from the date of expiration of the protection period, or from the date on which the prohibition decision was issued.[367]

Consequently, any interested person may apply to the Registrar for the cancellation of any trademark registered in the name of a third party if its registrant has not actually used it continuously for a period of three years preceding the application, unless proven that such lack of use has been due to special circumstances including import restriction or government measures impacting the commercialization in the country.

The above rule demands that a continuous three-year period takes place in which the trademark was not used in order for legal protection to lapse. The date of making the complaint is the date where such non-use should not have occurred. An exception to this is where the owner proves that such non-use was justifiable. The law in this regard is liberal and therefore if the owner of the trademark can prove that there was a special circumstance related to trade, government measure or any other justifiable reason that prevented him/her from using the trademark then the trademark will not be subject to cancellation.

As mentioned, use may take place by the owner of the trademark or any another person who might be authorized to do so by the rights holder such an employee, agent, or a licensee.

From this, it appears that the 2003 Saudi Trademark Royal Decree does not provide a strictly use obligation, since no fines or other legal sanctions are imposed for failure to use the trademark within a specified period of time.

In general, the expiration of a trademark registration implies that the trademark owner loses all rights derived from the prior extinguished registration. Therefore, if the owner of the non-renewed trademark wishes to register the same trademark again, he/she will be in the same position as any other new applicant.

A trademark registration may be cancelled due to non-use of the trademark for a period of three consecutive years as discussed in the previous section. Expiration of trademark registration has also been dealt with in the previous section.

366. *Ibid.*, Art. 27.
367. *Ibid.*, Art. 28.

§10. INFRINGEMENT AND REMEDIES

74. As explained in previous chapters, the 2002 Saudi Trademark Royal Decree contains a number of civil and criminal remedies which are applicable to IPRs infringements which have specific clauses related to trademark infringements too.

To start with, the 2002 Saudi Trademark Royal Decree contains a number of specific criminal penalties applicable in case of trademark infringement. According to this, Article 43 of the 2002 Saudi Trademark Royal Decree states that without prejudice to any harsher punishment, the following shall be punished with imprisonment for a period not exceeding one year and a fine not less than SAR 50,000 (approx. USD 15,000) and not exceeding SAR 1 million (approx. USD 266,378) or with one of these punishments:[368]

(1) Anyone who forges a registered trademark or imitates it in a way that misleads the public, and anyone who uses in bad faith a forged or an imitated trademark.[369]
(2) Anyone who puts or uses, in bad faith, a trademark owned by another on his products or services.
(3) Anyone who offers, puts up for sale, or sells or possesses with the intention of selling products carrying a forged, an imitated, or unlawfully put or used trademark, despite his/her knowledge thereof as well as anyone who offers to render services under such a trademark despite his/her knowledge thereof.

There are several court decisions which applied the above provisions in practice. For instance, it was decided that infringement has taken place through sale of products (mainly shoes wear) carrying the forged/imitated registered trademark (TEST) since the placement of the mark (VEST) on the product represented an infringement of the mark (TEST) because it is a famous mark in addition to the fact that the plaintiff acknowledged that he imported and stored the shoes in his store despite his lack of knowledge that it was forged. The court assumed that he should have known by taking into consideration the mark's fame and that the seller's shop was next to the shop of the other famous mark.[370] Also the same conclusion was reached in the case of the offering for sale the forged batteries under the mark (EVERPOWER) which attempted to confuse consumers with the famous (EVEREADY) batteries through the use of a similar logo.[371]

In addition, Article 44 of the 2002 Saudi Trademark Royal Decree states that without prejudice to any harsher punishment, the following shall be punished with imprisonment for a period not exceeding three months and a fine not less than SAR

368. Al Fehaidi explains that the act will be punishable under the Saudi legal regime and regardless of the number of times of the use of the forged mark even if it was for one time since this would be misleading. *See* Al Fehaidi, *ibid.*, at 178.

369. Al Fehaidi, opines that this would be difficult to prove since no cases were decided in Saudi till now under such circumstances. For more *see* Al Fehaidi, *ibid.*, at 184.

370. *See* the Decision number 5 /d/a/1 for the Year 2003 supported by the Decision Number 157/t/5 for the Year 2003.

371. *See* the Decision Number 33 /d/a/1 for the Year 2003.

20,000 (approx. USD 6,000) and not exceeding SAR 250,000 (approx. USD 66,000), or with one of these punishments:

(1) Anyone who uses an unregistered trademark in the cases specified in paragraphs (b, c, d, e) of Article 2 of the 2002 Saudi Trademark Royal Decree.
(2) Anyone who unlawfully inscribes on his/her trademarks or commercial papers a statement that would lead to the belief that they have been registered.

Moreover, Article 45 of the 2002 Saudi Trademark Royal Decree affirms that a repeat offender shall be punished with a punishment not exceeding twice the maximum punishment specified for the offence and closure of the place of business or the project for a period not less than fifteen days and not exceeding six months, in addition to publicizing the judgment at the expense of the offender in accordance with the conditions and procedures provided for in the 2003 Implementing Regulations.[372] Moreover, Article 47 of the 2002 Saudi Trademark Royal Decree provides that the public right of action shall be dropped after the expiration of a period of five years from the date of the commission of the offence without taking any act of investigation or prosecution. The fact that the public right of action is dropped shall not prejudice any private rights under such statute of limitations.

Importantly, Article 48 of the 2002 Saudi Trademark Royal Decree states that anyone who has suffered damage as a result of the commission of any of the offences provided for under the 2002 Saudi Trademark Royal Decree may claim appropriate compensation for the damages sustained, from the person responsible for the offence.

Article 49 of the 2002 Saudi Trademark Royal Decree provides a number of precautionary measures applicable in case of trademark infringement too. Based on this, an owner of a trademark may at any time, even prior to filing any civil or criminal lawsuit obtain – on the basis of a petition accompanied by an official document indicating the registration of the trademark – an order from the BoGs to take the necessary precautionary measures, especially the following:

(1) The preparation of a record of detailed description of the equipment and tools which are/or were used in committing the offence and the local and imported products or goods and papers on which the trademark in question was used.
(2) Seizure of the items referred to above provided that the seizure thereof shall not be effected until the claimant provides a security to be preliminarily estimated by the BoGs to compensate the party against whom the seizure is effected, if needed. It is permissible after the seizure is effected to contest the adequacy of the deposit made by the claimant in accordance with the conditions and procedures provided for in the 2003 Implementing Regulations. The order of the BoGs may

372. Article 46 of the 2002 Saudi Trademark Royal Decree states that a repeat offender under the provisions of the 2002 Saudi Trademark Royal Decree is anyone who has been convicted of any of the offences provided for herein and has again committed another, similar offence within a period of three years from the date on which a final judgment on the previous offence was rendered against him/her. The offences provided for in Arts 43 and 44 of 2002 Saudi Trademark Royal Decree shall be deemed similar as well.

include the assignment of one or more experts to assist the authority specified by the 2003 Implementing Regulations.

The precautionary measures taken by the trademark's owner shall be considered null and void if not followed by a civil or criminal lawsuit against the party against whom such measures were taken within a period of ten days from the date on which the measures provided for in Article 49 of the 2002 Saudi Trademark Royal Decree are taken.[373]

Moreover, the defendant may take measures against a bad faith plaintiff requesting compensation to which the defendant might be entitled as a result of the measures provided for under Article 49 of the 2002 Saudi Trademark Royal Decree, within a period of ninety days after expiration of the period provided for in Article 50 of the 2002 Saudi Trademark Royal Decree if the party making the seizure does not file his/her lawsuit or from the date on which a final judgment was rendered on the seizure lawsuit relating to the trademark. In all cases the security shall not be refunded to the seizing party except after rendering of the final judgment in the lawsuit convicting the party against whom the seizure is effected, or after expiration of the period fixed for the defendant without filing the lawsuit, unless the judgment rendered on the lawsuit of the seizure includes a decision relating to the issue of deposit.[374]

The BoGs may, in any civil or criminal lawsuit, render a judgment to confiscate the seized items or those items seized afterward, in order to deduct the value thereof from the damages or fines or to dispose of them in accordance with the conditions and procedures provided for in the 2003 Implementing Regulations. The BoGs may order the publicizing of the judgment in one or more newspaper(s) at the expense of the party against whom the judgment is rendered. It may also order the destruction of the forged or imitated trademarks or marks wrongfully placed or used, and order, when necessary, the destruction of the items carrying such trademarks even if a judgment of acquittal is rendered.[375] Moreover, the BoGs shall have jurisdiction to decide all civil and criminal lawsuits and disputes arising out of the implementation of the 2002 Saudi Trademark Royal Decree as well as the imposition of the penalties specified herein for the violation of the provisions.[376] The Bureau of Investigation and Prosecution shall represent the public right of action in the criminal case for violation of the provisions of the 2002 Saudi Trademark Royal Decree.[377]

Article 56 of the 2002 Saudi Trademark Royal Decree provides that the employees appointed by the Minister of Commerce shall have the powers of the judicial investigation officers as far as enforcement of the 2002 Saudi Trademark Royal Decree is concerned.

Notably, the 2003 Implementing Regulations provides further details on the above. Article 36 of the Implementing Regulations provides that the officials referred to in Article 56 of the 2002 Saudi Trademark Royal Decree who are appointed pursuant to a decision by the Minister of Commerce shall jointly or severally record all violations to the provisions of the 2002 Saudi Trademark Royal Decree and its 2003 Implementing

373. *Ibid.*, Art. 50.
374. *Ibid.*, Art. 51.
375. *Ibid.*, Art. 52.
376. *Ibid.*, Art. 53.
377. *Ibid.*, Art. 54.

Regulation hereof, regardless of whether such violations came into their knowledge through a complaint filed by a certain person or in the course of an inspection visit made by them to the market places or shops. A record of the occurrence of such violation shall be made and signed by the writer thereof as well as the owner of the shop or his/her substitute at the time said violation was recorded.

Article 37 of the 2003 Implementing Regulations further provides that for the purpose of performing the tasks entrusted to them, the officials referred to in the preceding article may do the following:

(1) Inspect shops for violations of the provisions of the 2002 Saudi Trademark Royal Decree.
(2) Seize the goods on which are affixed trademarks that are contrary to the provisions of the 2002 Saudi Trademark Royal Decree and collect three specimens thereof for submission purposes, when necessary, and send one specimen to the Bureau of Investigation and Public Prosecution. The remaining specimens shall remain seized pending determination of the penal action. A seizure record shall be made, signed by the official and the owner of the shop or his substitute. Said record shall specify the place wherein said seizure of goods was conducted, be it the trader's warehouse, a part of the trader's shop, or a warehouse designated for this purpose. In all events, it must be ascertained that said goods have not been seized by another official authority and that an undertaking to that effect has been taken from the owner of the shop. If, however, the owner of the shop declares that said goods are under seizure, he/she shall submit documents which prove that said seizure has been conducted. In all events, said goods shall be seized provided that coordination with the seizing authority has been made with the participation of a representative thereof.
(3) If deemed appropriate, conduct an immediate investigation with the violator after confronting him/her with the violation attributed. In all events, the violator shall be allowed to submit his/her defences in writing or such defences shall be recorded and attached to the seizure record, after entering therein the violator's name, nationality, capacity, residence address, business address and telephone numbers. The violator shall have the right to verify the identity of the official who reported said violation.

Furthermore, Article 38 of the 2003 Implementing Regulations provides that after investigating the violator, all violation papers, along with a specimen of the violation subject matter, shall be referred by the Deputy Minister for Internal Trade to the Bureau of Investigation and Public Prosecution, with a request to initiate a criminal action before the BoGs in accordance with Article 54 of the 2002 Saudi Trademark Royal Decree.

Furthermore, Article 39 of the 2003 Implementing Regulations explains that the officials appointed pursuant to a decision by the Minister of Commerce shall act as judicial investigation and recording officers and shall enforce the orders and judgments of the BoGs in accordance with Articles 49 and 52 of the 2002 Saudi Trademark Royal Decree. They may, for this purpose, seek assistance from the police departments.

In addition, Article 40 of the 2003 Implementing Regulations states that the Ministry of Commerce and Industry shall draft a notice of the judgment rendered against a repeating violator, in accordance with Article 45 of the 2002 Saudi Trademark Royal Decree, and it shall be published at the expense of the violator in a distinct place in two widely distributed newspapers, one of which is published in the province where the violator's head office is located, if any.

If seizure is conducted pursuant to an order issued in accordance with the provisions of Article 49 of the 2002 Saudi Trademark Royal Decree, the party on whom seizure is effected may contest the adequacy of the security provided by the seizer, by virtue of a petition filed with the BoGs within ten days from date of such seizure.[378]

In addition, additional provisions related to infringement of trademarks may also be found under the Royal Decree No. (M/19) Dated 23/4/1429H (corresponding to 29 April 2008) Concerning the Approval of the Anti-Commercial Fraud Law (hereinafter 'the 2008 Fraud Law'). Based on this, the following will also apply to:

(1) Any product that has been altered or tampered with in any way, causing it to lose some of its material or moral value, by means of discount, manufacturing or any other means and whether in its substance, nature, kind, type, shape, components, features, requirements, characteristics, origin or quantity in terms of weight, measure, measurement, number, capacity or calibre.
(2) Any product not conforming to the approved standard specifications.
(3) Defective product: Any product no longer fit for utilization, use or consumption as specified by the Regulations.

In addition, Article 2 of the 2008 Fraud Law provides that a person shall be considered a violator of the provisions of this law if he/she:

(1) Deceives or attempts to deceive by any means in any of the following:

    (a) Product's essence, nature, kind, type, components or essential characteristics.
    (b) Product's origin.
    (c) Product's quantity, whether in terms of weight, measure, size, number, capacity or calibre.

(2) Commits or attempts to commit fraud.
(3) Sells or offers a fraudulent product for sale.
(4) Seizes a fraudulent product with the intent to trade in.
(5) Manufactures, produces, sizes, sells or offers products not conforming to applicable standard specifications for sale.
(6) Uses canisters, vessels, packages, containers or stickers not conforming to applicable standard specifications, in preparing products for sale.
(7) Fills, packs, ties, distributes, stores or transports products not conforming to applicable standard specifications.

378. *See* the 2003 Implementing Regulations, Art. 41.

(8) Imports, manufactures, prints, seizes, sells or offers containers, packages or labels used in fraud for sale.
(9) Imports a fraudulent product.

With relation to such acts, Article 16 of the 2008 Fraud Law states that a person committing a violation provided for in Article 2 of the law shall be subject to a fine not exceeding SAR 500.00 (approx. USD 150,000), imprisonment for a period of not more than two years or to both penalties. Moreover, Article 17 of the 2008 Fraud Law provides that a person committing a violation provided for in Article 4 of this law shall be subject to a fine not exceeding SAR 50,000 (approx. USD 15,000), imprisonment for a period of not more than six months or to both penalties. Article 18 of the 2008 Fraud Law states that a fine not exceeding SAR 1 million (approx. USD 300,000), imprisonment for a period of not more than three years or both penalties shall be imposed in the following two cases:

(1) If the fraud or attempted fraud is combined with the use of false or non-standard weights, measurements, measures, stamps or other testing devices; the use of means that would affect badly on the process of weighing, measuring or testing a product, or if the fraudulent product or the materials are harmful to the health of humans or animals.
(2) If any of the violation(s) provided for in Articles 3, 7 and 9 of the 2008 Fraud Law is committed.

Article 19 of the 2008 Fraud Law further states that without prejudice to the penalties provided for in Article 18 of this law, any person disposing of impounded products shall be subject to a fine equal to their value. In addition and without prejudice to the penalties provided for under the 2008 Fraud Law, a judgment may be rendered to close the shop in violation for a period not exceeding one year for violations provided for in Article 2 of the 2008 Fraud Law.[379]

According to Article 21 of the 2008 Fraud Law, in all cases where fraud is established, the fraudulent product must be destroyed or disposed of in any appropriate manner, and the tools used in fraud or deceit shall be confiscated.

Article 22 further states that without prejudice to the aggrieved party's right to claim for damages arising from one of the violations provided for in the 2008 Fraud Law, a violator shall commit to withdraw the fraudulent product and repay the value thereof to the buyer in accordance with terms and procedures stipulated in the Regulations. The Bureau of Investigation and Public Prosecution may request the imposition of a travel ban on any person proven by the investigation to be in violation of the provisions of the 2008 Fraud Law until a final judgment is rendered. In case of conviction, the competent authority shall order the deportation of the expatriate from the country after enforcing the judgment. The convicted expatriate may not be allowed to return to the country for work.[380]

If a violator repeats a violation set forth under the 2008 Fraud Law within a period of five years from the date of the final judgment, he/she shall be subject to a

379. The 2008 Fraud Law, Art. 20.
380. *Ibid.*, Art. 23.

penalty not exceeding the double of the maximum penalty prescribed for the violation. If the violator further repeats the violation, the violator shall, in addition to the prescribed penalties, be banned from engaging in commercial activities for a period not exceeding five years.[381] A summary of the final judgment of conviction for a violation provided for in the previous articles shall be published in two daily newspapers at the convicted person's expense, provided that one of the newspapers is published in the area where the violation occurred or the nearest area thereto.[382]

The penalties provided for under the 2008 Fraud Law shall be imposed on any person participating in or instigating a violation.[383] In case of necessity or urgency, the Minister may order a provisional attachment of a product and withdraw it from the markets in case of suspected fraud, provided that the attachment order is referred to the BoGs within a period not exceeding seventy-two hours, as stipulated in the Regulations, to confirm or annul the attachment.[384]

In addition, to the above measures and remedies, there are several border measures which may be applied by virtue of the Regulations of Border Procedures for Protection of IPRs of Trademarks and Copyrights issued under the Ministerial Decision No. (1277) 15 *Jumada I* 1425H – 3 July 2004 (hereinafter 'the 2004 Border Measures Decision'). According to Article 2 of the 2004 Border Measures Decision, the Customs Authorities may suspend the clearance of goods suspected of bearing imitated trademarks upon having prima facie evidence to this effect, and they shall notify the importer and the trademark owner, if his/her address is known, of the suspension. However and without prejudice to the protection of confidential information, the right holder and importer may inspect samples of goods or works the clearance of which has been suspended in order to confirm the claim of the competent authorities.[385]

Upon suspending the clearance of goods on their own accord, the Customs Authorities may ask the trademark owner to provide, free of charge, any information or assistance, including technical know-how and facilities, in order to determine if the goods are counterfeits.[386]

The trademarks owner may, at any time, even prior to filing a civil or criminal lawsuit, and on the basis of a petition enclosed therewith an official trademark registration certificate, seek the issuance of a judicial order by the BoGs to seize the goods bearing a counterfeit of his/her trademark and suspend their clearance by Customs, in accordance with the procedures and conditions stipulated in Article 49 of 2002 Saudi Trademark Royal Decree.[387] The Customs' Suspension of Clearance of Infringing Goods or Works pursuant to an Order by the BoGs or a Decision by the Ministry of Culture and

381. *Ibid.*, Art. 24.
382. *Ibid.*, Art. 25.
383. *Ibid.*, Art. 26.
384. *Ibid.*, Art. 27.
385. The 2004 Border Measures Decision, Art. 3.
386. *Ibid.*, Art. 4. *See also* the Case Number 79/t/4 Year 1988 which defines counterfeiting as any the imitation of the trademark in a literal and exact manner without any change in its features in order to mislead consumers.
387. *Ibid.*, Art. 6. In determining the meaning of counterfeiting, the Saudi courts established that 'it is not necessary to achieve counterfeiting to have an identical copying but rather similarity which may lead consumers to mistakenly recognize the products'. *See* the Court Decision Number 125/t/4 for the Year 1988.

Information.[388] The Customs shall, pursuant to a preventive seizure order by the BoGs or a decision by the Ministry of Culture and Information, suspend the clearance of infringing goods or works.

Without prejudice to the execution of the seizure, the party against whom the preventive seizure has been issued may, within a period of ten days from the date of notification of the seizure, file a request either with the circuit handling the case at the BoGs or the competent department at the Ministry of Culture and Information to reconsider it by revoking the same or staying its execution.[389]

The seizure order issued by the BoGs or the preventive seizure decision issued by the Ministry of Culture and Information shall be deemed null and void unless the right holder follows it by filing a civil or criminal lawsuit against whom such an order has been issued, within a period of ten days from the date of its issuance.[390] If the rights holder does not submit to the Customs Authorities, within the ten days period from his/her notification of the preventive seizure order or decision, proof of his filing a civil or criminal lawsuit with the BoGs or with the competent committee at the Ministry of Culture and Information, the Customs Authorities shall clear the goods and works subject of seizure, if other conditions of import and export have been complied with.[391]

The 2004 Border Measures Decision includes some provisions related to the disposal of infringing goods as well. Based on this, Article 11 of the 2004 Border Measures Decision states that the Customs Authorities shall be entrusted with the execution of judgments and decisions issued by the competent bodies for the confiscation or destruction of infringing goods and works, and they shall have the power to dispose of the same through non-commercial outlets, unless otherwise adjudicated by the judicial authority or as directed by the competent administrative authority. Moreover, the Customs Authorities shall undertake not to allow the re-exportation of goods bearing counterfeit trademarks without altering their condition or subjecting them to another customs procedure, other than in exceptional circumstances.[392]

The 2004 Border Measures Decision includes further an opposition procedure as well. Article 13 of the 2004 Border Measures Decision states that the parties concerned may challenge the decisions issued by the Customs Authority, in respect of the application of the Decision, before the BoGs within a period of sixty days of notification in writing or through publication, if notification is not possible.

§11. Impact of Regional Agreements on Trademark Protection in Saudi Arabia

75. As mentioned earlier, there were few regional agreements which had a major impact on Saudi Arabia's trademark protection regime. The most important agreement in this regard is the GCC 2006 Unified GCC Trademark Law. Following is a brief description of the trademark related-provisions included under this agreement.

388. *Ibid.*, Art. 7.
389. *Ibid.*, Art. 8.
390. *Ibid.*, Art. 9.
391. *Ibid.*, Art. 10.
392. *Ibid.*, Art. 12.

I. The 2006 Unified GCC Trademark Law

76. As been explained, the objective of intellectual property harmonization and other laws has been a long-standing project for the six GCC states of Bahrain, Kuwait, Oman, Qatar, Saudi Arabia and the United Arab Emirates (UAE), with a GCC Patent Law being in place since 1992 and a GCC Customs Law being in place since 2003.[393] In the field of trademarks protection, the concept of a harmonized trademark law which applies across the GCC states dates back to the 1980s. More recently, a draft Unified GCC Trademark Law was published in 2006 in the GCC Official Gazette, although this law was not activated in practice.[394] However, in 2013, a further revision of the proposed law was undertaken.[395] In the case of the 2006 Unified GCC Trademark Law, the Supreme Council of the GCC issued a Resolution during the thirty-third GCC Session held in December 2012 requesting its Member States to implement and put into practice the GCC Trademark Law into their respective national laws '*Within a period of six months as from the date on which the Commercial Co-operation Committee approves the Implementing Regulations of the [Trade Mark] Law*' (the Implementing Regulations).[396]

It has been observed elsewhere that the need for an Implementing Regulations to be prepared was already set out in Article 52 of the 2006 Unified GCC Trademark Law itself,[397] which states that the Commercial Co-operation Committee (a division of the GCC General Secretariat) is responsible for issuing the Implementing Regulations. With relation to Saudi Arabia, the Royal Decree No. M/94 (issued on 23 May 2014) states that the Cabinet agrees to ratify the 2006 Unified GCC Trademark Law and that a royal decree has been drafted (but not published) to complete this ratification process.

However and as observed, the Royal Decree No. M/94 does not specify when exactly the 2006 Unified GCC Trademark Law will be implemented in Saudi Arabia, and whether it is going to be implemented without amendment. It does not also clarify how the implementation of the GCC Trademark Law in Saudi Arabia will affect any existing conflicting Saudi laws. There is also no mention of repealing Saudi Arabia's current Trademark Law. Based on this, there was a need to enact further legislation in Saudi Arabia in order to enable the 2006 Unified GCC Trademark Law to come into force and to repeal the current Saudi Trademark Law.[398] This took place by virtue of the Royal Decree No. M/51 of 24 May 2014 approving the GCC Trademark Law published in the official Gazette on 1 July 2016 (hereinafter 'the 2016 Royal Decree').

It has been remarked by practitioners that 'The introduction of the GCC Trade Mark Law and its Implementing Regulations will possibly have more impact in Saudi Arabia than in any other of the GCC states. This is because the new Law and Implementing Regulations contain a number of provisions that are not present in the old Saudi Trade

393. For more *see* http://www.clydeco.com/insight/updates/view/ip-newsletter-article-october-2015-the-gcc-trade-mark-law.
394. It should be approved locally by a law in each member state and published in the official Gazette in each member too.
395. For more *see* Clyde & Co, *ibid.*
396. For more *see* Clyde & Co, *ibid.*
397. For more *see* Clyde & Co, *ibid.*
398. For more *see* Clyde & Co, *ibid.*

Mark Law (which is repealed by the GCC Trade Mark Law) and it also introduces some important procedural changes.'[399] The 2006 Unified GCC Trademark Law aims towards creating unity between Member States on issues including the registrability of trademarks, the registration process and the enforcement of trademark rights. However, the law does not provide for a single or unified (unitary) filing, registration or enforcement systems within all GCC states. Each GCC state will continue to maintain its own and independent Trademarks Office/Registrar which will continue to receive applications and register trademarks nationally. In order to register a trademark in all six GCC states, it will still be necessary to file six separate national trademark applications

Some of the key proposed provisions of the 2006 Unified GCC Trademark Law (as echoed under the 2016 Royal Decree) include the following:

(1) The Definition of a trademark: The proposed definition of a mark expressly includes some forms of non-traditional trademarks under its coverage, such as colour, combinations of colour, sounds and smells. This represents an improvement when compared to the current 2002 Saudi Trademark Royal Decree which does include reference to some of these types such as sound and smell trademarks.
(2) Priority claims: The person(s) defined as having the right to register their trademarks in the GCC states are defined (under Article 5 of the 2006 Unified GCC Trademark Law and the 2016 Royal Decree) as including any 'persons holding the nationality of, or residing in, a foreign country that is a signatory to a multinational treaty to which one of the GCC Member States is a party'. This provision can be read in conjunction with Article 11 of the 2006 Unified GCC Trademark Law which allows for a period of six-month-priority period to be claimed where a person has applied for a trademark registration in a country that is a signatory to a multinational treaty to which one of the GCC states is a party.
(3) Multi-class filings: At present, it has been observed that it is only possible to file applications covering a single class in each of the GCC Member States. None of the GCC states allows for multi-class applications to be filed independently. The initial 2006 Unified GCC Trademark Law expressly states that a trademark application may not include more than one class. However, this statement has been deleted from the 2013 draft. The implication of this change is that, potentially, it may become possible to file multi-class applications in the GCC states.
(4) Examination and opposition procedures: At present, the practice across most of the national Trademarks Offices in the GCC region is not to take into consideration goods and/or services in different classes when examining a trademark application. This practice also often applies in trademark opposition proceedings. However, the 2013 draft of the GCC Trademark Law introduces (under Article 9) a statement that 'goods or services listed in the same class may not necessarily indicate similarity. Likewise, goods or services listed in different classes may not necessarily be dissimilar'.

---

399. *See* Clyde & Co, Saudi Arabia: Saudi Trade Mark Office Adopts GCC Trade Mark Law - Legal And Practical Implications, 3 Oct. 2016, available at http://www.mondaq.com/saudiarabia/x/532042/Trademark/Saudi+Trade+Mark+Office+Adopts+GCC+Trade+Mark+Law+Legal+And+Practical+Implications

(5) The GCC Trademark Law applies new official fees as follows:[400]

- Registering a trade mark (from filing through to registration): Decreased by 7%, from USD 1,865 to USD 1,735;
- Renewing a trade mark: Increased by 8%, from USD 1,600 to USD 1,735;
- Opposing a trade mark: Increased from zero to USD 270.

(6) Treatment of well-known marks: The protection afforded to well-known marks is given additional coverage under the 2006 Unified GCC Trademark Law and the 2016 Roya Decree by a prohibition (under Article 3) against registering marks which constitute a 'reproduction, an imitation, or a translation of a well-known mark or an essential part thereof' in relation to identical/similar goods and/or services. The 2006 Unified GCC Trademark Law also prohibits the registration of such marks in relation to dissimilar goods and/or services where the use of the mark would indicate a connection between those goods and/or services and the owner of the well-known mark, and would be likely to damage his/her interests.

(7) Partial assignment and cancellation of trademarks: The current national trademark laws in the GCC states generally treat a trademark as an asset which cannot be divided and based on that a trademark registration may not be partially cancelled or assigned in part. The 2006 Unified GCC Trademark Law adopts a more flexible approach by stating for a trademark to be assigned in whole or in part.[401]

(8) GIs, collective and certification marks, public agency and professional instruction marks: as discussed, under the 2002 Saudi Trademark Law, very limited protection is provided to the above-mentioned forms of trademarks. The 2006 Unified GCC Trademark Law goes further and includes a dedicated part to the protection of GIs, collective and certification marks, public agency and professional instruction marks.[402]

(9) Rights granted and Exclusivity: The 2006 Unified GCC Trademark Law expressly provides (under Article 17) that 'the owner of a registered trademark shall have the exclusive right to use its mark and to prevent third parties from using its mark, or any identical or similar mark' in relation to identical or similar goods or services and in a manner which is likely to mislead the public. Importantly, the law also provides that a likelihood of misleading the public will be presumed when a mark identical to a registered trademark is used in relation to identical goods or services. This removes the need for a trademark owner to establish confusion where an identical mark is being used in relation to identical goods. In these circumstances, the burden of proof will transfer to the defendant to show that its use of the mark does not cause confusion (which is likely, at the very least, to be an extremely difficult task).

400. *See* Clyde & Co, ibid.

401. *See* the 2006 Unified GCC Trademark Law, Art. 27.

402. Intellectual Property Newsletter, Clyde and Co. Licensing provisions in the draft GCC Trade Mark Law. By Rob Deans and Joycia Young, Partners, Clyde & Co LLP. 1 Feb. 2015. Available at http://www.clydeco.com/insight/updates/view/ip-newsletter-article-february-2015-licensing-provisions-in-the-draft-gcc-tuary 2015.

(10) Infringements, border measures and Enforcement: The 2006 Unified GCC Trademark Law sets out several provisions dealing with trademark infringements and penalties. As with the current Saudi Law, the GCC Trademark Law focuses on combating the counterfeiting of trademarks. The 2006 Unified GCC Trademark Law, as drafted, appears to cover both registered and unregistered trademarks, and it allows action to be taken against identical and similar marks being used in relation to the same or similar goods or services.[403] The law also restricts the use of trademarks which would:[404]

- Indicate a connection with the goods or services of the holder of a registered mark.
- Damage the interests of the holder of a registered mark.
- Diminish the value of the goods or services distinguished by a registered mark.

The GCC Trademark Law allows (under Articles 42 and 43) for criminal penalties to be applied in infringement cases:

- In the case of a first infringement – a fine of up to SAR 100,000 (approx. USD 26,000) plus three months imprisonment.
- In the case of a second infringement – a fine of up to SAR 200,000 (approx. USD 52,000) plus six months imprisonment and closure of premises.

In addition (pursuant to Article 41 of the 2006 Unified GCC Trademark Law), damages may be awarded in civil claims which may include a recovery of profits from the infringer. The Court may order (under Article 41.3c) the infringer to disclose the identity of any other parties involved in any aspect of the infringement. The GCC Trademark Law also includes substantial provisions (at Articles 38 and 39) relating to the enforcement of trademark rights through Customs. These provisions appear to supplement the existing GCC Common Customs Law together with relevant local laws.

As many have already observed, the introduction of the 2006 Unified GCC Trademark Law is a significant development. It will give rise to numerous improvements in the protection of trademarks in the GCC region. The important issue is to ensure that a detailed interpretation and application of the law in practice is followed.[405]

403. *See* the 2006 Unified GCC Trademark Law, Art. 42.

404. *Ibid., see* Arts 42, 3.11 and 3.12.

405. For more *see* GCC Trademark Law Coming Soon, September 2014, Saba Al Sultani, & Rob Deans, Partner, Clyde & Co LLP, Dubai, UAE. http://www.wipo.int/wipo_magazine/en/2014/05/article_0010.html.

§12. Overlapping and Relation to Other Intellectual Property Laws

77. As in the case of the majority of Arab states, trademark law and practice are one of the most vibrant areas of intellectual property protection in the Kingdom of Saudi Arabia. The Saudi trademark protection regime is widely influenced and largely shaped by the requirements of the TRIPS Agreement and the provisions of the 2006 Unified GCC Trademark Law.

Chapter 5. Trade Names

§1. Sources: Legislation

78. The protection of trade names is one of the oldest forms of protection known in the region. With relation to this, some form of protection was available in the region before the arrival of Islam.[406] The protection of trade names was even further emphasized under Islamic principles too.[407]

Trade names are governed in Saudi Arabia under the Law of Trade Names issued by the Royal Decree No. M/15 12 Sha'ban 1420 / 20 November 1999 (hereinafter 'the 1999 Trade Names Law').[408] The 1999 Trade Names Law repealed the Trade Name Registration Law No. 30 of 1953. The Trade Names Law was published in the Official Gazette and came into force after ninety days of the date of publication.[409]

In addition to the above legislation, trade name protection is governed by the multilateral industrial property agreements which Saudi Arabia acceded to including the Paris Convention for the Protection of Industrial Property and the TRIPS Agreement.

It is notable to highlight that unlike some other jurisdictions,[410] the Saudi Arabian legislature differentiates and separates between both, the protection of trademark and trade names.

§2. The Protection of Trade Names

79. The 1999 Trade Names Law stipulates that every merchant must have a trade name to be recorded in the Commercial Register to be able to conduct his/her activities in the country. This name shall consist of the name of the merchant as recorded in the Civil Register, a novel appellation or both. It may include data relating to the type of commercial activity. In all cases the name must be suitable, not misleading, nor inconsistent with Islamic *Shariah* or public interest.[411]

Notably, Al Fuzan differentiates between a trade name and a personal name under the Saudi legal regime. One particular area of difference lies in the fact that the personal name is always undertaken by an individual while a trade name may also be undertaken by an entity in this regard.[412] The same approach applies in the case of

406. Al Fuzan, Mohammed, Al Netham Al Kanoni Lil Esm El Tejari wa al Alameh el Tajjarayeh, Maktakeh al Kanon wa al Ektesad, al Riyadh. First Edition, 2013, 17.

407. *Ibid.*

408. Law No. 9 for the year 2006. No 116 for the year 2003 published on p. 4616 of the Official Gazette Number 4677, dated 30 Sept. 2004.

409. The 1999 Trade Names Law, Art. 20.

410. For example, *see* the Argentine law. *See* G Cabanellas, *IPRs in Argentina* (The Hague: Kluwer Law International, 1997).

411. The 1999 Trade Names Law, Art. 1.

412. Al Fuzan, *ibid.*, at 33.

other GCC countries when compared to Saudi Arabia. Differences are also evident between trade names and trademarks under the Saudi legal regime, in essence that the use of a trademark often refers to the products and services provided by the merchant unlike the case with a trade name which refers to the name of the merchant/company itself.[413]

The 1999 Trade Names Law does not define which signs may be used and protected as trade names. In general, any name used to identify an activity qualifies as a trade name. This would include individual names, surnames, corporate names and any other names with or without any specific meaning. As a general principle, a trade name may be registered to distinguish any activity regardless if it was commercial, for profit or not.

In addition, the 1999 Trade Names Law provides that subject to the provisions of the Saudi Companies' Law, the name of the company shall be its trade name and may include a novel appellation or data relating to the type of commerce/activities in which the company is engaged in.[414]

With relation to this, Article 3 of the 1999 Trade Names Law states that the trade name shall consist of Arabic or Arabized words, and may not include foreign words. Notably, the article provides a number of exceptions to this rule, these include:

(1) Names of foreign companies registered abroad.
(2) Companies with well-known international names.
(3) Companies of mixed capital, to be specified by a decision issued by the Minister of Commerce.

The application for registration of a trade name shall be submitted to the Commercial Register Office. If more than one merchant or company applies to register the same name, priority shall be given to the first one who used it publicly.[415] In case the application for registration of the name is approved, it must be published in the manner specified by the implementing regulations. The Commercial Register Office may reject the application pursuant to a reasoned decision within a period not exceeding thirty days.[416]

Upon registration of the name in the Commercial Register no other merchant may use it in the Kingdom in connection with the same commercial activity in which the owner of the registered name is engaged. If the commercial name applied for is similar to a commercial name already registered in the Commercial Register, the merchant shall add to that name something to distinguish it from the name already registered.[417]

Article 7 of the 1999 Saudi Trade Names Law stipulates that the merchant, whether an individual or a company must post his/her trade name clearly on the front of his/her place of business as well as all his/her printed materials. Where there is a difference between the trade name of the individual merchant and his/her name as

413. Al Fuzan, *ibid.*, at 37.
414. The 1999 Trade Names Law, Art. 3.
415. *Ibid.*, Art. 4.
416. *Ibid.*, Art. 5.
417. *Ibid.*, Art. 6.

registered in the Civil Register, the merchant shall record his name as registered in the Civil Register fully in all his/her printed materials and he/she shall sign the same in all his/her commercial transactions.

The trade name shall not be disposed of independently of the place of business, and any disposition of the place of business does not include its trade name unless otherwise agreed to in writing. In this case the person to whom the name is transferred shall add to it a statement signifying the transfer of ownership. If the predecessor agrees to the use of the original trade name without any addition, he/she shall be responsible for the obligations of the successor entered into under this name if the successor fails to meet them.[418]

Whosoever succeeds to own a trade name incidental to transfer of ownership of a place of business shall also succeed his/her predecessor's rights and obligations undertaken under this name. Nevertheless the predecessor shall remain responsible jointly with the successor for the performance of these obligations. Any agreement to the contrary is not binding on third parties unless recorded in the Commercial Register and third parties are given notice, by registered mail, and is published in the Official Gazette and another Saudi newspaper, provided that no one objects to it within a period not exceeding thirty days after the date of delivery of the notice or the date of publication in the newspaper whichever earlier. A lawsuit for the responsibility of the successor for the obligations of the predecessor shall not be heard after the expiration of a period of five years from the date of transfer of ownership of the place of business.[419]

In case of transfer of the place of business without its trade name, the predecessor shall be responsible for the obligations arising prior to the transfer of ownership of the place of business unless there is an agreement providing, in addition to that, for the joint responsibility of the successor for these obligations accordingly.[420]

§3. Infringement and Remedies

80. The Saudi legal regime contains several legal, civil and administrative remedies and options available in case of infringement of a trade name. To start with, civil liability arises in case where the use of the trade name took place by any other person and therefore compensation for damages suffered by its owner shall be awarded.

Moreover, if the trade name is used by other than its owner or is used by its owner in a way that violates the law, those concerned may request the Minister of Commerce to prevent its use or strike it off the Commercial Register if already registered. They may also resort to the BoGs for compensation if appropriate.[421]

Without prejudice to any more severe penalty provided for under another law, anyone who uses a trade name contrary to the provisions of the 1999 Saudi Trade Names Law shall be punished with a fine that may not exceed SAR 50,000 (approx. USD 15,000). The penalty may be doubled in the event the violation is repeated.[422]

418. *Ibid.*, Art. 8.
419. *Ibid.*, Art. 9.
420. *Ibid.*, Art. 10.
421. *Ibid.*, Art. 11.
422. *Ibid.*, Art. 12.

Notably, legal protection is also afforded under the unfair competition law of the country if the use (passing off) of the trade name leads to unjust enrichment on the part of the infringer as a result of misleading consumers.[423]

The officers of the Commercial Register, each in his/her area of competence, shall investigate and record violations of the 1999 Saudi Trade Names Law and the decisions issued for its implementation.[424]

Investigating violations of the 1999 Saudi Trade Names Law and the imposition of penalties shall be vested in a committee formed in pursuant to a decision of the Minister of Commerce composed of three members, at least one of whom is a law specialist.[425]

The representative of the public prosecution in the Ministry of Commerce and Industry and its branches, each in accordance with its powers, shall be charged with the responsibility of prosecuting violations of the provisions in the 1999 Saudi Trade Names Law before the Committee.[426]

The protection provided pursuant to provisions of the 1999 Saudi Trade Names Law expires when the commercial registration of the merchant, whether an individual or a company, is cancelled, and whatever the reason may be. It also expires when the name is stricken off the Commercial Register by a decision of the Minister of Commerce, if it appears that the registration was effected in violation of the provisions of the 1999 Saudi Trade Names Law.[427]

The parties concerned may object before the Minister of Commerce decisions of the Commercial Register Office and to the decisions of the Committee empowered to impose penalties within a period of thirty days from the date of notice of the decision. The refusal of the Commercial Register Office to make a decision which the Office should have made in accordance with the laws and regulations or its failure to act shall be deemed a decision.

Within a period of thirty days from the date of notification of the Minister's decision, the parties concerned may also file a grievance with the BoGs against the decisions of the Minister of Commerce made in connection with their objections or which were made pursuant to Article 11 or 16 of the 1999 Saudi Trade Names Law. In case no decision is made by the Minister in connection with the objection or the application submitted to him, within a period not exceeding sixty days of the date of filing the objection or the application, the party objecting or the applicant may file a grievance with the BoGs against the decision of the Commercial Register Office or against the decision of the committee empowered to impose penalties, or in connection with his/her application, within a period of thirty days of the date of expiration of the period specified for the Minister to make his/her decision.[428]

Notably, Article 18 of the 1999 Saudi Trade Names Law states that the BoGs shall have jurisdiction to decide all lawsuits and disputes arising from the implementation of the 1999 Saudi Trade Names Law and that the Minister of Commerce shall issue

423. *See* the Saudi Unfair Competition Law Number 25 for the year 2004.
424. The 1999 Saudi Trade Names Law, Art. 13.
425. *Ibid.*, Art. 14.
426. *Ibid.*, Art. 15.
427. *Ibid.*, Art. 16.
428. *Ibid.*, Art. 17.

the regulations and decisions necessary for the implementation of the provisions of this law.[429]

§4. Overlapping and Relation to Other Industrial Property Laws

81. The protection for trade names has been established for some time in the country. Some of the provisions and principles in the trade names area are influenced by the trademark and unfair competition protection regimes in the country.

429. *Ibid.*, Art. 19.

Chapter 6. Industrial Designs

§1. SOURCES: LEGISLATION

82. The protection of industrial designs in Saudi Arabia is governed by the Law of Patents, Layout Designs of Integrated Circuits, Plant Varieties and Industrial Designs (hereinafter 'the 2004 Saudi Patent Law')[430] and its 2004 Implementing Regulations. As mentioned previously, this is a comprehensive law adopting a holistic approach which also governs patents and trademark protection. Based on this, the 2004 Saudi Patent Law and its 2004 Implementing Regulations provide protection for all types of industrial property rights including industrial designs.

In addition to the 2004 Saudi Patent Law and its 2004 Implementing Regulations, industrial designs are also protected by the rules included under international intellectual property agreements which Saudi Arabia is a member of, including the rules provided under the Paris Convention for the Protection of Industrial Property and the provisions of the TRIPS Agreement.

§2. SUBJECT MATTER OF PROTECTION

83. Designs extend to cover a wide-ranging domain of activities. As Bently and Sherman state, these include industrial designs, urban planning, graphic design, fashion design, graphic design and packaging design.[431]

Article 1 of the 2004 Saudi Patent Law defines an industrial design as 'A composition of two-dimensional lines or colours, or any three-dimensional shape that gives an industrial product, or a product of traditional crafts, a special appearance provided that this is not only for functional or technical purpose including textile designs.'

It is apparent from the definitions that the law is concerned with the ornamental appearance and composition of the design and not with the functional and technical aspects of the product. The 2004 Saudi Patent Law also provides that protection will be awarded regardless if the product was used for a functional or technical purpose.

§3. CONDITIONS OF PROTECTION

84. The 2004 Saudi Patent Law contains a special chapter (Chapter 5) dedicated to the protection of industrial designs. Article 59 of the 2004 Saudi Patent Law states the main conditions needed for awarding protection.

430. Issued by the Royal Decree No. (M/27) dated 17 Jul. 2004 and was published in the Official Gazette (Om Alqura) in 7 Aug. 2004, and became effective as of 5 Sept. 2004.
431. L. Bently & B. Sherman, *Intellectual Property Law* (New York: Oxford University Press, 2004), 593.

Further, Article 59 of the 2004 Saudi Patent Law and Article 43 of the 2004 Implementing Regulations establish the basic elements of the subject matter to be protected under the law in relation to industrial designs. This includes:

(1) The industrial design certificate shall be granted, if it is novel[432] and has features that distinguish it from other known industrial designs. The industrial design shall be deemed novel if it was not disclosed to the public through publication anywhere in the world a tangible form, by use or by any other way, prior to the date of filing the registration application or the priority application. Disclosure of the industrial design to the public shall have no effect if it occurs during the priority period. The 2004 Implementing Regulations determines the other cases of disclosure which have no effect, as well as the provisions governing temporary protection of industrial designs.
(2) It shall be visible.
(3) It shall have features distinguishing it from known industrial designs.
(4) It shall not solely be for a functional or technical purpose.
(5) It shall not violate the provisions of Article 4 of the 2004 Saudi Patent Law.[433]
(6) It shall not include trademarks owned by others or flags or official emblems.
(7) The right to it shall be held by the applicant or the owner.

More specifically, Chapter 5 of the 2004 of the Saudi Patent Law contains reference to the relevant provisions with relation to the application and granting of industrial designs in the country. In general the following shall apply:

(1) The industrial design or model must be independently created. Although this requirement is not explicitly stated under the 2004 Saudi Patent Law, it is presumed that the Registrar will pay special attention to 'individual character' of the design during the examination process.[434] This requirement necessitates that for an industrial design or model to be legally protected in any given country, some effort must be exerted and invested by its creator in its creation for it to materialize.
(2) Appearance, presentation and appeal. In general, the definition of industrial designs and models provides that the ornamental aspects of the design must be visible and apparent.
(3) Public interest, *Shariah* and morality considerations. The 2004 Saudi Patent Law explicitly excludes from the ambit of registration any industrial design or model that violates *Shariah* or if the commercial exploitation of the industrial design is harmful to life, to human, animal or plant health, or substantially harmful to the environment.[435]

432. Absolute universal novelty is stipulated by the design law. However, applications are examined as to formalities only.
433. These are related to the situations of prohibiting the granting of an industrial design that violates *Sahriah* or if the commercial exploitation of the industrial design is harmful to life, to human, animal or plant health, or substantially harmful to the environment.
434. *See* generally Bently & Sherman, *Intellectual Property Law*.
435. The 2004 Saudi Patent Law, Art. 4.

§4. Formalities: Procedures for Obtaining Protection

85. Legal protection for industrial designs under the 2004 Saudi Patent Law is achieved through registration in a special national registry, known as the 'Registrar', positioned at the King Abdulaziz City for Science and Technology (Saudi Patent Office).[436] Registration is initiated by the applicant by means of a written application to be filed with the Registrar, on the form designated for this purpose. The application for registration of an industrial design shall be filed with the Registrar and shall contain a request, drawings, photographs or other adequate graphic representations of the article embodying the industrial design and an indication of the kind of products for which the industrial design is to be used. Notably, the registration process follows the same one designated for patent applications in the country.[437]

As a general rule, an application for a certificate of industrial design may include more than one industrial design provided that all of them are of the same class, according to the International Classification of Industrial Design (Locarno Classification), or the same group or the same structure. Applications with multiple figures will not be allowed. The applicant shall pay the fees prescribed for each industrial design.[438]

The application shall include the specified Form in addition to any other relevant attachment as well as figures (pictures and drawings) for the industrial design requested to be protected.[439] The number of industrial designs included in the application shall be specified as well in the application. Payment of the fees for the filing of each application shall be made at the time of applying.[440]

The application itself should include all relevant details, including the name of applicant,[441] the name of agent,[442] in addition to a declaration containing the name of the applicant or the agent and his/her signature shall be given in this part. The seal/stamp of the authorized agent, if any, shall be added. It shall be stated that the applicant

436. For more *see* http://www.kacst.edu.sa/en/innovation/patents/Pages/Home.aspx.

437. For more *see* Ch. 2 on patents and utility models. Notably, it was decided that the Directorate shall protect fifteen types in the first year of the application of the 2004 Saudi Patent Law, and a catalogue thereof shall be issued. New classes shall be catalogued each year according to need and capacity. For more *see* the 2004 Implementing Regulations, Art. 28.

438. The 2004 Implementing Regulations, Art. 24.1.

439. *See* the Saudi Patent Office, Form No. (401) 'Application for a Certificate of an Industrial Design' and Form No. (401-A).

440. The 2004 Implementing Regulations, Art. 24.2 and 5.

441. For individuals, the name shall be identical to the name in the identification document in the following order: first name, father's name, grandfather's name and family name. As for establishments and companies, it shall be identical to the official name. If there is more than one applicant, the first applicant's data shall be recorded in this part, and data relating to the remaining applicants shall be recorded in the attachment designed for that purpose. Communication between the Directorate and the applicants shall be through the first applicant if there is no agent.

442. The name of the agent shall be given, and he shall be authorized by a power of attorney issued by a notary public if the principal is in the Kingdom. If the principal is outside the Kingdom, it is necessary to have a power of attorney approved by the competent authorities and certified by the Kingdom's diplomatic missions abroad. The agent shall attach proof that he is licensed to practise such a profession in the Kingdom.

or the agent is responsible for all the consequences of not providing the correct information.[443]

Moreover, the number of the industrial design included shall be specified in the application in accordance with the form and will also include the name of designer and the[444] technical information covering the description of the industrial design,[445] the type of products and finally the classification.[446]

In addition, the application should include the drawings or photographs showing the complete parts of the industrial design, taking into consideration that the scope of protection is determined on the basis of the figures enclosed at the time of filing the application.[447] Therefore, the following guiding notes shall be observed:

- The figures shall be in colour(s), if protection of certain colours in the industrial design is desired.
- If there arc figures or parts in the industrial design whose protection is not sought, they shall be drawn in broken lines.
- When more than one figure for an industrial design is submitted in one application Form No. (401-A), the scope of protection covers the common elements in these figures.
- Figures shall be on size A4 paper and shall measure 40 × 40 millimetre as a minimum, and 252 × 165 millimetre as a maximum. A page may contain more than one figure.
- Figures shall be clear and indicate the distinctive features of the industrial design whose protection is sought, since these figures shall be published as enclosed.
- Figures shall not contain any words for the purpose of description or otherwise.
- Pages of figures shall be numbered consecutively for each separate industrial design (Form No. (401-A)), mentioning the total number of pages; for example, 1/4, 2/4, 3/4, 4/4 ... (page number/total number of pages). This shall be under the top margin in the centre of the page.
- Figures for each industrial design shall be numbered consecutively; for example, 1–1, 1–2, 1–3, ... (industrial design number – figure number). This shall be under the figure.
- Figures shall be submitted in one original and two true copies which may be directly duplicated. An electronic copy shall also be enclosed.

443. The 2004 Implementing Regulations, Art. 25.
444. The name of the designer shall be identical to the name in the identification document in the following order: first name, father's name, grandfather's name and family name. If there is more than one designer, the first designer's data shall be recorded in this part, and data relating to the remaining designers shall be recorded in the attachment designed for that purpose.
445. The industrial design shall be given in writing by describing each enclosed figure (picture or drawing) or by giving as brief a general description as possible. An additional sheet of paper may be attached if the assigned space is not sufficient.
446. *See* the 2004 Implementing Regulations, Art. 26. 1-2. Classification of the industrial design shall be mentioned in accordance with the International Classification of Industrial Designs (the Lokarno Classification).
447. *Ibid.*, Art. 27.

Article 34 of the 2004 Implementing Regulations deals more specifically with the registration and examination process for industrial designs. Based on this, registered applications shall be examined to ensure that they satisfy the formal conditions provided for in Articles 8 and 10 of the 2004 Saudi Patent Law and the relevant articles under Part Two of the 2004 Implementing Regulations for each subject of protection. If it is found from the formal examination that some of the prescribed conditions are not satisfied, the applicant shall be requested to satisfy them within a period not exceeding ninety days from the date of notification. If the applicant fails to perform what is requested from within the said period, his/her application shall be deemed null and void. Notably, the process shall follow the same one applicable for the granting of patents.[448]

The 2004 Implementing Regulations also deal with the case of amendment or changes to the application. Based on this, amendments or additions to the application for protection, made by the applicant or at the Directorate's request, may not exceed what was disclosed in the application at the time of filing, provided that the prescribed fees are paid. Moreover, amendments to any figure included in an application for a certificate of an industrial design entails that the date of amendment be deemed the date of filing. The applicant for an industrial design may cancel or add any element of protection, provided that this does not lead to any change in the concept of the integrity of the invention. The 2004 Saudi Patent Law further allows an applicant for protection to correct writing or calculation mistakes in the application and/or he/she may request the introduction of changes to the data given in the application without any additional charges. Moreover, an applicant for protection may withdraw his/her application unless it has been finally decided upon. The request for withdrawal shall be final and unconditional. If the application for protection is submitted by several persons, a request for withdrawal may not be accepted unless approved and signed by them all.[449]

If an applicant for a patent divides his/her application to several divisional applications, either on his/her own or in response to a request by the Directorate, as a result of the substantial examination which shows that the application includes more than one invention, he/she shall specify the invention included in the original application. The applicant may also file the other inventions which are separated as independent applications governed by the provisions for a new application. They shall keep the original application filing date and enjoy the right of priority, if any.[450]

The 2004 Saudi Patent Law provides for several types of priority claims for industrial designs.[451] The general rule is that the priority period for the industrial design shall be six months.[452] Moreover, the Saudi legal regime provides that if the industrial design has been displayed in an official exhibition or was otherwise previously disclosed to the public, the necessary documents showing date of display or disclosure shall be enclosed. If the applicant is a national of one of the countries of the Paris Union or a resident in one of them and desires to claim priority of an application which was

448. *See* Ch. 2 on patents and utility models.
449. The 2004 Implementing Regulations, Art. 32.
450. *Ibid.*, Art. 33.
451. *Ibid.*, Art. 26.3.
452. *See* the 2004 Saudi Patent Law, Art. 10.

previously filed in one of the Union countries, then the data relating to the priority application (the country, the number of application and the date of filing) and the number of the certificate and date, if any, and the classification, if any, shall be given. An approved copy of the previous application and a translation thereof shall be enclosed within a period not exceeding three months.

The granting process is stipulated under the 2004 Saudi Patent Law. Based on this, and upon ascertaining that the application for protection has satisfied the prescribed conditions, the Directorate shall notify the applicant thereof and require him/her to pay the grant and publication fees within a period of three months. Upon payment, the Directorate shall issue the protection document and publish that in the Gazette. If the applicant does not pay the due fees within the specified period, the application shall be rejected. Moreover, if it appears to the Directorate that the application for the protection document does not satisfy the prescribed conditions, it shall issue a reasoned decision rejecting the application and this shall be notified to the applicant and published in the Gazette accordingly.

According to the available statistics of the Saudi Patent Office, 677 industrial design applications were filed in 2014, 1036 industrial designs were granted, 80 applications were rejected and 198 industrial designs lapsed in 2014.[453]

The following table contains breakdown of the fees applicable in the country with relation to industrial designs.[454]

No.	*Fees*	*Individual* (SAR)	*Corporations* (SAR)
(1)	Registration Application	150	300
(2)	Change or Transfer of Ownership	75	150
(3)	Amendment or Addition to the Application	50	100
(4)	Obtaining a Copy of the Application or Certificate	150	300
(5)	Registration of Licence Contracts	150	300
(6)	Grant of Compulsory Licence	1500	3,000
(7)	Grant and Publication	175	350
(8)	**Annual fees**		
(8/1)	1st year	150	300
	2nd Year	150	300
	3rd Year	300	600
	4th Year	300	600
	5th Year	450	900

453. For more *see* http://www.kacst.edu.sa/en/innovation/patents/pages/statistics.aspx.
454. Fees are quoted in Saudi Riyals.

No.	*Fees*	*Individual* (SAR)	*Corporations* (SAR)
	6th Year	450	900
	7th Year	600	1,200
	8th Year	600	1,200
	9th Year	750	1,500
	10th year	750	1,500

§5. Ownership and Transfer: Assignment and Licences

86. Ownership of the rights granted with in regard to industrial models and designs is vested with the creator or to whomever the right passes to thereafter.

Article 5 of the 2004 Saudi Patent Law contains the rules applicable to industrial design ownership. Accordingly and as a general rule, the right to an industrial design shall belong to the inventor whose name was stated in the application.

The 2004 Saudi Patent Law also deals with the situation of joint ownership of industrial designs. Based on this, if two or more persons have jointly come up with an industrial design, the right to the industrial design shall belong to them equally unless they have agreed otherwise.[455] However the 2004 Saudi Patent Law further elaborates that no one shall be deemed a partner unless he/she contributes to the subject matter of protection, and his/her efforts are only confined to assistance in its execution.[456]

Where the same industrial design was made by more than one person independently of each other, the person whose application has the earliest filing date or, if priority is claimed, the earliest validly claimed priority date shall have the right to the industrial design, as long as the said application is not withdrawn, abandoned or rejected. In order to establish the right of preference, the Registrar shall take into account the matter claimed in the applications. Clearly, the Saudi legal regime adopts the 'first to file' approach in this regard.[457]

Regardless of the above, Article 5.e of the 2004 Saudi Patent Law provides that the person who develops the subject matter of protection shall have the right to state his/her name in that capacity in the protection document.

If the inventor of the industrial design is an employee, the law provides several scenarios in this regard. To start with, as a general rule, the employer shall be the owner of the protection document of the industrial design, unless the work contract stipulates otherwise, where its subject matter results from the execution of a contract, or an obligation providing for exerting efforts to develop it, or if the employer proves that the employee would not have developed the subject matter of the protection had he not used facilities, means or data made available through his/her employment.[458] This however shall be without prejudice to the employee's right to receive a special award

455. The 2004 Saudi Patent Law, Art. 5.b.
456. *Ibid.*, Art. 5.c.
457. *Ibid.*, Art. 5.d.
458. *Ibid.*, Art. 6.a.

to be agreed upon with the consent of both parties, or assessed by the Committee in light of the various circumstances of the contract of employment, and the economic importance of the subject matter of the protection. Any special agreement depriving the employee of this right shall be null and void.[459]

For the above purpose, the law further states that an application for a protection document of an industrial design filed by the employee within two years from the date of termination of employment shall be deemed as if submitted during the employment.[460] These provisions will also apply to government employees.[461]

Notably, Article 6.e of the 2004 Saudi Patent Law contains some provisions related to the special case where the subject matter of protection developed relates to national security. In such a case, it shall be governed by the provisions stipulated in the 2004 Implementing Regulations.

Article 7 of the 2004 Saudi Patent Law states that if the subject matter claimed in the application or in the protection document is derived from a subject matter owned by a person other than the applicant or the owner of the protection document, then this person may request the Committee to transfer the ownership of the application or protection document to him. The case for the transfer application shall not be heard after the elapse of five years of granting the protection unless the applicant's bad faith is established.

Article 16 of the 2004 Saudi Patent Law deals with the issue of assignment of industrial designs. Based on this, the law provides that any action resulting in the assignment of the protection application or the protection document itself must be in writing, signed by the two parties, and approved by an authority acceptable to the Directorate. No transfer of title, relating either to the protection application or the protection document itself shall be effective vis-à-vis a third party, except after filing the change application, paying the required fees, and recording it in the Directorate registers.

If several parties participated in filing one protection application or in the ownership of one protection document each one of them may assign his/her right in the application or the protection document to any of the partners, to all of them, or to a third party. The Directorate shall publish the transfer of title in the Gazette.

Moreover, if the protection document is disposed of to others in accordance with any act of disposition, or the right to exploit it is transferred to others for any reason, the owner of the protection document shall inform the party to whom the disposition is made or the party to whom the right of exploitation is officially transferred, of any legal measure taken in connection with the protection document, whether taken by him or by others against him.[462]

Moreover, Article 21 of the 2004 Saudi Patent Law deals with the situation of industrial design licensing. Based on this, the owner of the protection document may grant a contractual licence to others to perform all or some of the acts of exploitation

459. *Ibid.*, Art. 6.b.
460. *Ibid.*, Art. 6 c.
461. *Ibid.*, Art. 6 d.
462. *Ibid.*, Art. 17.

stipulated in the special provisions, for each protected subject matter.[463] A licence contract shall not be valid vis-à-vis a third party unless the specified fee is paid and it is registered in the records of the Directorate. This licence shall not deprive the owner of the protection document from exploiting the subject matter himself/herself or granting another licence for the same protected subject matter, unless the first licence contract states otherwise.[464]

Interestingly, the law grants the Directorate some role with relation to licensing. Based on this, the Directorate may instruct the parties to the licence contract to amend it in order to prevent abusing the right in the protection document or any other negative effect on competition or the acquisition of technology and its dissemination.[465] This is needed to correct any imbalance in the deal or the anti-competitive impact.

The licence gives the licensee the right to perform all acts and enjoy all privileges assigned to the holder of the protection document related to the subject of protection throughout the country during the whole period of protection, unless it is otherwise stated in the licence contract. The licensee shall not assign the rights and privileges licensed to him/her by the owner of the protection document, unless it is expressly stated in the licence contract.[466]

§6. Scope of Exclusive Rights

87. Article 60 of the 2004 Saudi Patent Law provides that the owner of rights related to industrial model or design has an exclusive property right over the model or design. Accordingly, the owner shall have the right to initiate an action before the Committee against any person who infringes the industrial design by exploiting it for commercial purposes without his/her consent within the country through manufacture, sale or importation of a product that includes or represents a wholly or substantially copied industrial design.

By contrast, it appears that it would be permissible under the law to undertake any of the above actions or activities as long as they are undertaken for non-commercial purposes. Notably, this is in line with the obligations and requirements of the TRIPS Agreement.[467]

§7. Limitations of the Scope of Protection

88. In general, if an industrial model or design has been successfully registered, there are no specific limitations on the scope of the exclusive rights derived from such registration. There are no requirements or obligations as to working, producing, or

463. Notably, Art. 1 of the 2004 Saudi Patent Law defines a contractual licence as 'A contract under which the owner of the protection document grants a third party some or all of his rights to exploit the protection document for a specified period against a specified fee.'
464. The 2004 Saudi Patent Law, Art. 21.
465. *Ibid.*, Art. 22.
466. *Ibid.*, Art. 23.
467. *See* the TRIPS Agreement, Art. 26.1.

manufacturing the industrial model or design in the country during a specific period of time. The Saudi contains exceptions such as those usually available for non-commercial, research or experimental use which may also be found under other legal regimes.[468]

The 2004 Saudi Patent Law states under Article 24 the City may grant a compulsory licence to a third party to exploit an invention covered by a certificate of design upon an application submitted to it. Notably, the same conditions which apply to granting of compulsory licences to patents apply to those in the case of industrial designs.

Finally, Article 46 of the 2004 Implementing Regulations provides a number of cases where the invalidation of an industrial design may take place as follows:

(1) In the case of any violation of the provisions of Articles 2, 4 and 59 of the 2004 Saudi Patent Law.
(2) In case of request for the invalidation in case where it turns out that the protection document was issued to a person other than the person who developed the subject matter of protection.

§8. Duration of Protection

89. The term of protection of an industrial design or model shall be for a period of ten years from the filing date of the application for registration.[469]

This protection awarded to industrial designs and models expires when the above protection term lapses or if the registration was annulled by a court decision for failure to meet the requirements of the law as discussed.

§9. Infringement and Remedies

90. The 2004 Saudi Patent Law contains several remedies applicable in the case of industrial designs infringement. As mentioned, Article 60 of the 2004 Patent Law states that the owner of the industrial design certificate may initiate an action before the Committee against any person who infringes the industrial design by exploiting it for commercial purposes without his/her consent within the country through manufacture, sale or importation of a product that includes or represents a wholly or substantially copied industrial design.

Moreover, Article 61 of the 2004 Patent Law further states that without prejudice to what Article 34 of the law stipulates,[470] any party that violates any of the provisions provided for in the 2004 Saudi Patent Law shall be punished with a fine not exceeding

468. *See* the 2004 Saudi Patent Law, Art. 24.

469. *Ibid.*, Art. 19.d.

470. Which states that: '*Any act of exploitation provided for in the special provisions governing each of the protection subject matters, performed by any person in the Kingdom without a written consent of the owner of the protection document recorded with the Directorate, shall be deemed an infringement on the subject matter of protection.*'

SAR 50,000 (approx. USD 15,000), and the maximum limit shall be doubled in case of repetition.

§10. Overlapping and Relation to Other Industrial Property Laws

91. The 2004 Saudi Patent Law includes several provisions applicable to patent protection which are at the same time also applicable to industrial designs protection in the country. Accordingly, the applicable provisions and principles under the 2004 Saudi Patent Law in relation to inventions of industrial designs arising from the employment relationship are also applicable. Also, the conditions provided in the case of licensing, assignment and transfer of ownership.

Chapter 7. Plant Variety Protection

§1. Sources: Legislation

92. Prior to the year 2004, Saudi Arabia did not grant legal protection to plant varieties. The pace of regulation in this particular area was relatively slow due to the country's preoccupation with reforming and upgrading other IPRs including patents, trademarks and copyright.

This however is unsurprising. As Price indicates, such rights received 'little attention or action from Gulf States, and there is little indication of external pressure upon them within the context of the WTO to comply with their TRIPS obligations at this stage'.[471] Moreover, Price states, Saudi Arabia has adopted a hybrid approach that borrows both from the patent protection approach and the sui generis option. It dedicates five articles within its patent law specifically to the protection of new plant varieties, but also provides forte general patent provisions to apply equally to new plant varieties.[472]

Prompted by its WTO's accession and the need to meet its requirements,[473] in 2004, Saudi Arabia introduced a number of provisions dedicated to the protection of plant varieties under the 2004 Saudi Patent Law. The conditions and procedural aspects for relevant applications are explained under the 2004 Implementing Regulations.

Plant variety protection in Saudi Arabia under the said law is mainly shaped by the rules of the TRIPS Agreement since the country is not a member of the Convention for the Protection of New Varieties in Plant (UPOV). As stated, the 2004 Saudi Patent Law is supplemented by the 2004 Implementing Regulations dealing with several formal and procedural aspects of the law.

§2. Scope of Protection

93. The authority entrusted with plant variety protection in the country is the Directorate of Patents at KACST.[474] In general, the rights granted to a plant variety include:

(1) Producing or propagating it.
(2) Conditioning it for purposes of propagation.
(3) Exporting it.
(4) Importing it.
(5) Offering it for sale, selling it or any other sort of marketing.

471. D. Price, *The Development of Intellectual Property Regimes in the Arabian Gulf States: Infidels at the Gates* (New York: Routledge, 2009), 128.

472. *Ibid.*, at 129.

473. *See* M. Kunal, 'TRIPS and Developing Countries: The Impact on Plant Varieties and Traditional Knowledge', *Trade Law Review* 12, no. 6 (2006).

474. *See* http://www.kacst.edu.sa/en/innovation/patents/pages/plant_varieties.aspx.

(6) Stocking it for any of the above purposes.

In addition to the above, the rights holder shall have right to initiate an action against any person who infringes the patented variety in the country without his/her consent. Notably,

§3. Subject Matter of Protection

94. A plant variety is defined under the 2004 Saudi Patent Law to include a plant grouping within a single botanical taxon of the lowest known rank which, irrespective of whether the conditions for the grant of a breeders right are fully met, can be defined by the expression of the characteristics resulting from a given genotype or a combination of genotypes distinguished from any other plant grouping, by the expression of at least one of the said characteristics, and considered as units with regard to its suitability for being propagated without change.

In addition, Article 1 of the 2004 Saudi Patent Law defines the plant breeder as the person who breeds, discovers or develops a new plant variety.

§4. Conditions of Protection

95. Under the Saudi legal regime, the conditions for the protection of plant variety include the following:

(1) The plant variety must be new. According to the 2004 Saudi Patent Law, a plant variety is new if, at the date of filing the application or the date of the claimed priority, propagating or harvested materials of the variety have not been sold or otherwise made available to others by the breeder or with his consent, for the purposes of exploiting the variety.
(2) The variety must be distinctive. A plant variety is distinct if it is clearly distinguishable from any other variety whose existence is a matter of common knowledge at the time of filling the application or the time of the claimed priority.
(3) Uniformity. According to the 2004 Saudi Patent Law, the variety should be uniform. In this regard, the variety shall be deemed to be uniform if, subject to the variation that may be expected from the particular features of its propagation, it is sufficiently uniform in its basic characteristics.
(4) Stability. According to the 2004 Saudi Patent Law, the variety shall be deemed to be stable if its basic characteristics remain unchanged after repeated propagation or at the end of each given propagation cycle.
(5) Listing and naming. It is presumed that the variety must belong to a plant species that is included in the plant varieties catalogue issued by the concerned authorities. A plant variety is denominated by specifying its genus and species. The denomination of the plant variety may consist of one word or a group of words and numbers or a group of letters and numbers with or without meaning, provided that the constituents of the denomination make it possible to identify the variety.

§5. Formalities: Procedures for Obtaining Protection

96. Full legal protection is obtained in the country by the registration of the plant variety with the Directorate of Patents at KACST.[475]

Article 20 of the 2004 Implementing Regulations explains the process and conditions of granting protection to plant varieties. Based on this, an application should be made on the designated application form, titled 'Application for a Plant Patent', and the technical description of the variety according to the forms of each plant genus protected by the 2004 Implementing Regulations, as well as any relevant attachments.

The same article further contains reference to the needed requirements. Based on this, the application may not include more than one protection application of one variety.[476]

Article 21 of the 2004 Implementing Regulations further provides the conditions needed for the filling of thc 'Application for a Plant Patent'. Accordingly, the specified form shall be filled out in a clear manner and to include the name of the applicant, the name of the plant breeder and the data relating to priority and disclosure in English language. The form shall also include the name of the plant variety or the suggested denomination. If there is no denomination, a suggested denomination of the variety or a temporary one that refers to the plant breeder shall be submitted instead. The denomination of the plant variety may consist of one word or a group of words and numbers or a group of letters and numbers with or without a specific meaning, provided that the constituents of the denomination make it possible to identify the variety.

In addition, the form shall include the genus and species, namely to include the scientific name of the variety shall be mentioned by specifying its genus and species in Latin, in italics or underlined, according to the conventions of writing a scientific name. If there is a common or a commercial name for the variety it shall be given in Arabic, English or Latin.

There are specific provisions related to the name of applicant. Based on this, in case of individuals, the name shall be identical to the name in the identification document in the following order: first name, father's name, grandfather's name and family name. As for establishments and companies, it shall be identical to the official name. If there is more than one applicant, the first applicant's data shall be recorded in this part, and the data relating to the remaining applicants shall be recorded in the form designed for that purpose. Communication between the Directorate and the applicants shall be through the first applicant if there is no agent.

In addition, the application should include the name of the plant breeder. The name of the plant breeder shall be identical to the name in the identification document in the following order: first name, father's name, grandfather's name and family name.

475. Link http://www.kacst.edu.sa/en/innovation/patents/pages/plant_varieties.aspx.

476. White size A4 paper shall be used, and the paper must be clean and free from amendments, cancellation and carbon stains: (1) The technical description of the variety shall be submitted in one original and two true copies;(2) The denomination of the plant variety mentioned in the technical description of the variety shall be identical to the denomination mentioned in the form and the official documents;(3) The documents submitted shall be original or certified by the competent authorities; (4) Application fees shall be paid at the time of filing the application; (5) The applicant.

If there is more than one breeder who actually participated in the breeding of the plant, data relating to the first breeder shall be written in this part and the data relating to the remaining breeders shall be recorded in the form designed for that purpose.

The name of the agent shall be stated, and the agent shall be authorized by a power of attorney issued by a notary public if the principal is in the country. If the principal is outside the country, it is necessary to have a power of attorney approved by the competent authorities and certified by the country's embassies abroad, and the agent shall attach proof that he/she is licensed to practice such a profession in the Saudi Arabia.[477]

If the plant variety was previously disclosed or sold or the propagating materials were previously sold, the documents showing the date and reasons for disclosure shall be attached. In the case of a priority claim, there shall be mentioned the name of the state, date and number of application, date of publication and the number of the plant patent (the number of granting the patent to the plant breeders) and its date, if any. A certified copy of the previous application and a translation thereof shall be attached within three months. Data relating to other previous filings shall be given in the designated form.

A declaration should also be made with the application. In this part shall be written the name of the applicant or the agent and his/her signature. The seal of the authorized agent, if any, shall be added. It shall also be stated that the applicant or the agent is liable for all the consequences of not providing the correct information

When submitting the technical description of the variety it shall include the following details:[478]

(1) Denomination of the variety.
(2) Specification of the plant classification (by giving both its Latin and local denomination).
(3) Full disclosure of the origin of the variety and the method of breeding.
(4) A detailed description of the consecutive stages of the choice and propagation processes which were used to breed the variety.
(5) Proof of the uniformity of the variety showing the degree of variation in any of its characteristics.
(6) Statement of the stability of the variety showing the number of cycles of propagation during which none of the distinguishing features has undergone any change and the changes noted during the propagation process, and its repetition, together with a repetition of the noted or expected confusion.
(7) Statement that the variety is distinct showing clearly how it is distinguished from other varieties descending from the same species. If there is similarity between the variety and other varieties the applicant shall specify these varieties with a detailed description of the differences among them. Samples of propagation

477. The attachments include labels of attachments to the form (technical specification of the variety and any other attachments) and the number of their pages shall be recorded in numbers and letters, in accordance with the general conditions of the technical specifications of the variety. In case of a priority claim, any attachments in this respect shall be indicated.
478. The 2004 Implementing Regulations, Art. 22.

materials or other plant samples of the variety or a photograph shall be provided, if this helps show the distinctiveness of the variety very clearly.

(8) Illustrations of the variety, if they are necessary to identify it, along with a brief description thereof, if any.
(9) A picture of the plant or its main parts, especially decoration or unknown plant.

The applicant shall provide the Directorate with a copy of the examination and the research reports, along with requested copies of the previously filed applications or plant.

Moreover, the applicant for a variety registration may claim application priority in Saudi Arabia. According to Article 10.a of the 2004 Saudi Patent Law, the applicant may benefit from the priority given to a previous application filed during the priority period specified for each of the subject matters of protection (in this case plant variety), from the filing date of the previous application, provided that it is accompanied by a written declaration stating the date and number of the previous application and the place where it was filed by him/her or their predecessor. The applicant shall also submit a copy of the previous application approved by the authority where the protection application was submitted, within a period not exceeding ninety days from the date of filing the application with the Directorate. More specifically, Article 10.b of the 2004 Saudi Patent Law provides that the priority period for plant varieties shall be twelve months.

However, Article 20 of the 2004 Saudi Patent Law adopts a worldwide approach in this regard with some exceptions related to prior use of a plant variety. Based on this, it provides that if a person, in good faith, exploits a plant variety before the date of filing the plant variety, anywhere in the world, such a party shall be entitled – despite the issuance of the protection document – to continue to perform these acts without expanding them. This right shall not be assigned or transferred to others except with all parts of the firm or one of them including goodwill.

Article 29 of the 2004 Implementing Regulations elaborates more specifically on this situation. Accordingly, any previous filing at a national or regional office in the countries of the Paris Union or the UPOV shall be recognized as giving rise to the right of priority.

Notably, the periods of priority shall start from the date of filing the first application. The day of filing shall not be included in the period. If the last day of the priority period is an official holiday or a day in which the Directorate is not open for receiving applications, the period shall be extended until the first following working day.

The applicant claiming the privilege of priority may defer providing the Directorate with the number of the previous application and the classification code of the application for the plant patent for a grace period not exceeding three months from the date of filing the application. If an applicant claiming the privilege of priority fails to submit a certified copy of the previous application and a translation thereof within the prescribed grace period, his/her right of priority shall be forfeited, and this shall be recorded in the registers of the Directorate.

In addition, Article 31 of the 2004 Saudi Patent Law states that filing an application for a plant patent in another country or the registration of a variety in a list of varieties the marketing of which is permitted in that state is deemed to render the variety being the subject of the application a matter of common knowledge as from the date of application, provided that the application leads to the grant of a breeder's right or entry in the catalogue. The variety is also deemed a matter of common knowledge if it is currently exploited or has been registered in a register of varieties kept by a professional association recognized by the Directorate or included in a reference collection.

Notably, prior to the completion of the registration process, the variety should undergo a technical examination in order to ensure that the variety is distinct, uniform and stable in accordance with the following:[479]

(1) Applications for which no filings were previously made outside the country shall be examined by the Directorate or by any national or foreign institution specified by the Directorate, in accordance with 'the Directory of the International Union for the Protection of Plant Varieties' for performing the examination of distinctiveness, uniformity and stability. As for unlisted varieties they shall be examined according to available resources.
(2) As for applications for which filings were previously made outside the country and were or would be examined abroad, the Directorate may benefit from the results of the examination and adopt them if the examination was performed in environmental conditions compatible with the environmental conditions of the country.

Notably, it was reported in June 2009,[480] pursuant to Ministerial Resolution no. 10/M/159489 dated 28 January 2009, fifteen new species have been introduced to the national list of approved plant varieties in Saudi Arabia. With the new additions, the national list now includes the following varieties:

National List (Listed by Common Name)	
Apple (*New*)	Cauliflower
Mango (*New*)	Peas
Orange (*New*)	Garlic
Lemon (*New*)	Wheat
Olive (*New*)	Barley
Melon (*New*)	Persem
Beet (*New*)	Date Palm
Okra (*New*)	Watermelon
Pepper (*New*)	Grapes
Beans (*New*)	Potatoes
Carrots (*New*)	Tomatoes
Eggplant (*New*)	Cucumber

479. *Ibid.*, Art. 37.
480. Available at http://www.sabaip.com/en/News/Saudi-Arabia-New-Plant-Varieties-Introduced.

National List (Listed by Common Name)	
Corn	Onion
Peach	Apricots
Squash and Cucurbits	Roses

A maintenance fee is due annually and is payable during the first three months of each year following the year the plant variety application was filed. The following table provides a list of the due fees accordingly.

No.	*Fees*	*Individuals (SAR)*	*Corporations (SAR)*
(1)	Registration Application	500	1,000
(2)	Change or Transfer of Ownership	500	1,000
(3)	Amendment or Addition to the Application	100	200
(4)	Obtaining a Copy of the Application or Certificate	50	100
(5)	Registration of Licence Contracts	500	1,000
(6)	Grant of Compulsory Licence	2,500	5,000
(7)	Grant and Publication	500	1,000
(8)	**Annual fees**		
(8/1)	1st Year	500	1,000
	2nd Year	500	1,000
	3rd Year	750	1,500
	4th Year	750	1,500
	5th Year	1,000	2,000
	6th Year	1,000	2,000
	7th Year	1,250	2,500
	8th Year	1,250	2,500
	9th Year	1,500	3,000
	10th Year	1,500	3,000
	11th Year	1,750	3,500
	12th Year	1,750	3,500
	13th Year	2,000	4,000
	14th Year	2,000	4,000
	15th Year	2,250	4,500
	16th Year	2,250	4,500

No.	*Fees*	*Individuals (SAR)*	*Corporations (SAR)*
	17th Year	2,500	5,000
	18th Year	2,500	5,000
	19th Year	2,750	5,500
	20th Year	2,750	5,500
	21st year to 25th year for the protection of trees and vines	3,500	7,000

According to available figures, no filed applications for plant varieties were made in 2014 in the country. In 2013, ten applications were filed, while in 2012, five applications were filed for the protection of plant varieties in Saudi Arabia.[481]

§6. Ownership and Transfer: Assignment, Licences and Compulsory Licences

97. In general and as established elsewhere, the exclusive property right in the plant variety shall be vested with the breeder or to whom the variety right passes on thereafter. In case where more than one person participated jointly in creation of the plant variety, the property of the plant variety shall belong to all the persons participating in its breeding, provided that it is registered equally and jointly between them, unless the parties agree otherwise. However, the property right shall be granted to the first breeder to file an application, if the breeding was independently and separately made by more than one person. If the breeding was a result of an employment contract, which requires the employee to carry out such breeding, the property right shall be granted to the employer, unless otherwise stipulated by the contract of employment between the parties.

Article 5 of the 2004 Saudi Patent Law provides that the protection document shall be a personal right of the person in whose name it was issued. This right may be transferred by inheritance, as well as with or without consideration. However, if the subject matter of protection is a joint work of several persons, they shall be equally entitled to the right, unless they have agreed otherwise.

The 2004 Saudi Patent Law further verifies that no one shall be deemed a partner unless he/she contributes to the subject matter of protection, and his/her efforts are only confined to assistance in its execution. However, if more than one person has independently developed the same subject matter of protection, the protection document shall be granted to the first applicant (first to file). The person who develops the subject matter of protection shall have the right to state his/her name in that capacity in the protection document.

Article 6 of the 2004 Saudi Patent Law deals with employment relationships. Based on this, the employer shall be the owner of the protection document, unless the work contract stipulates otherwise, where its subject matter results from the execution

481. *See* http://www.kacst.edu.sa/en/innovation/patents/pages/statistics.aspx.

of a contract, or an obligation providing for exerting efforts to develop it, or if the employer proves that the employee would not have developed the subject matter of the protection had he/she not used facilities, means or data made available through his/her employment. This shall be without prejudice to the employee's right to receive a special award to be agreed upon with the consent of both parties, or assessed by the Committee in light of the various circumstances of the contract of employment, and the economic importance of the subject matter of the protection. Any special agreement depriving the employee of this right shall be null and void. An application for a protection document filed by the employee within two years from the date of termination of employment shall be deemed as if submitted during the employment. Notably, this shall also be applicable to government employees.

If the subject matter of protection developed relates to national security, it shall be governed by the provisions stipulated in the 2004 Implementing Regulations.

Moreover, Article 7 of the 2004 Saudi Patent Law provides that if the subject matter claimed in the application or in the protection document is derived from a subject matter owned by a person other than the applicant or the owner of the protection document, then this person may request the Committee to transfer the ownership of the application or protection document to him/her. The case for the transfer application shall not be heard after the elapse of a period of five years of granting the protection unless the applicant's bad faith is established.

Notably, the law contains a number of provisions specifically applicable in the case of compulsory licensing for plant varieties. Article 25 of the 2004 Saudi Patent Law states that the City may grant a compulsory licence to a third party to exploit a plant variety patented by a plant patent, upon an application submitted to it in accordance with the following:

(1) The compulsory licence is necessary to protect public interest.
(2) The applicant for the compulsory licence being able financially and technically.
(3) Failure of the applicant to obtain a licence from the owner of the plant patent at reasonable terms.
(4) The elapse of a period of three years between the date of granting the plant patent and the date of applying for the compulsory licence.
(5) The compulsory licence shall not be restricted to performing all or some of the acts referred to in Article 56 of the 2004 Saudi Patent Law to meet the needs of the local market.
(6) The owner of the patent shall be awarded a fair compensation. The Committee shall determine the amount of compensation, and the licensee shall undertake to pay it.
(7) The City may instruct the owner of the plant patent to provide the holder of a compulsory licence with the required quantity of propagation material for the use of the compulsory licence in a reasonable fashion.

Notably, in other than exceptional circumstances, the compulsory licence shall not be granted for a period less than two years or more than four years. The City may extend the term for additional periods, upon verifying that the grounds for granting the compulsory licence still exist. There were no cases of compulsory licensing reported in the country up-to-date.

§7. Scope of Exclusive Rights

98. Article 56 of the 2004 Saudi Patent Law defines the exclusive rights of the plant variety owner. Accordingly, the plant owner of the protection document may initiate an action before the Committee against any person who infringes the patented variety by exploiting the propagating material of the patented variety without his/her consent inside the country.

The following shall be deemed to be exploitation of the propagating material of the patented variety:

(1) Producing or propagating it.
(2) Conditioning it for purposes of propagation.
(3) Exporting it.
(4) Importing it.
(5) Offering it for sale, selling it or any other sort of marketing.
(6) Stocking it for any of the above purposes.

Notably, the below referred to rights shall also include harvested material of the variety, including the whole plant or part thereof obtained by unlawful use of the propagating material of the variety. This applies where the owner of the protection document of the plant patent was not given a reasonable chance to exercise his/her rights in relation to the propagating material of the said variety.

These rights shall in addition extend to the varieties derived essentially from the protected variety if it is not possible to distinguish such varieties clearly, in accordance with Article 55.b of the 2004 Saudi Patent Law, from the said protected variety, or that the production of these varieties requires the repeated use of the said protected variety.

However, these rights do not extend to acts performed for non-commercial personal purposes or for experimental purposes or for purposes of breeding new varieties.[482]

The rights conferred by the plant patent shall not be restricted by any measure taken to regulate the operations of producing the materials of plant varieties, their monitoring, marketing, importation and exportation.[483]

§8. Limitations of the Scope of Protection

99. The 2004 Saudi Patent Law contains several limitations on the exclusive rights granted with regard to plant varieties.

To start with, Article 56 the 2004 Saudi Patent Law provides that the owner of the plant patent is obligated to do the following:

482. The 2004 Saudi Patent Law, Art. 56.
483. *Ibid.*, Art. 57.

(1) Maintain the protected variety or, when necessary, its hereditary components for the whole duration of the term of protection.
(2) Provide the City, upon its request, and within the specified period, with information, documents or necessary materials to prove his/her maintenance of the variety.
(3) Propose a suitable denomination for the variety, within the specified period, in case its denomination was cancelled by the City.
(4) Provide the City when necessary, upon its request and within the specified period, with reasonable samples of the protected variety or its hereditary components for the following purposes.
(5) Establishing or renewing the official sample of the variety.
(6) Undertaking a comparative test of other varieties for purposes of protection.

In case the owner of the plant patent does not observe any of these obligations, the plant variety patent shall be forfeited after notifying the owner of the necessity of fulfilling his/her obligation and giving him/her a reasonable grace period to fulfil the obligation(s) he/she has violated. In all cases the forfeiture of the plant variety patent shall be entered in the register and published in the Gazette. The Regulations shall specify the grace periods stated in this case.

§9. Duration of Protection: Nullification and Cancellation

100. Plant variety protection in Saudi Arabia is granted for a period of twenty years beginning from the date of the filing of the application. However, the protection period for trees shall be twenty-five years.[484]

In addition to the natural expiration of protection term, the exclusive rights on registered plant varieties may be nullified for any of the following reasons:

– If the applicant or the owner of the protection document fails to pay it within a maximum period of three months from its due date, the applicant/owner shall be liable to pay double the amount. If the applicant owner fails to pay after being warned during the three months period following the expiration of the first three months, the application or the protection document shall cease to be valid, and this shall be recorded in the Register and published in the Gazette.

More specifically, the 2004 Implementing Regulations provide that the grounds for invalidating a protection document fully or partially are as follows:

(1) For plant patents, violation of the provisions of Articles 4, 54 and 55 of the 2004 Saudi Patent Law.
(2) Invalidation may also be requested if it turns out that the protection document was issued to a person other than the person who developed the subject matter of protection.[485]

484. *Ibid.*, Art. 19.c.
485. The 2004 Implementing Regulations, Art. 46.

§10. Infringement and Remedies

101. Infringement of the exclusive rights of plant varieties is subject to civil and criminal penalties as prescribed under the 2004 Saudi Patent Law. Based on this, provisional, civil, customs and criminal measures provided in the law shall apply in respect of the enforcement of plant breeders' rights.

More specifically, Article 61 of the 2004 Saudi Patent Law provides that without prejudice to what Article 34 of the 2004 Saudi Patent Law stipulates, any party that violates any of the provisions provided for in this law shall be punished with a fine not exceeding SAR 50,000 (approx. USD 15,000), and the maximum limit shall be doubled in case of repetition.

Notably, Article 34 of the 2004 Saudi Patent Law states that any act of exploitation provided for in the special provisions governing each of the protection subject matters, performed by any person in the country without a written consent of the owner of the protection document recorded with the Directorate, shall be deemed an infringement on the subject matter of protection. At the request of the owner of the protection document, and any party with interest, the Committee shall grant an injunction to prevent the infringement in addition to the necessary damages, and it may impose a fine upon the infringer not exceeding SAR 100,000 (approx. USD 30,000). The maximum fine shall be doubled in case of repetition. If the Committee sees that the infringement calls for the punishment of imprisonment, the infringer shall be referred from the start to the BoGs. The Committee may take the necessary prompt measures it deems necessary to prevent the damages resulting from the infringement.

The decision issued by the Committee in this case shall be published in the Official Gazette, the Gazette and two daily newspapers, at the expense of the party against whom the decision is issued. The provision of this article shall be applied, without prejudice, to any harsher punishment provided for in any other law.

§11. Overlapping and Relation to Other Intellectual Property Laws

102. Plant varieties are protected under the 2004 Saudi Patent Law and its 2004 Implementing Regulations. Based on this, protection is provided through a sui generis regime rather than an independent one in Saudi Arabia.

Chapter 8. Layout-Designs of Integrated Circuits

§1. Sources: Legislation

103. Legal protection of topographic integrated circuits (hereinafter 'semiconductors') is provided in Saudi Arabia through sui generis protection under the law issued on 19/7/1425 H (4/9/2004 AD), namely the Law of Patents, Layout Designs of Integrated Circuits, Plant Varieties and Industrial Designs (hereinafter 'the 2004 Saudi Patent Law'). The related provisions are in compliance with the requirements of the TRIPS Agreement in this field.

In general, integrated circuits protection in Saudi Arabia is also influenced by the rules and principles established under several international intellectual property agreements in this area including those provided under the Paris and Rome Conventions, and the TRIPS Agreement.[486] In addition, the 2004 Saudi Implementing Regulations of the Law of Patents, Layout Designs of Integrated Circuits, Plant Varieties and Industrial Designs (the 2004 Implementing Regulations) supplement the rules of the 2004 Saudi Patent Law.

§2. Subject Matter of Protection

104. Article 1 of the 2004 Saudi Patent Law states that 'Layout-Design' is synonymous with 'topography' and means the three-dimensional disposition, however expressed, of the elements, at least one of which is an active element, and of some or all of the interconnections of an integrated circuit, or such a three-dimensional disposition prepared for an integrated circuit intended for manufacture. For the purpose of this, a protected layout-design is a design that is awarded protection in line with the requirements and stipulations of the 2004 Saudi Patent Law.

In conjunction with the above, it is noted that the Saudi legislature defined 'integrated circuits' and 'layout-designs' each separately rather than collectively. Based on this, Article 1 of the 2004 Saudi Patent Law states that an integrated circuit means 'A product in its final or intermediate form in which the elements, at least one of which is active, and some or all of the interconnections are integrally formed in or on a piece of material, and the purpose of this is to perform an electronic function.' The same article further defines layout-design as 'three dimensional disposition of the elements – at least one of which is active – and of some or all of the interconnections of an integrated circuit, or such a three dimensional disposition prepared for an integrated circuit intended for manufacture'.

486. TRIPS Agreement, Art. 35 provides that members agree to provide protection to the layout-designs (topographies) of integrated circuits (referred to in this agreement as 'layout-designs') in accordance with Arts 2 through 7 (other than para. 3 of Art. 6), Art. 12 and para. 3 of Art. 16 of the Treaty on Intellectual Property in Respect of Integrated Circuits and, in addition, to comply with the following provisions.

§3. CONDITIONS OF PROTECTION

105. In order to be granted legal protection, a layout-design must be registered in the country. Chapter 3 of the 2004 Saudi Patent Law lays down the foundations of legal protection for layout-designs of integrated circuits in the country. Accordingly, legal protection may be obtained for layout-designs of integrated circuits in the country if a number of conditions were met, these include:

(1) Prior commercial use. An application for registration of a layout-design of an integrated circuit may be filed in Saudi Arabia, if the design has not been commercially exploited before or was subject to commercial exploitation for a period not exceeding two years in any part of the world.[487]

In addition, Article 50 of the 2004 Saudi Patent Law provides that the certificate of layout-design shall be granted, if the layout-design is original; i.e., a result of its creator's own intellectual effort, and is not commonplace among creators of designs and manufacturers of integrated circuits at the time of its creation. As to a design that consists of a combination of elements and interconnections that are commonplace, it shall be deemed original under the law if the whole combination is original. As seen from the above, emphasis on the 'originality' factor is explicitly made in this regard and is measured with reference to the creator's own intellectual effort and not with reference to commonplace among creators of layout-designs and manufacturers of integrated circuits at the time of its creation.

§4. FORMALITIES: PROCEDURES FOR OBTAINING PROTECTION

106. Layout-designs and integrated circuits are registered in the country based on an application made to Registrar at the King Abdul Aziz City for Science and Technology (otherwise known as the Saudi Patent Office). Registration is based on a written application submitted to the Registrar on the form designated for this purpose. The application must contain all the required information, samples and drawings needed.

Legal protection of layout-designs is granted in accordance with Articles 18 and 19 of the 2004 Implementing Regulations. Accordingly, an application shall be made to the Registrar and shall include the following:

- Form No. (201) titled as the form for the 'Application for a Certificate of a Layout Design of an Integrated Circuit' where the information shall be recorded in accordance with Article 19 of the 2004 Saudi Patent Law.
- A brief and accurate description of the design, including the information that defines the electronic function performed by the integrated circuit.
- A clear drawing or picture of the design. Parts of the drawing or picture related to the method of manufacturing the integrated circuit may be excluded, provided that the remaining parts are sufficient to explain and identify the design.

487. The 2004 Saudi Patent Law, Art. 49.

– Any other relevant attachments.

In addition to the above, the 2004 Implementing Regulations stipulates that a sample of the integrated circuit shall be enclosed if it is the subject of commercial exploitation, if requested by the Directorate. Moreover, the designated application form should include details related to the name of design, date and place of first commercial exploitation, the name of applicant,[488] name of design innovator,[489] name of agent,[490] and any other relevant attachments in addition to the declaration.

The process for making the application is also explained under the 2004 Saudi Patent Law and the 2004 Implementing Regulations. Based on this, Article 8 of the 2004 Saudi Patent Law provides that the application for granting protection document shall be submitted to the Directorate in the prescribed form. The 2004 Implementing Regulations further specifies the information and documents required to be enclosed with the application. If the applicant is not the party which developed the subject matter of protection, his/her name must be stated and the document proving the transfer of title of the design's subject matter to him/her must be enclosed, and the Directorate may, in this case, send a copy of these documents to the party which developed the subject matter of protection. After satisfying the requirements and payment of the specified fee, the application shall be registered.

Article 9 of the 2004 Saudi Patent Law provides that the applicant may introduce the amendments he/she deems fit in the application, provided that these amendments shall introduce no change to what was disclosed in the original application itself.

Moreover, Article 10 of the 2004 Saudi Patent Law states that the applicant may benefit from the priority given to a previous application filed during the priority period specified for each of the subject matters of protection, from the filing date of the previous application, provided that it is accompanied by a written declaration stating the date and number of the previous application and the place where it was filed by him/her or his/her predecessor. The applicant shall also submit a copy of the previous application approved by the authority where the protection application was submitted,

488. Article 19 of the 2004 Implementing Regulations states that: '*For individuals, the name shall be identical to the name in the identification document in the following order: first name, father's name, grandfather's name and family name. As for establishments and companies, it shall be identical to the official name. If there is more than one applicant, data relating to the first applicant shall be recorded in this part, and the data relating to the remaining applicants shall be recorded in the attachment designed for that purpose, (Form No. (201-A)). Communication between the Directorate and the applicants shall be through the first applicant if there is no agent.*'

489. The name shall be identical to the name in the identification document in the following order: first name, father's name, grandfather's name and family name. If there is more than one innovator, the data relating to the first innovator shall be recorded in this part and the data relating to the other innovator shall be recorded in the special attachment designed for that purpose.

490. The name of the agent shall be stated, and he shall be authorized by a power of attorney issued by a notary public if the principal is in the Kingdom. If the principal is outside the Kingdom, it is necessary to have a power of attorney approved by the competent authorities and certified by the Kingdom's embassies abroad, and the agent shall attach proof that he/she is licensed to practise such a profession in the Kingdom.

within a period not exceeding ninety days from the date of filing the application with the Directorate.

Article 12 of the 2004 Saudi Patent Law states that the Directorate shall examine the registered applications in terms of formalities. If it appears, from the examination process, that some of the legally prescribed conditions are not satisfied it may instruct the applicant to satisfy them within a maximum period of ninety days from the date of notification. If the applicant does not fulfil what was requested within the said period, his/her application would be considered as if it had never been filed.

In addition, if the Directorate finds that the application has satisfied the stipulated conditions, it shall issue a decision granting the protection document. The said decision shall be published in sequence as regard to its issuance by the Directorate.[491] However, if the Directorate finds that the applicant does not qualify for the protection document, it shall issue a decision stating the reasons for the rejection, and the applicant shall be notified thereof.[492]

Notably, the applicant may withdraw the application at any time unless it has been finally decided upon. However, such withdrawal shall not give the right to recover the fees paid or any other expenses.[493]

The 2004 Saudi Patent Law provides under Article 16 that any action resulting in the assignment of the protection application or the protection document itself must be in writing, signed by the two parties, and approved by an authority acceptable to the Directorate. No transfer of title, relating either to the protection application or the protection document itself shall be effective vis-à-vis a third party, except after filing the change application, paying the required fees, and recording it in the Directorate registers.

Finally, it should be noted that if several parties participated in filing one protection application or in the ownership of one protection document each one of them may assign his/her right in the application or the protection document to any of the partners, to all of them, or to a third party. The Directorate shall subsequently publish the transfer of title in the Gazette.

The following table contains breakdown of the fees applicable in the country with relation to layout-designs.[494] Fees payable under the provisions of this law shall be determined in accordance with the following table.[495]

No.	*Fees*	*Individuals (SAR)*	*Corporations (SAR)*
(1)	Registration Application	500	1,000
(2)	Change or Transfer of Ownership	500	1,000
(3)	Amendment or Addition to the Application	250	500
(4)	Obtaining a Copy of the Application or Certificate	50	100

491. The 2004 Saudi Patent Law, Art. 14.a.
492. *Ibid.*, 14.b.
493. *Ibid.*, Art. 15.
494. Fees are quoted in Saudi Riyals.
495. The 2004 Saudi Patent Law, Art. 42.

No.	*Fees*	*Individuals (SAR)*	*Corporations (SAR)*
(5)	Registration of Licence Contracts	500	1,000
(6)	Grant of Compulsory Licence	2,500	5,000
(7)	Grant and Publication	150	1,000
(8)	**Annual fees**		
(8/1)	1st year	500	3,100
	2nd Year	750	1,500
	3rd Year	1,000	2,000
	4th Year	1,250	2,500
	5th Year	1,500	3,000
	6th Year	1,750	3,500
	7th Year	2,000	4,000
	8th Year	2,250	4,500
	9th Year	2,500	5,000
	10th year	2,750	5,500

§5. Ownership and Transfer: Assignment, Licences and Compulsory Licensing

107. As a general rule, the rights holder is the creator of a protected layout-design or his/her successor in title. Article 50 of the 2004 Saudi Patent Law identifies the owner of the layout-design in an explicit manner. In this regard, the 2004 Saudi Patent Law states that the certificate of layout-design shall be granted, if the layout-design is original; i.e., a result of its creator's own intellectual effort.

The rights in a protected layout-design may be assigned or transferred by succession. Where several persons have jointly created a layout-design, the right shall belong to them jointly.

The 2004 Saudi Patent Law provides that the protection document shall be a personal right of the person in whose name it was issued. This right may be transferred by inheritance, as well as with or without consideration. If the subject matter of protection is a joint work of several persons, they shall be equally entitled to the right, unless they have agreed otherwise. The 2004 Saudi Patent Law further explains that no one shall be deemed a partner unless he/she contributes to the subject matter of protection, and his/her efforts are only confined to assistance in its execution. If more than one person has independently developed the same subject matter of protection, the protection document shall be granted to the first applicant. The person who develops the subject matter of protection shall have the right to state his/her name in that capacity in the protection document.

Article 6 of the 2004 Saudi Patent Law provides that the employer shall be the owner of the protection document, unless the work contract stipulates otherwise, where its subject matter results from the execution of a contract, or an obligation providing for exerting efforts to develop it, or if the employer proves that the employee would not have developed the subject matter of the protection had he/she not used facilities, means or data made available through his/her employment. This shall be without prejudice to the employee's right to receive a special award to be agreed upon with the consent of both parties, or assessed by the Committee in light of the various circumstances of the contract of employment, and the economic importance of the subject matter of the protection. Any special agreement depriving the employee of this right shall be null and void.

Notably, an application for a protection document filed by the employee within a period of two years from the date of termination of employment shall be deemed as if submitted during the employment. This shall also apply to government employees. If the subject matter of protection developed relates to national security, it shall be governed by the provisions stipulated in the 2004 Implementing Regulations as been highlighted under Chapter 2.

Moreover, Article 7 of the 2004 Saudi Patent Law provides that if the subject matter claimed in the application or in the protection document is derived from a subject matter owned by a person other than the applicant or the owner of the protection document, then this person may request the Committee to transfer the ownership of the application or protection document to him/her. The case for the transfer application shall not be heard after the elapse of a period of five years period from the granting the protection unless the applicant's bad faith is established.

Moreover, the 2004 Saudi Patent Law contains a number of clauses applicable to the issuance of compulsory licensing for layout-designs in the country. Article 24 of the 2004 Saudi Patent Law states that the City may grant a compulsory licence to a third party to exploit a layout-design covered by a certificate of design upon an application submitted to it, according to the following:

(1) The application shall be submitted after the elapse of a period of four years from the date of filing the layout-design application or three years from the date of granting the layout-design, whichever expires later, without the owner of the protection document exploiting his/her layout-design or having exploited it in an inadequate fashion, unless he/she justifies that with a legitimate excuse.

(2) The applicant for the compulsory licence must prove that he/she has exerted – over a reasonable period of time – efforts in order to obtain a contractual licence on the basis of reasonable commercial conditions, and for a reasonable financial compensation. However, this provision and the provision of the preceding paragraph do not apply where the applicant is a government body or a person authorized by it, and the aim was to meet public interest – especially security, health, nutrition or the development other vital sectors of the national economy – or to meet a state of emergency or other very compelling circumstances, or where the aim thereof was public non-commercial purposes. In the latter case, and upon knowledge of the existence of a layout-design, their holder shall be promptly informed.

(3) The compulsory licence is basically granted to make the layout-design available in the local markets. But this provision does not apply where the aim of the licence is to prevent or restrict practices against which a decision or judgment is issued declaring them to be acts of unlawful competition.
(4) The decision granting the licence shall specify the scope and term of the licence, according to the purpose for which it was granted. The licence shall be subject to termination if the conditions for which it was granted cease to exist and their recurrence is not likely, with due regards to the lawful interests of the licensee.
(5) The licence shall not be exclusive.
(6) Each application shall be independently decided.
(7) The owner of the protection document or the holder of a certificate of a design shall be awarded a fair compensation. The Committee shall determine the amount of the compensation, and the licensee undertakes to pay it.
(8) If the compulsory licence is related to a semi-conductor technology, the purpose of the licence shall be for public non-commercial purposes only or to control acts concerning which a decision or judgment is issued declaring them to be acts of unlawful competition.

In addition, Article 26 of the 2004 Saudi Patent Law states that the beneficiary of the compulsory licence may not assign it to others, unless the assignment includes all or part of the firm benefiting from the licence or its goodwill. The City's approval of the assignment is required; otherwise, it shall be null and void. If the City approves such assignment, the assignee becomes liable for the obligations assumed by the first beneficiary prior to the approval of the assignment. Moreover, the City may amend the decision to grant the compulsory licence if need arises. The owner of the protection document or the beneficiary of the compulsory licence may request the City to make this amendment if its prerequisites are fulfilled. The reasons for the decision of the City to amend the licence or to reject the request must be stated.[496]

In addition, the City shall cancel the compulsory licence in the following cases:

(1) If the beneficiary of the licence fails to exploit it in a way that satisfies the Kingdom's needs, within a period of two years from the grant of the licence, renewable for an equal period, if it is proved that there is a legitimate cause.
(2) If the beneficiary of the compulsory licence fails to pay the due fees within a period of ninety days from the due date, including the compensations to which the owner of the protection document is entitled, as stipulated in the decision granting the licence.
(3) If the beneficiary of the compulsory licence fails to observe any condition necessary for granting of the licence.

Article 29 of the 2004 Saudi Patent Law states that the beneficiary of the compulsory licence may relinquish the licence by a written request to the City. However, the relinquishment becomes effective from the date of approval of the City.

In general, the decisions of compulsory licence, its amendment, withdrawal, transference to others and relinquishment shall be entered in the records of the

496. The 2004 Saudi Patent Law, Art. 27.

Directorate, published in the Gazette and notified to the owner of the protection document.[497] Notably, the owner of the protection document may relinquish it by submitting a written request to the City. The relinquishment may be confined to one or more of the stated elements of protection. However, relinquishment of the protection document, in case of compulsory licence, shall only be accepted with a written consent of the beneficiary of the licence, or the proof of the existence of compelling circumstances justifying this relinquishment. The relinquishment shall be registered and published in the Gazette, and it shall not be effective against a third party except from the date of publication.[498]

The Saudi legal regime allows for an opposition procedure. Accordingly, any party with interest may challenge the decision of granting of a protection document before the Committee, and seek total or partial revocation, relying upon the violation of the stipulated conditions for granting the protection document. The owner of the protection document shall include the beneficiary of the licence as a party to the lawsuit; otherwise, the latter may interfere on his/her own behalf. The Committee may order to enter any party with interest, and the 2004 Implementing Regulations shall specify the grounds upon which the request for the revocation of any protection document shall be based.[499] A judgment of total or partial invalidity of the decision granting the protection document renders the decision null and void from the date of issuance, within the scope of what is nullified. However, the decision to nullify the protection document shall not imply a refund of the sums paid for the licence to exploit it, unless the licensee proves that what he/she has gained, as a result of the licence, is not equal to what he/her has paid, in which case he/she may recover the amount exceeding the gain he/she received. The decision of annulment of granting the protection document shall be published after its issuance, and shall be effective vis-à-vis a third party from the date of publication.[500]

Any act of exploitation provided for in the special provisions governing each of the protection subject matters, performed by any person in the country without a written consent of the owner of the protection document recorded with the Directorate, shall be deemed an infringement on the subject matter of protection. At the request of the owner of the protection document, and any party with interest, the Committee shall grant an injunction to prevent the infringement in addition to the necessary damages, and it may impose a fine upon the infringer not exceeding SAR 100,000 (approx. USD 30,000). The maximum fine shall be doubled in case of repetition. If the Committee sees that the infringement calls for the punishment of imprisonment, the infringer shall be referred from the start to the BoGs. The Committee may take the necessary prompt measures it deems necessary to prevent the damages resulting from the infringement.[501] The decision issued by the Committee in this case shall be published in the Official Gazette, the Gazette and two daily newspapers, at the expense of the party against whom the decision is issued. The provision of this article shall be applied, without prejudice, to any harsher punishment provided for in any other law.

497. *Ibid.*, Art. 30.
498. *Ibid.*, Art. 31.
499. *Ibid.*, Art. 32.
500. *Ibid.*, Art. 33.
501. *Ibid.*, Art. 34.

The law calls for the creation of a committee consisting of three law specialists and two technical experts whose grade shall not be lower than grade twelve. The members shall be nominated by the President of the City. The formation of the Committee shall be pursuant to a resolution by the Council of Ministers for a term of three years renewable for one time only. The resolution shall appoint one of the law specialists as chairman of the Committee.[502]

Article 36 of the 2004 Saudi Patent Law states that the Committee shall have jurisdiction over the following:

(1) All disputes and appeals against decisions issued in connection with protection documents.
(2) Penal lawsuits for violations of the provisions of the 2004 Saudi Patent Law and its 2004 Implementing Regulations.

The litigants shall be notified of the lawsuits filed with the Committee, in accordance with the provisions of the 2004 Implementing Regulations.

Decisions of the Committee shall be issued by majority vote, provided that the grounds for the decisions are stated, and their text is read in a public session. The Committee shall not refuse to issue a decision in the lawsuit on the ground that there is no provision to govern the dispute in the Law or the Implementing Regulations. In that case the Committee shall refer to the general rules observed in the country. An appeal against any decision issued by the Committee may be brought before the BoGs within a period not exceeding sixty days from the date of notification of the decision.[503] The Committee may contact the government bodies concerned and request any explanation and information it deems necessary. The City shall provide the Committee with all documents and papers relating to applications or subject matters of protection in dispute, whenever requested to do so by the Committee.[504]

The Committee may seek the assistance of different expert bodies for whatever it deems necessary of the technical matters referred to it, and it shall determine the litigants liable for the expenses incurred.[505]

Reviewing of the protection documents and any related information registered with the Directorate may be allowed free of charge. Any person may obtain copies therefrom, upon payment of the required fees.[506]

Employees of the Directorate and members of the Committee shall not disclose technical information relating to the protection applications of which they become cognizant in their capacity to any person, unless such person is officially authorized to receive that information in accordance with the rules applicable in the country. They shall also not disclose such information to the public, or use it in any way. This undertaking continues after the end of their service.[507]

---

502. *Ibid.*, Art. 35.
503. *Ibid.*, Art. 37.
504. *Ibid.*, Art. 38.
505. *Ibid.*, Art. 39.
506. *Ibid.*, Art. 40.
507. *Ibid.*, Art. 41.

Employees of the Directorate and members of the Committee may not obtain any of the protection documents or deal in any of the rights relating to them during their service and for two years after the end of service.

§6. Scope of Protection

108. Rights owner of layout-designs has an exclusive property right to protect the layout-design from abuse and infringement. Article 47 of the 2004 Saudi Patent Law provides the parameters of legal protection granted to layout-designs in the country. In this regard, legal protection shall have the effect that the following acts shall be unlawful if performed without the authorization of the right holder:

(1) If it is a product: Its manufacture, sale, offering for sale, use, storage or its importation for any of these purposes.
(2) If it is a process: The use of the process, or performing any of the acts referred to in the previous paragraph, in relation to the product which is directly obtained by the use of this process.

However, the owner of the protection document's right shall not preclude others from exploiting the protected subject matter in non-commercial activities relating to scientific research. Notably, the above is in line with the requirements of Article 36 of the TRIPS Agreement.[508]

§7. Limitations of the Scope of Protection

109. Once a layout-design has been registered, there are no specific limitations on the scope of the exclusive rights derived from such registration. In this regard, the 2004 Saudi Patent Law does not introduce or contain any requirement or obligation as to working, producing, or manufacturing the layout-design in or outside the country during a specific period of time.

However, the law provides a number of exceptions in the area of reproducing layout-designs. As mentioned, the law contains some exceptions against the legal rights arising from the ownership of semi-conductors. Based on this, the effect of protection of a layout-design under the 2004 Saudi Patent Law shall not preclude others from exploiting his/her invention in non-commercial activities relating to scientific research.

§8. Duration of Protection

110. Article 19.b the 2004 Saudi Patent Law sets out the protection term of layout-designs to be for a period of ten years. Based on this, the ten-year protection

508. *See* C. Correa, *Intellectual Property Rights, the WTO and Developing Countries* (London: Zed Books, 2000).

of a layout-design shall commence from filing the application or ten years from the date of start of its commercial exploitation anywhere in the world. In any case, the protection period may not exceed fifteen years from the date of creation of the design.

As seen, Saudi Arabia is in compliance with the requirement of Article 38 of the TRIPS Agreement in this regard which provides Member States with two options when it comes to calculating the commencement date of protection as following:

The first option, in members requiring registration as a condition of protection, the term of protection of layout-designs shall not end before the expiration of a period of ten years counted from the date of filing an application for registration or from the first commercial exploitation wherever in the world it occurs.

Second option, member may provide that protection shall lapse after a period of fifteen years from the creation of the layout-design.

§9. Cancellation of Registration

111. Article 46.2 of the 2004 Implementing Regulations provides that the rules applicable to invalidation of layout-designs.

According to Article 46.2 of the 2004 Implementing Regulations, bases for invalidating a protection document for a layout-design fully would be in the case of the violation of the provisions of Articles 2, 4, 49 and 50 of the 2004 Saudi Patent Law. In addition, the same article further provides that invalidation may also be requested if it turns out that the protection document was issued to a person other than the person who developed the subject matter of protection.

§10. Infringement and Remedies

112. The infringement of the exclusive rights of the owner of a layout-design results in civil and criminal penalties and remedies. Based on this, Article 61 of the 2004 Saudi Patent Law further states that protection against unfair competition shall also apply independently of, and in addition to, any legislative provisions protecting layout-designs.

Based on this, and without prejudice to what Article 34 of the 2004 Saudi Patent Law stipulates, any party that violates any of the provisions provided for in this law shall be punished with a fine not exceeding SAR 50,000 (approx. USD 15,000), and the maximum limit shall be doubled in case of repetition.

§11. Overlapping and Relations to Other Industrial Property Laws

113. The protection of layout-designs is a relatively new legislative tool in the country. Therefore there has been minimal level of activity undertaken in this area in the country.

Chapter 9. Trade Secrets/Confidential Information

§1. Sources: Legislation

114. Prior to 2005, the protection against trade secrets was provided in Saudi Arabia under the Royal Decree No. 30 for the Year 2000 for the Protection Trademarks, Trade Secrets and Protection from Unfair Competition. However, in 2005, the Regulations for the Protection of Confidential Commercial Information were issued by virtue of the Minister of Commerce and Industry's Decision No. (3218) dated 25/03/1426H (4 May 2005) hereinafter 'the 2005 Confidential Information Regulations'.[509]

Protection against unfair competition has been established in many legal regimes for some time including the protection of trade secrets and confidential information. As been observed, reliance on trade secrets protection rather than patent protection may enable an inventor or business owner to have permanent control over the use and utilization of the technology and/or invention but at the same time would not prevent third parties from reverse engineering or development attempts of the technology.[510]

In the Arab World, the protection of undisclosed commercial information and trade secrets is protected either under independent legal codes or under the framework of other laws and legislations.[511] The Saudi legal regime adopts the latter approach in this regard. Thus, the 2005 Confidential Information Regulations provides legal framework and protection for confidential information in accordance with the standards required by the TRIPS Agreement and Paris Convention.[512]

§2. The Protection of Trade Secrets and Unfair Competition

115. Article 1 of the 2005 Confidential Information Regulations provides a list of cases where commercial secrets are treated as such. Based on this, any information shall be deemed a commercial secret in any of the cases stated below:

(1) If it is usually not known in its final form, or in any of its minute constituents or if it is not usually easily obtainable by those engaged in this type of business.
(2) If it is of commercial value due to its confidentiality.
(3) If the rightful owner takes reasonable measures to maintain its confidentiality under its current circumstances.

509. As amended by Decision No. (431) dated 01/05/1426H (8 Jun. 2005) authorized by the Council of Ministers Decision No. (50) dated 25/02/1426H (4 Apr. 2005).
510. For more *see* H. MacCueen et al., *Contemporary Intellectual Property: Law and Policy*, 2nd edn. (New York: Oxford University Press, 2010).
511. For example, trade secrets are protected in Jordan under the Trade Secrets Law No. 7 for the year 2003, while in Qatar it is protected under the Trade Secrets Law No. 5 for the year 2005.
512. Article 10*bis* of the Paris Convention provides protection from unfair competition, including by acts contrary to honest practises in commercial and industrial matters.

(4) The rightful owner shall be any person entitled to disclose, use or retain a commercial secret.
(5) The rightful owner may keep the information in his/her possession and refrain from disclosing it.
(6) The rightful owner may take the necessary measures to prevent any person from using the commercial secret protected in accordance with the 2005 Confidential Information Regulations.

Moreover, Article 3.1 of the 2005 Confidential Information Regulations provides that obtaining, using or disclosing any commercial secret in a way that is inconsistent with honest commercial practices and without the consent of the rightful owner shall be deemed an abuse of the commercial secret. In all cases, it may not be disclosed in a way inconsistent with its reality.

Notably, Article 3.2 of the 2005 Confidential Information Regulations further verifies that for the purposes of implementing the provisions Article 3.1 of the Regulations, the following, in particular, shall be deemed violations of honest commercial practices:

(1) Breach of contracts relating to commercial secrets.
(2) Breach of confidentiality of entrusted information or encouraging its breach.
(3) A person obtaining the commercial secrets from a third party if such a person knows or is capable of knowing that the third party has obtained the same as a result of a violation of honest commercial practices.

Notably, Article 3.3 of the 2005 Confidential Information Regulations provides some exceptions to the above rule. Based on this, reaching a commercial secret, independently or through reverse engineering, shall not be deemed, in particular, a violation of honest commercial practices to that effect.

The 2005 Confidential Information Regulations further explain that the competent authorities shall protect the commercial secrets submitted to them against disclosure and protect them against unfair commercial use. The said authorities may not disclose them unless disclosure is deemed necessary for the protection of the public interest.[513]

Notably, where an official competent authority requires the submission of information about secret tests or any data obtained as a result of substantial efforts, as a precondition for approving the marketing of drugs or chemical agricultural products in which new chemical substances are used, the said authority shall undertake to protect such information against unfair commercial use, for a minimum period of five years from the date of obtaining the approval.[514] This is in compliance with the TRIPS Agreement approach in this area. More specifically, Saudi legislature adopts a similar line to that adopted by the TRIPS Agreement. As such, Article 39.2 of the TRIPS Agreement states that natural and legal persons shall have the possibility of preventing information lawfully within their control from being disclosed to, acquired by, or used

513. The 2005 Confidential Information Regulations, Art. 4.
514. *Ibid.*, Art. 5.

by others without their consent in a manner contrary to honest commercial practices so long as such information:[515]

(1) is secret in the sense that it is not, as a body or in the precise configuration and assembly of its components, generally known among or readily accessible to persons within the circles that normally deal with the kind of information in question;
(2) has commercial value because it is secret; and
(3) has been subject to reasonable steps under the circumstances, by the person lawfully in control of the information, to keep it secret.

The competent registration authority – during the protection term of commercial secrets – may permit third parties to use the undisclosed data of secret tests submitted by another applicant in the following cases:[516]

(1) If the product first registered in the country has not been subject of trading within a reasonable period of time determined by the registration authority, after approving its marketing.
(2) If this is required by a pressing necessity determined by the competent authority to protect the public.

The 2005 Confidential Information Regulations contains another set of exemptions form the ambit of legal protection. Based on this, the 2005 Confidential Information Regulations shall not protect commercial secrets inconsistent with Islamic *Shariah*, public order and public morality.[517]

From the above, it becomes clear that the Saudi legal regime does not specify the acts which may represent or amount to unfair competition practises but rather provides general definition of what may constitute such.

It is clear that protection of trade secrets and unfair competition is protected without any formalities in Saudi Arabia. Such protection is granted for an indefinite period of time which is in line with international practises.

§3. Infringement and Remedies

116. Article 8 of the 2005 Confidential Information Regulations states that any person harmed as a result of violating the provisions of these Regulations may file a lawsuit before the competent judicial authority to claim compensation for damages

515. For the purpose of this provision, 'a manner contrary to honest commercial practices' shall mean at least practices such as breach of contract, breach of confidence and inducement to breach, and includes the acquisition of undisclosed information by third parties who knew, or were grossly negligent in failing to know, that such practices were involved in the acquisition.
516. The 2005 Confidential Information Regulations Art. (6).
517. *Ibid.*, Art. 7.

sustained.[518] In addition, the penalties available under unfair completion law shall also be applicable.

Interestingly, the statute of limitations does not apply in relation to infringements of unfair competition nature in Saudi Arabia.

In addition to the measures available under the 2005 Confidential Information Regulations, some of the provisions included under the Penal Law on Dissemination and Disclosure of Classified Information and Documents (promulgated by Royal Decree No. M/35 of 8/5/1432H (12 April 2011) may also apply (hereinafter 'the 2011 Saudi Penal Law'). Based on this, Article 1 of the 2001 Saudi Penal Law defines classified documents as all media types which contain classified information the disclosure of which prejudices the State's national security, interests, policies or rights, whether produced or received by its agencies. It also defines classified information as any information an employee obtains – or is privy to by virtue of office – the disclosure of which undermines the State's national security, interests, policies or rights.[519]

Article 3 of the 2011 Saudi Penal Law further states that in application of the provisions of this law, the following shall be deemed a public employee:

(1) Any person employed by the government or by any agency of a public corporate personality, whether permanently or temporarily.
(2) Any person assigned by a government entity or any other administrative authority to carry out a certain task.
(3) Any person employed by companies or sole proprietorships which manage, operate or maintain public facilities or provide public services, as well as those employed by companies to whose capital the State contributes.
(4) An arbiter or expert designated by the government or by any other judicial authority.
(5) Chairmen and members of board of directors of companies provided for in paragraph (3) of this Article.

Accordingly, Article 5 of the 2011 Saudi Penal Law states that without prejudice to any harsher punishment prescribed by law, the following acts shall be punished by imprisonment for a period not exceeding twenty years or a fine not exceeding SAR 1 million (approx. USD 300,000) or by both:

(1) Disseminating or disclosing classified information or documents.
(2) Entering or attempting to enter a place without authorization, with the intent of obtaining classified information or documents.
(3) Obtaining classified information or documents by illicit means.
(4) Possessing or becoming privy – by virtue of office – to official classified information or documents and disclosing, communicating or disseminating the same without a lawfully justified cause.

518. *Ibid.*, Art. 8.

519. The Regulations of Classified Documents and Lists – issued by the National Center for Documents and Archives – shall, in coordination with relevant entities, determine the titles, level of classification and subject matter of said documents.

(5) Wilfully destroying or misusing classified documents, knowing that such classified documents relate to the State's security or public interest, with the intent of undermining the State's military, political, diplomatic, economic or social status.
(6) Failing to maintain confidentiality of information or documents.

Article 6 of the 2001 Saudi Penal Law provides that any person participating in any of the articles stipulated in this law shall be subject to the punishments provided for in Article 5, and any person who knowingly agrees to, instigates or assists in commitment of the crimes shall be deemed an accomplice if such crimes are committed on the basis of such agreement, instigation or assistance.

When enforcing the punishment stipulated in Article 5 of the 2011 Saudi Penal Law, proportionality between crime and punishment as well as extenuating or aggravating circumstances shall be taken into consideration. The following shall be deemed aggravating circumstances:[520]

(1) If the crime is committed during wartime.
(2) If the crime is committed – in any form or manner and by any means – for the sake of a foreign state or any person working therefor, either directly or indirectly.
(3) If the classified information or document is important and of high level of confidentiality.

Finally, under the 2001 Telecommunications Act, violations may result in penalties of up to SAR 5,000,000 (approx. USD 1,500,000). Under the 2007 Anti-Cyber Crime Law, unlawful access to data that jeopardizes internal or external security or the national economy may result in up to ten years in prison and fines up to SAR 5,000,000 (approx. USD 1,500,000).

§4. Overlapping and Relations to Other Industrial Property Laws

117. Evidently, the protection of undisclosed information and trade secrets in Saudi Arabia is subject to a complex set of regulatory requirements. The protection regime is also impacted by the requirements of the 2011 Saudi Penal Law, the Telecommunications Act of 2001 and the Anti-Cyber Crime Law of 2007. Moreover, Saudi Arabia has several other laws which contain provisions protecting confidential information or trade secrets such as the Companies Law, the Labor Law, the Banks Control Law and the procedural rules of the Communications and Information Technology Commission.

520. The 2011 Saudi Penal Law, Art. 7.

Chapter 10. Geographical Indications and Appellations of Origin

§1. Sources: Legislation

118. GIs are also protected under the 2002 Saudi Trademark Royal Decree. Accordingly, GIs may be registered as trademarks in Saudi Arabia provided that they meet definitions established by the 2002 Saudi Trademark Royal Decree. For instance, Article 2 of the 2002 Saudi Trademark Royal Decree provides that the following signs, emblems, flags and others listed below shall not be considered or registered as trademark:[521]

– Signs without any specific distinction and which are descriptions of characteristics or which are no more than common names which are by custom given to the products or services.
– Geographical names if their use is liable to create confusion as to the source of the products or services or their origin or liable to monopolize notice of origin or name the source without rightful justification.[522]

However, geographical names cannot be registered as trademarks 'if their use is liable to create confusion as to the source of the products or services or their origin or liable to monopolize notice of origin or name the source without rightful justification'. In accordance with Article 38 of the 2002 Saudi Trademark Royal Decree, the Minister of Commerce may permit the registration of a mark which is owned jointly by natural or legal persons who are undertaking the control of specific products or services or inspection thereof as regards their origin, ingredients, method of manufacture or performance, or descriptions or any of the characteristics thereof. However, the 2002 Saudi Trademark Royal Decree provides that geographical names may not be registered if their use causes misconceptions as to the source of the products or services or origin thereof, or if their use would entail a monopoly of the source or the name of the origin without any rightful or proper justification.[523] Once a GI application is filed, it will be examined to determine its applicability for registration in the country. If the Registrar objects in writing to certain aspects of the mark during the examination process, a period of thirty days will be granted to the applicant to comply with the Registrar's request.

Once the application is formally rejected, a complaint or appeal against the rejection can be filed before the Minister of Commerce, within a period not exceeding

521. Myra E.J.B. Williamson, 'Geographical Indications, Biodiversity and Traditional Knowledge: Obligations and Opportunities for the Country of Saudi Arabia', *Arab Law Quarterly* 26, no. 1 (January 2012): 99–119.
522. The 2002 Saudi Trademark Royal Decree, Art. 2. f.
523. *Ibid.*, Art. 2.f.

sixty days from the date of notification of the rejection. The Minister's decision may be appealed before the BoGs (First Instance Court).[524] The trademark or service mark applications accepted for registration are published in the country's Official Gazette. Publication is an invitation to any interested party to oppose the registration of trademarks conflicting with their interests. An opposition to the registration of a trademark or service mark should be filed within the term of the opposition period, i.e., ninety days from the date of publication of the notice in the Official Gazette.[525] The case should be filed before the BoGs (the First Instance Court). It is considered to be an offence to forge or to imitate registered trademarks in any way that misleads the public, or uses a trademark owned by someone else on his products or services or offers or presents for sale or sells.[526]

It should be noted that the country has excluded from the scope of protection some types of GIs with regard to Article 23 of the TRIPS Agreement. These are related to the additional protection of GIs with regard to alcohol and alcoholic beverages, which was also deleted from the list of classification of goods and services attached to the trademark system in the country. According to official sources, the justification for this was provided to the WTO members in terms of their conflict with Islamic law and established *Shariah* principles. All member countries accepted these justifications which meet the requirements of the (TRIPS) agreement.[527]

524. *Ibid.*, Art. 8.
525. *See* generally Al Fuzan, Mohammed, Al Netham Al Kanoni Lil Esm El Tejari wa al Alameh el Tajjarayeh, Maktakeh al Kanon wa al Ektesad, al Riyadh. First Edition, 2013.
526. For more *see* the Technical–Legal study on geographical designations for olive oil and table olives, available at http://www.cimdol.com/FichaAmpliada.asp?id_documento=8927&MarcaClave=&IdUsuario=13715280. In conjunction, *see also* the 2002 Saudi Trademark Royal Decree, Art. 43.
527. For more *see* http://www.mci.gov.sa/en/Agencies/TechnicalAffairs/Departments/Sharq/Pages/1-4-3.aspx.

Selected Bibliography

Al Fehaidi, Abdullah, Al Alamat Al Tejareyeh, First Edition. 2011 Dar Al Hadarah Lilnasher wa Al Tawzee, Saudi Arabia.

Al Fuzan, M. Netham Hemayet Hukok Al Mualef fi al Mamlaka al Arabia al Saudia (AL Kanon Wa Al Ektsad Library), Riyadh, Saudi Arabia, first edition 2009.

Al Fuzan, M. Al Netham Al Kanoni Lil Esm El Tejari wa al Alameh el Tajjarayeh (AL Kanon Wa Al Ektsad Library), Riyadh. First Edition, 2013.

Al Sharq Al Awsat, 5 Dec. 2010, issue 11695, at http://archive.aawsat.com/details.asp?section=19&article=598144&issueno=11695#.VaVdgfmqqko, visited 14 Jul. 2015.

Al Sultani, S. & Rob Deans, Partner, Clyde & Co LLP, Dubai, UAE. http://www.wipo.int/wipo_magazine/en/2014/05/article_0010.html.

Al-Darwish, A., et al. *Saudi Arabia: Tackling Emerging Economic Challenges to Sustain Strong Growth.* Middle East and Central Asia departmental paper series. (Washington, D.C.: International Monetary Fund, 2015.

Aljabre, A. 'Understanding Software Piracy in Saudi Arabia and the Need for Change'. *Journal of Emerging Trends in Computing and Information Sciences* 3, no. 11 (November 2012).

Arif, Afida Mastura Muhammad. 'An Analysis of Copyright Protection in Saudi Arabia'. *International Journal of Law and Management* 56, no. 1 (2014): 38–49.

BBC. http://www.bbc.com/news/world-middle-east-14702705.

Bently, L. & B. Sherman. *Intellectual Property Law.* New York: Oxford University Press, 2004.

Cabanellas, G. *IPRs in Argentina.* The Hague: Kluwer Law International, 1997.

Clyde & Co. Monthly Insights/Updates, March 2015 letter. Available at http://www.clydeco.com/insight/updates/view/trade-mark-protection.

Clyde & Co. A unified GCC Trade Mark Law – half way there, and ready for 2015? 1 November 2014, Available at http://www.clydeco.com/insight/updates/view/ip-newsletter-article-november-2014-a-unified-gcc-trade-mark-law-half-way-t.

Clyde & Co. Intellectual Property Newsletter, Licensing provisions in the draft GCC Trade Mark Law. By Deans, R. & J. Young, Partners, Clyde & Co LLP. 1 Feb. 2015. Available at http://www.clydeco.com/insight/updates/view/ip-newsletter-article-february-2015-licensing-provisions-in-the-draft-gcc-tuary 2015.

Correa, C. 'International Dimension of the Research Exception'. SIPPI Project, AAAS (Washington, DC, 2005). Available at http://sippi.aaas.org/intlexemptionpaper.shtmli.

Correa, C. *Intellectual Property Rights, the WTO and Developing Countries.* London: Zed Books, 2000.

El Said, M. 'The Road from TRIPS-Minus to TRIPS to TRIPS-Plus: Implications of IPRs for the Arab World'. *The Journal of World Intellectual Property* 8, no. 1 (2005).

El Said, M. *IPRs in Jordan.* The Netherlands: Kluwer Law International, 2009.

El Said, M. *IPRs in Lebanon.* The Netherlands: Kluwer Law International, 2011.

El Said, M. *IPRs in Oman.* The Netherlands: Kluwer Law International, 2013.

El Said, M. 'The Compatibility of Modern Intellectual Property Protection Norms with Islamic Principles: Lessons from History'. *W.I.P.O. Journal* 4, no. 1 (2012): 121–128.

El Said, M. *The Development of Intellectual Property Protection in the Arab World.* Lewiston: Edwin Mellen Press, 2008.

Garrison, C. 'Exceptions to Patent Rights in Developing Countries', paper submitted to the International Centre for Trade and Sustainable Development, ICTSD Project on IPRs and Sustainable Development, issue 17 (Geneva, August 2006). Also *see* C. Correa, 'International Dimension of the Research Exception', SIPPI Project, AAAS (Washington, DC, 2005). Available at http://sippi.aaas.org/intlexemption paper.shtmli.

GCC Patent Office at http://www.gccpo.org/.

Global Britannia. http://global.britannica.com/topic/history-of-Arabia. Last visited 7 Feb. 2016.

Heald, P. 'Trademarks and Geographical Indications: Exploring the Contours of the TRIPS Agreement'. *Vanderbilt Journal of Transnational Law* 26, no. 2 (1996).

King Abdul Aziz City http://www.kacst.edu.sa/en/innovation/patents/pages/plant_varieties.aspx.

Kunal, M. 'TRIPS and Developing Countries: The Impact on Plant Varieties and Traditional Knowledge', *Trade Law Review* 12, no. 6 (2006).

Lyons, J. *The House of Wisdom: How the Arabs Transformed Western Civilization.* New York, Bloomsbury Press, 2009.

Selected Bibliography

MacCueen, H., et al. *Contemporary Intellectual Property: Law and Policy.* 2nd edn. New York: Oxford University Press, 2010.

McClure, D. 'Trademarks and Unfair Competition: A Critical History of Legal Though'. *Trademark Reporter* 69 (1979).

National Geographic, at http://science.nationalgeographic.com/science/prehistoric-world/precambrian/.

Oxford Business Group, http://www.oxfordbusinessgroup.com/analysis/long-game-new-development-plan-shows-clear-commitment-education-and-private-sector.

Patent Office of the Cooperation Council for the Arab States of the Gulf, at http://www.gccpo.org/DefaultEn.aspx.

Price, D. *The Development of Intellectual Property Regimes in the Arabian Gulf States: Infidels at the Gates.* New York: Routledge, 2009.

Price, D. 'Politics, Piracy and Punishment: Copyright Protection in the Arabian Gulf'. *The Journal of World Intellectual Property* 14, no. 3–4 (2011).

Saba IP, available at http://www.sabaip.com/en/News/Saudi-Arabia-New-Regulations-for-Entering-PCT-National-Phase-.

Saudi Arabia Ministry of Culture and Information, available at http://www.info.gov.sa/copyrights/English/eDefault.aspx.

Saudi Arabia Ministry of Economy and Planning, available at http://services.mep.gov.sa/themes/BlueArc/.

Saudi Arabia Ministry of Foreign Affairs, available at http://www.mofa.gov.sa/sites/mofaen/EServ/VisitingSaudiArabia/aboutKingDom/Pages/KingdomGeography46466.aspx.

Saudi General Authority of Statistics, available at http://www.stats.gov.sa/en/english.

Shanker, D. 'The Paragraph 6 Solution of the Doha Public Health Declaration and Export under the TRIPS Agreement'. *Journal of World Intellectual Property* 7, no. 3 (2004): 365–400.

Torremans, P. *Holyoak and Torremans Intellectual Property Law.* New York: Oxford University Press, 2005.

UNDP. *Human Development Report 2013: The Rise of the South.* New York, UNDP, 2013.

Williamson, Myra E.J.B. 'Geographical Indications, Biodiversity and Traditional Knowledge: Obligations and Opportunities for the Country of Saudi Arabia'. *Arab Law Quarterly* 26, no. 1 (January 2012): 99–119.

World Bank, http://data.worldbank.org/country/saudi-arabia.

WTO, the Working Party on the Accession of the Kingdom of Saudi Arabia, WT/ACC/SAU/61, 1 Nov. 2005.

Selected Bibliography

Index

The numbers here refer to paragraph numbers.

Index

Index

Index

Made in the USA
Monee, IL
13 September 2026

62974265R00116